LEADERSHIP: *Oliphant Cartoons & Sculpture from the Bush Years*

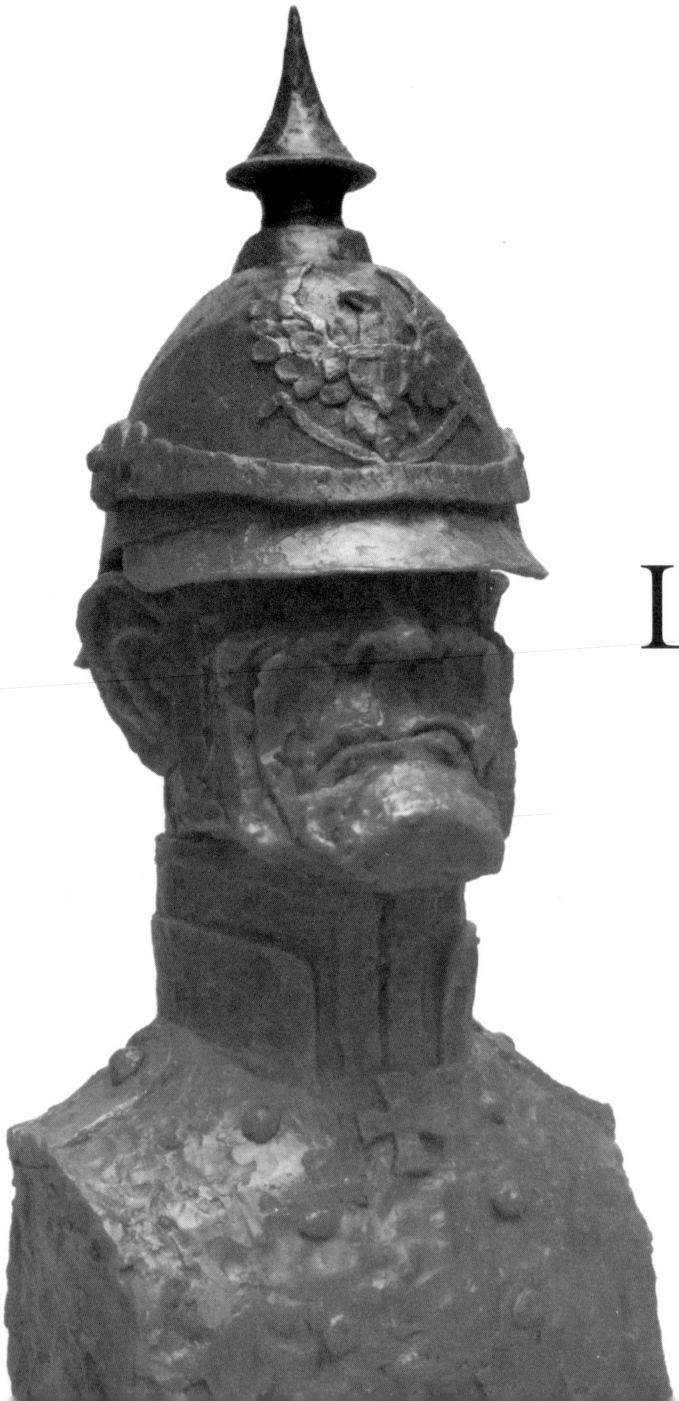

LEADERSHIP

Oliphant

Oliphant Cartoons & Sculpture from the Bush Years

Andrews McMeel
Publishing, LLC

Kansas City

This catalogue accompanies the exhibition *Leadership: Oliphant Cartoons & Sculpture from the Bush Years* at the Telfair Museum of Art in Savannah, Georgia, opening January 31st through April 4th, 2008. The exhibition will then travel to other American museums.

Cover:
102. **Leadership—Bush, Cheney, and a Horse,** 2007
Watercolor and colored inks on archival paper
12 × 16 inches

Frontispiece:
97. **Rumsfeld,** 2007
Bronze, 22½ × 9 × 9 inches

 For information, write Andrews McMeel Publishing, LLC, 4520 Main Street, Kansas City, Missouri 64111.

07 08 09 10 11 BID 10 9 8 7 6 5 4 3 2

ISBN-13: 978-0-7407-2674-3
ISBN-10: 0-7407-2674-9

Library of Congress Control Number: 2007925934

Oliphant cartoons appear courtesy of the artist and Universal Press Syndicate.

Design: Marcus Ratliff
Composition: Amy Pyle

www.andrewsmcmeel.com

For Jim Idema, In Memoriam.

And for Susan Corn Conway,
whose dedication and talent
make things happen.

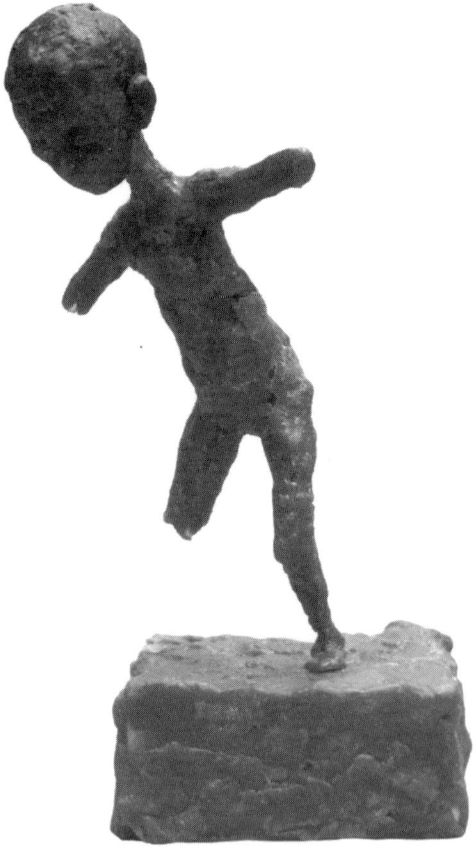

98.
Memorial for a Small War, 2007
Bronze, $8\frac{3}{4} \times 4 \times 4\frac{1}{2}$ inches

Contents

9   **Foreword**   by P. J. O'Rourke

15   **Cartoons and Sketches**

120   **Exhibition Checklist**

125   **Afterword**   by Wendy Wick Reaves

128   **Acknowledgments**

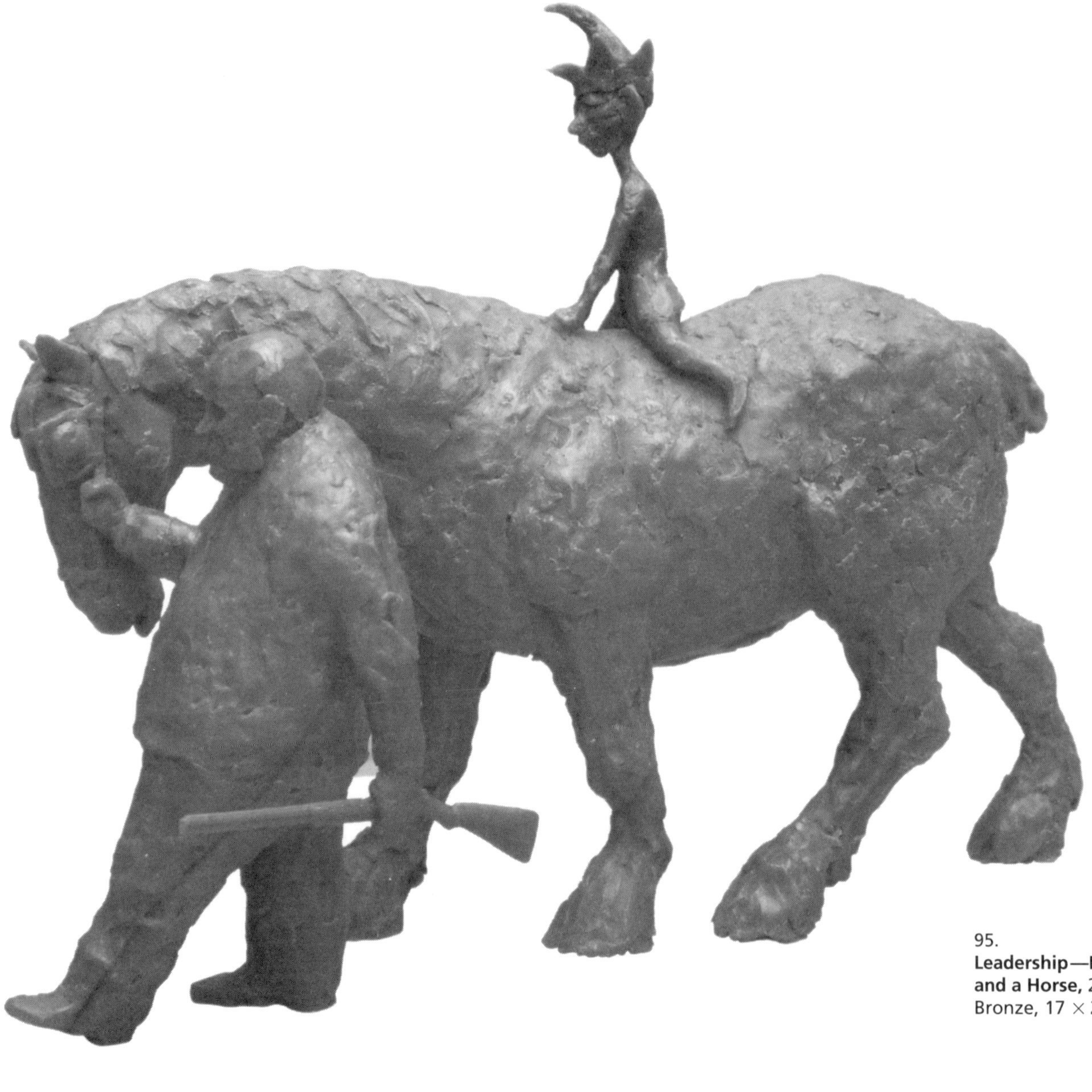

95.
Leadership—Bush, Cheney, and a Horse, 2007
Bronze, 17 × 26 × 13 inches

Foreword   by P. J. O'Rourke

Just a dash of ink and a dab of words or a splish and a splash of clay and the whole of our human folly is revealed by Pat Oliphant. Is Pat such a genius that he's able to show us our idiocy at a glance? Or are we such idiots that a glance is all it takes?

Let us quickly decide that Pat is a genius. Otherwise we'll feel bad about ourselves. Oliphant has a uniquely sensitive perception of evil, malfeasance, and greed. He is able to see things that we can't see. At least I hope so. Because if we've been looking right at evil, malfeasance, and greed and not noticing them, or if we've been complacently accepting evil, malfeasance, and greed without so much as making wry comments to a miniature penguin, then we're jerks.

To paraphrase a well-known jerk whom Pat used to draw frequently before the jerk died and went to hell, "I am not a jerk." And you, esteemed reader, aren't a jerk either. Besides, it's not our fault that we're jerks. Taking blame for things is out-of-date and second millennial. Feeling good about ourselves is the new first commandment. The deep thinkers of the twenty-first century—Barack Obama, SpongeBob SquarePants, and Paula Abdul, to name some if not

all of them—tell us that we should get audaciously stuffed with hope, go soak our heads in confidence, and binge on good feelings about ourselves until we're ready to pop.

Behold the important twenty-first century personages whom Pat Oliphant portrays in this exhibition, some of whom have popped already. What a mess. But, mess or no, these personages are feeling good about themselves. Pride? Hah! That's projecting an assured campaign persona to the electorate. Wrath? Nonsense! A troop surge in Baghdad is vital to the cause in our war against... um... everybody. And don't call it avarice or envy or even lobbying. Call it "a rewarding private-sector position after many years of sacrifice in a public-service career." Or call it "spending more time with the family" if the important personage popped in a really messy way. Whatever, huge book contracts are on offer to these important personages along with lecture fees lucrative enough to make them all feel good about themselves no matter how big and icky they were as pustules upon the body politic. Gosh, what nostalgia one feels for the mere sloth of the Reagan era when the chief executive snoozed his way

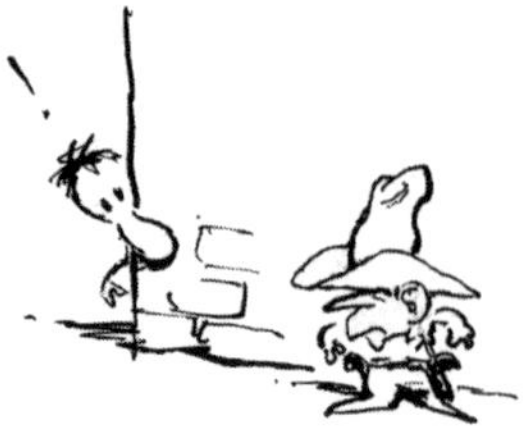

through cabinet meetings or for the simple lust and gluttony of the Clinton administration. But I digress.

The point here is that there's nothing illustrated in this exhibition that most Americans wouldn't gladly do if Pat Oliphant—with his uniquely sensitive perception of evil, malfeasance, and greed—wasn't showing us that these things stink. Pat is all that stands between us and idiocy and jerkdom (and, alas, lucrative lecture fees). Pat takes the raw material of our sin and forges it into seething indignation. As with so much of the manufacturing sector, America no longer produces seething indignation. We've had to outsource it to an Aussie wetback.

Actually Pat Oliphant claims to be American himself these days (and the Bush family claims to be Texan). But let's not drop a dime on Pat. Let's not call the Department of Homeland Security and turn him in. Pat arrived from Adelaide in 1964 before Homeland Security had been created to guard our borders against terror, presumably including that terror we have of feeling bad about ourselves. And, anyway, as I already pointed out, Pat doesn't make us feel bad about ourselves the way he would if we were jerks, which, as I also already pointed out, isn't our fault. Try this experiment: Gather a group of run-of-the-mill Americans, such as the would-be '08 Republican presidential candidates who participated in the first TV debate (Americans don't get any more run-of-the-mill than this), and ask them, "How many of you don't believe in evolution?" NBC did perform this experiment and three Republican candidates raised their hands, and it definitely wasn't their fault because when they lowered their hands their knuckles dragged on the ground. Everybody who watched the debate thought, "Wow, this is like an Oliphant cartoon!" And that's one way Pat makes us feel good about ourselves. He's a genius, and we noticed. This makes us junior or assistant geniuses.

Being a genius, Pat has a number of brilliant techniques to differentiate Good from Bad. For one thing he has developed a philosophy that can be drawn. It is almost impossible to draw Existentialism or Logical Positivism or Kant's Critique of Pure Reason. Cutting a picture of Neo-Platonism out of the newspaper and putting it on your refrigerator door with a decorative magnet will give you some idea of how brilliant Pat's technique is.

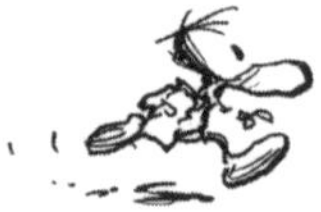

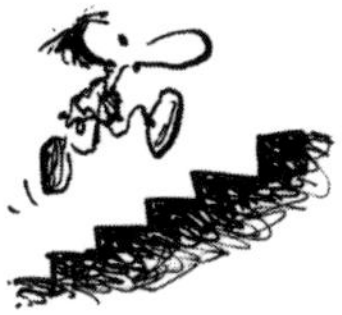

Pat draws Bad large and unattractive and doing things that aren't nice. He draws Good very small in a corner making wry comments to a miniature penguin. The miniature penguin, by the way, is named Punk.

Some people have a theory that Punk is God because Punk says the kind of things that God must say when politics put God into an exasperated celestial editorial cartoonist mood, which must be pretty often. For instance, in a cartoon that Pat drew at the time of the 2001 presidential inauguration, Hillary and Bill are shown absconding from the White House with the silver, the china, and the kitchen sink. Smally drawn Good says, "Well, the Clinton legacy is secure." And Punk says, "Just so they never come back." However, an omniscient God should have foreseen the '08 Hillary campaign. And, for that matter, so should have Pat.

Other people think Punk is God because in Oliphant cartoons where Bad is doing things that really, really aren't nice, such as descending in the form of the Four Horsemen of the Apocalypse on the women and children of Sudan, Punk is nowhere to be found. I say who can blame him. Although I'm not sure that "God—who can blame him?" is sound theology. Anyway Punk never comes back in the next cartoon with a new commandment like "Feel good about yourself."

Personally I don't think God talks to Pat or manifests himself as Punk, as long as Pat and Punk keep taking their meds. I think the secret to Pat's uniquely sensitive perception of evil, malfeasance, and greed is that deep down inside he's an old softie, a kindhearted fellow, a nice guy, too damn nice, wouldn't swat a fly, wouldn't so much as lift a finger, wouldn't lift a finger no matter what, even if he can lick everybody in the room with one hand tied behind... etc. Pat himself will say something to this effect from time to time.

Then there is the matter of Pat's balanced approach to the issues of the day. Some critics have claimed that Pat leans to the left. But he has been known to stagger to the right as well, and also to go facedown, and to fall over backwards too. Taken altogether and mathematically averaged Pat's stance is balanced. Furthermore it is the stance that the issues of the day demand. That is, I've noticed that along

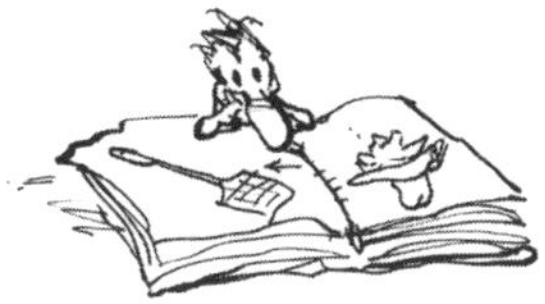

about six p.m. I myself begin to lean to the left, stagger to the right, and go facedown. The difference is that by the cocktail hour Pat—who is on an old-fashioned newspaper deadline—is finished with his job while I—a self-unemployed freelancer—am just beginning mine.

This is why Pat's work shows greater moral clarity than my work. That and the fact that Pat has morals. I don't. I'm a Republican. I was full of morals during the Clinton-Lewinsky scandal, but then I invested all my moral capital in the rising political stock of George W. Bush, Dick Cheney, and the Iraq War, and now I'm ethically broke. But I'm digressing again.

You can tell Pat has morals because he's a vegetarian. Not that there's anything particularly moral, as far as I'm concerned, about eating innocent fruits and helpless vegetables and nuts and berries that have done no harm to anyone. But the true purpose of having morals is to annoy people. Fussing about food gives Pat an opportunity to annoy people three times a day, making sure that the Welsh in the Welsh rarebit were organic free-range Welsh and so forth. Meanwhile it's only once a day that I open my newspaper and see a dash of ink and a dab of words about George W. Bush, Dick Cheney, and the Iraq War and get annoyed that I'm morally bankrupt. Except, excuse me, I almost forgot that I'm not annoyed by Pat's morals or vegetarianism. Because he's a genius, and just being in the presence of genius makes us feel good about ourselves. Doesn't it?

Pat's rule about vegetarianism is that he won't consume "anything with a face." He is fibbing. There is a face right on a bottle of Old Granddad. Furthermore I've seen Pat tuck into a lobster with a mug that was more intelligent, sensitive, and decent looking than any politico Pat skewers.

Pat agrees. He says to imagine a restaurant with a big tank up front and swimming in the tank is Vladimir Putin, Al Sharpton, and Mark Foley. Nobody who walked into that restaurant would ever be able to eat again. But this is a rare example of Pat agreeing about anything to do with politics. Usually there's no winning a political argument with Pat Oliphant.

I might say something like, "Politicians are asses."

He'll say, "The ass is a noble, patient, long-suffering animal."

I'll say, "I'm talking anatomy—what the special interests are kissing."

He'll say, "You want lobbyists to kiss politicians on the *lips*?! That's *truly* disgusting!"

"You're right," I'll say. "They're not asses, they're snakes."

"You're wrong," he'll say. "Show me a snake with a hand to grasp from the poor or a foot to tread on the helpless."

"Call them bloodsucking leeches," I'll say.

"You're giving poor, wiggling little *Hirudo medicinalis* a bad name. He's been thought for centuries to have curative powers. Indeed, you're insulting the whole animal kingdom."

"Then they're troglodytes! Neanderthals!"

And Pat will say, "I see no evidence of transcendent and redeeming art on the cave walls of their politics."

The transcendent and redeeming art—that would be the stuff Pat does. Well, to tell the truth, I don't know enough about art (or transcendence or redemption) to go that far. But Pat's cartoons are awful damn good.

Most political cartoonists lampoon important personages by emphasizing a few prominent physical characteristics, mostly so we'll know who the hell it is they're drawing. The meaning of a political cartoon where Nancy Pelosi and Kim Jung Il look exactly alike is confusing, even when each is carefully labeled. Most political cartoonists are also making fun of those important personages. Don Imus has a hat

that's ha! ha! ha! ha! But Pat Oliphant's cartoons serve a different purpose.

Pat's heightenings, embellishments, enhancements, and hyperboles illustrate what the imps and fiends of hell will be doing to these future denizens of the netherworld's VIP lounge.

If an Oliphant character is gross in size it's not for the purpose of Oliver Hardy risibility. The villain has grown with the flesh of pride, with the obesity of power. He's gained the weight necessary to make a wonderful, splattering fry-up when he's dipped into the boiling pitch. If an Oliphant character is all arms and legs, gangling in awkward stretches and tangles, it's not for the sake of a Stan Laurel pratfall. This is a prefiguring of torture on the rack, where the bastard will be yanked and stretched to cover the full distance between his avowed principles and his actual practices. Pat doesn't draw George W. Bush's ears big to make us laugh at George. This is the size to which demons will need to stretch those auditory apparatuses to make George hear a single word of reproof.

Pat Oliphant makes us feel good about ourselves—comparatively speaking. Surely we'll go to a better part of hell than his important personages. And it's nice to have those personages suffering the agonies of eternal damnation right there on our refrigerator attached with decorative magnets.

There is, however, one small worry. Pat could run out of important personages to attack with seething indignation or he could get tired of attacking them. Then he might turn his uniquely sensitive perception of evil, malfeasance, and greed on us and start drawing cartoons about the way *we* behave. Worse yet, it might occur to Pat that this is a free country and a democracy and that the asses and arses and snakes and leeches and Neanderthals that he's been drawing owe their power and position to you and me— we who are drawn very small in a corner making wry comments to a miniature penguin. Then we won't feel good about ourselves at all.

But do not panic. I have a plan. Let's hold a lot of art exhibitions in prestigious venues featuring Pat's work and ensuring his reputation as a genius. We'll turn Pat into a National Treasure.

Nobody listens to National Treasures. In fact usually we assume they're already dead, like that National Treasure Senator Joe Lieberman. Oh? He isn't? Well you get the idea. What we do is praise Pat Oliphant so loudly that we can't hear anything that Pat says to us. That way we're safe from finding out that we're idiots and jerks and it's nobody's fault but our own. This is an ancient method of dealing with people who have a uniquely sensitive perception of evil, malfeasance, and greed. It dates back at least to St. Simeon Stylites in Syria in the fifth century A.D. St. Simeon Stylites was a mighty prophet, revealing the whole of human folly, forging a whole bunch of seething indignation—his era's equivalent of a hard-hitting editorial cartoonist. He spent the last thirty-five years of his life living on top of a sixty-foot pillar being revered as a National Treasure. What was he doing on top of the sixty-foot pillar? We chased him up there.

P. J. O'Rourke is an author whose latest book, On the Wealth of Nations, *has been published by Grove/Atlantic Press.*

Cartoons and Sketches

1.
The Departure
January 24, 2001

The Clintons, seen here leaving 1600 Pennsylvania Avenue in January 2001, took with them most items that were not nailed down. Nothing so well became their term in office as the manner of their leaving.

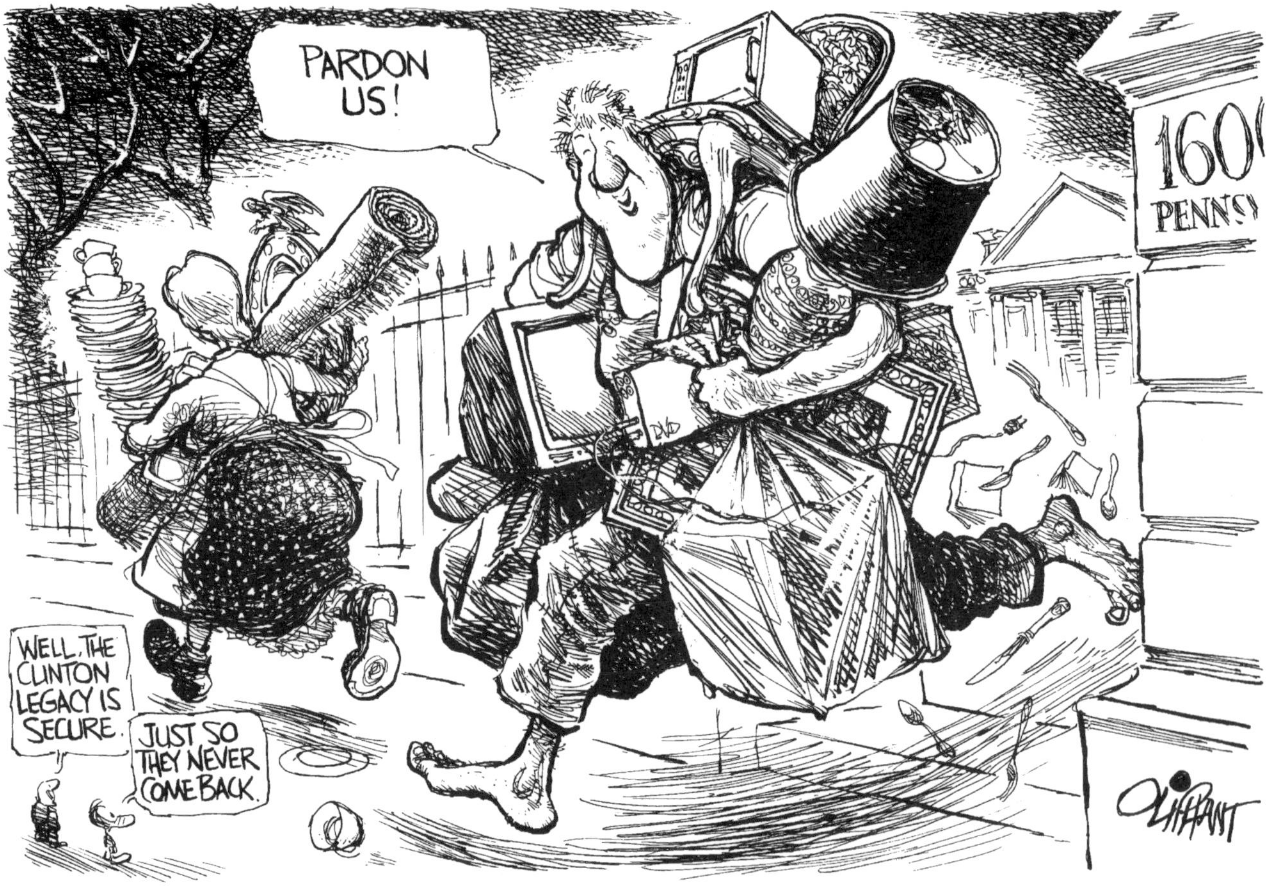
PARDON US!
1600 PENNS
WELL, THE CLINTON LEGACY IS SECURE.
JUST SO THEY NEVER COME BACK.
DVD
OLIPHANT

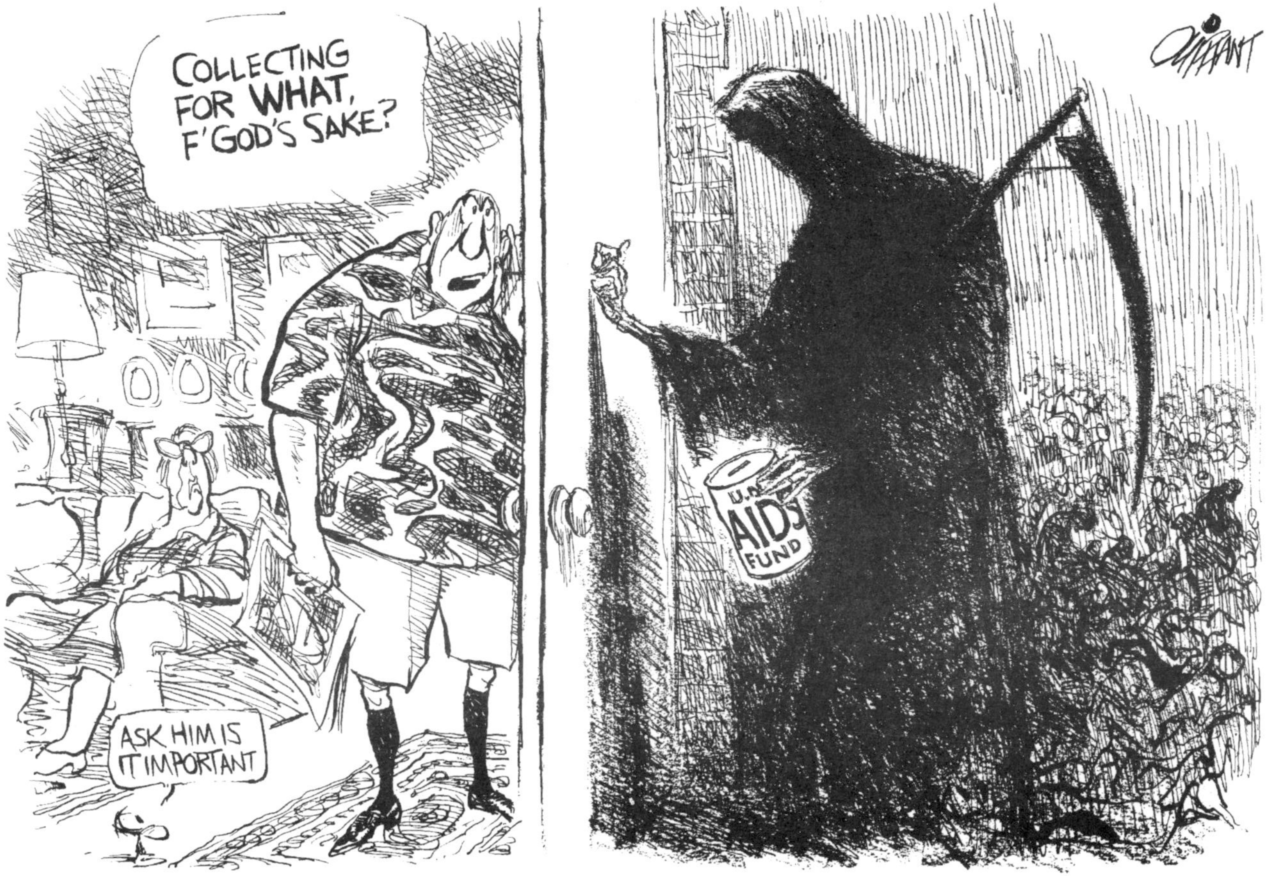
COLLECTING FOR WHAT, F'GOD'S SAKE?
ASK HIM IS IT IMPORTANT
AIDS
FUND

2.
Knock, Knock
June 26, 2001

An intrusion from the world outside.

3.
Nine Eleven
September 13, 2001

The World Trade Center in
New York was destroyed by
terrorists.

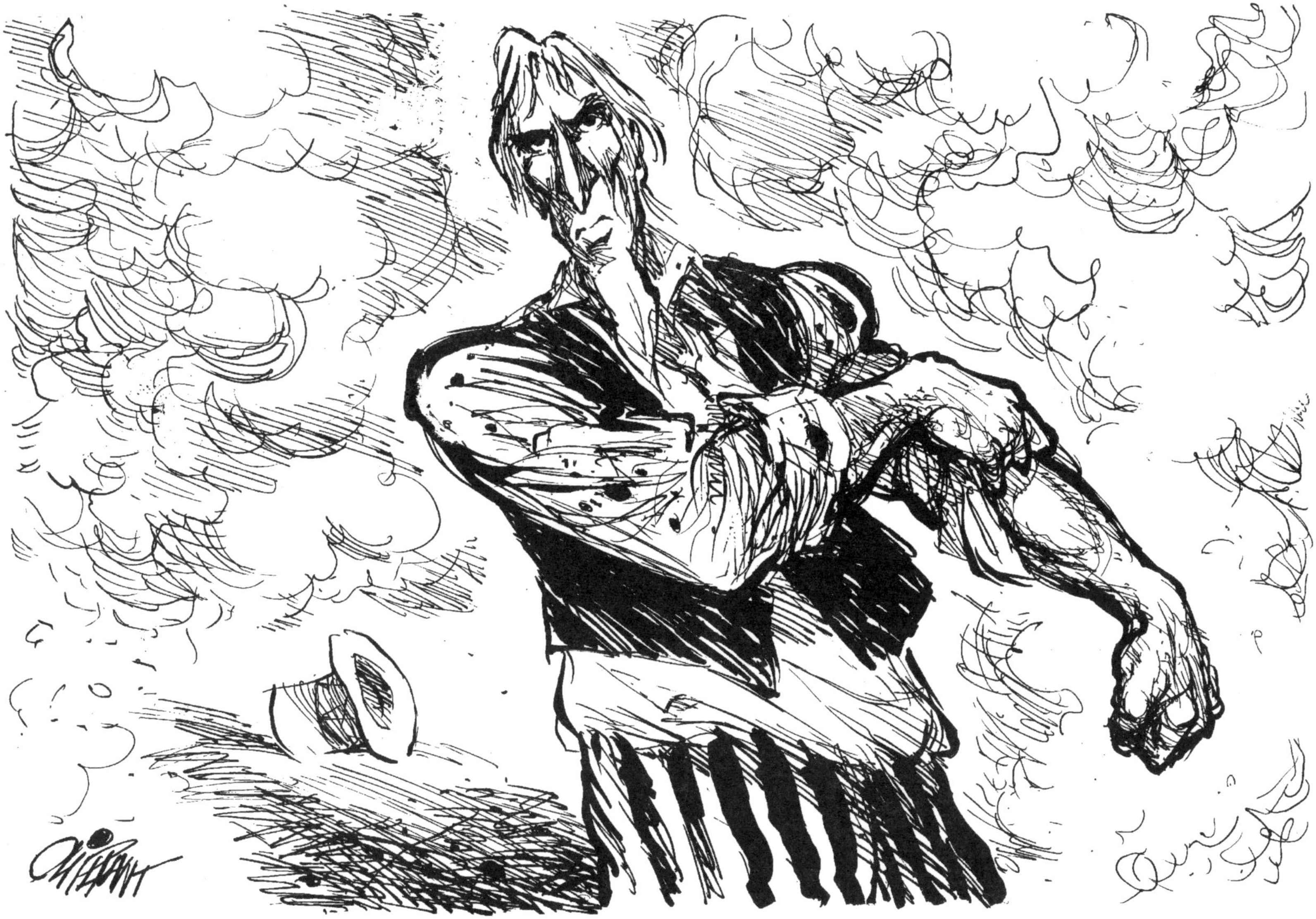

4.
Celebration of Spring
March 20, 2002

The revelations of sexual abuse committed by a large section of the Roman Catholic Church clergy, shocking as they were, came as no real surprise to those who had heard rumors of such things for many years. Those revelations, and the subsequent investigations, set the stage for a whole plethora of cartoons on the subject. Cartoons need villains for targets, and these need not always be politicians. And the depiction of evil in a drawing is always aided by massed areas of black, counterpoint to large areas of light; or, in this case one could say, masses of priests played opposite large areas of altar boys.

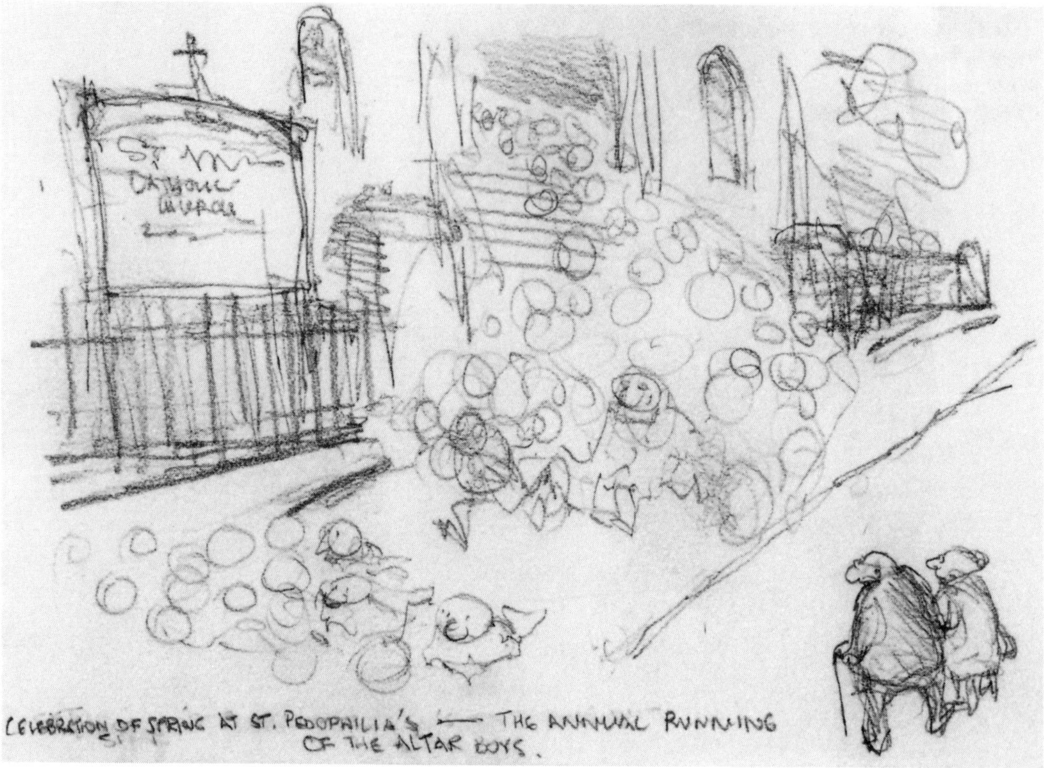
CELEBRATION OF SPRING AT ST. PEDOPHILIA'S ← THE ANNUAL RUNNING
OF THE ALTAR BOYS.

Preliminary sketch for
Celebration of Spring
Graphite on paper

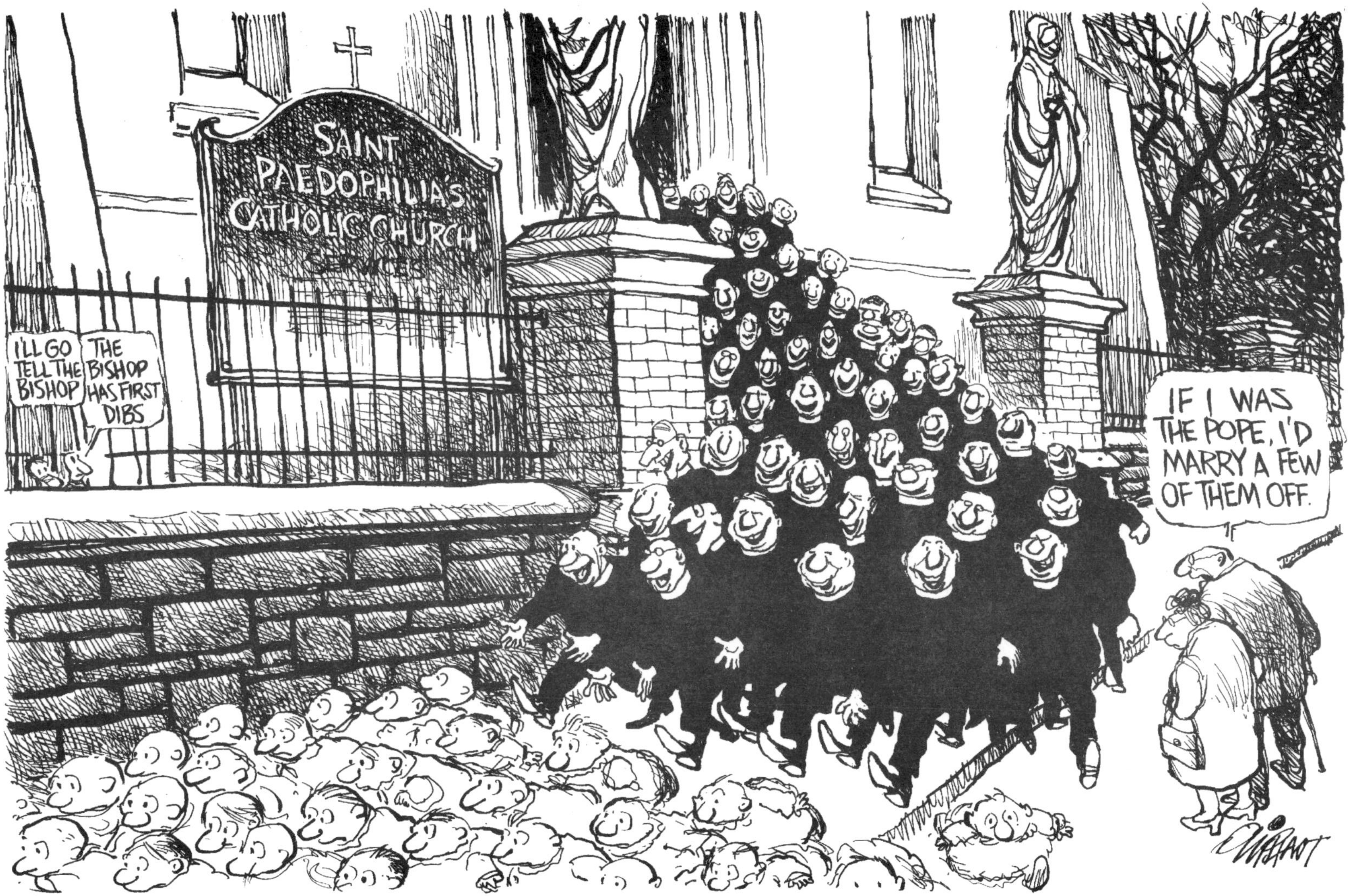
SAINT PAEDOPHILIA'S CATHOLIC CHURCH
SERVICES
I'LL GO TELL THE BISHOP
THE BISHOP HAS FIRST DIBS
IF I WAS THE POPE, I'D MARRY A FEW OF THEM OFF.

CELEBRATION OF SPRING AT ST. PAEDOPHILIA'S—THE ANNUAL RUNNING OF THE ALTAR BOYS.

5.

Stop Arguing and Charge

August 27, 2002

Against the admonitory advice of more thoughtful souls, George W. Bush prepared to charge blindly into a battle in Iraq, which was to become his own Little Bighorn.

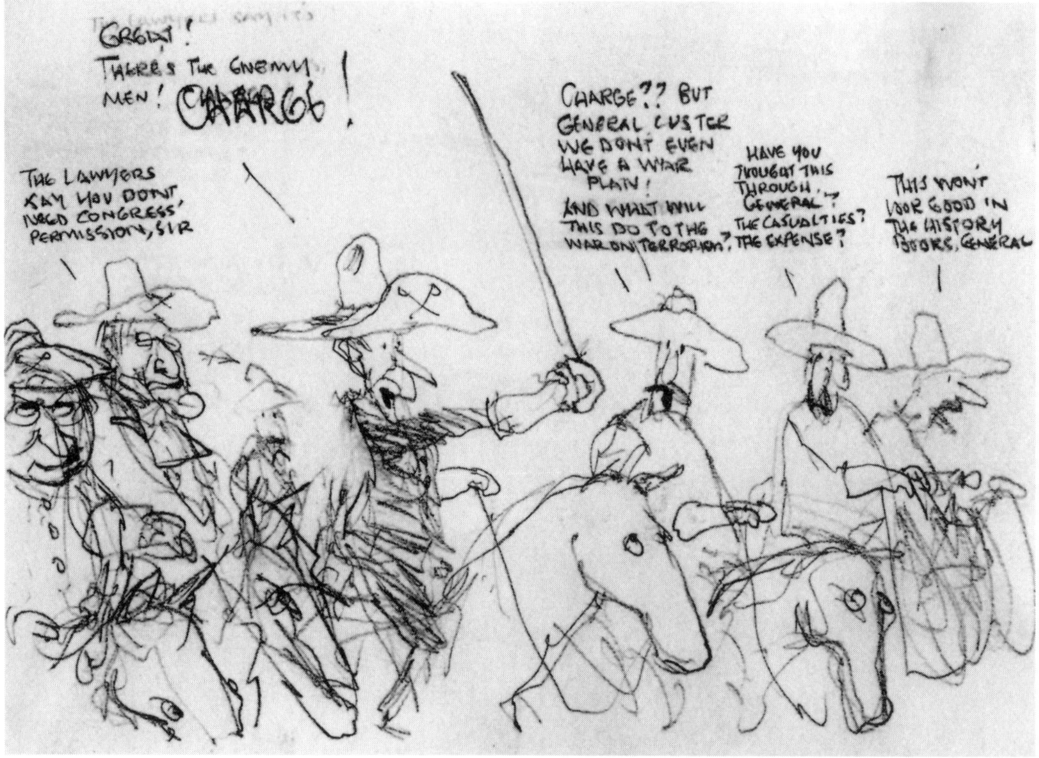

GREAT! THERE'S THE ENEMY MEN! CHARGE!
THE LAWYERS SAY YOU DON'T NEED CONGRESS' PERMISSION, SIR
CHARGE?? BUT GENERAL CUSTER WE DON'T EVEN HAVE A WAR PLAN! AND WHAT WILL THIS DO TO THE WAR ON TERRORISM?
HAVE YOU THOUGHT THIS THROUGH, GENERAL? THE CASUALTIES? THE EXPENSE?
THIS WON'T LOOK GOOD IN THE HISTORY BOOKS, GENERAL

Preliminary sketch for
Stop Arguing and Charge
Graphite on paper

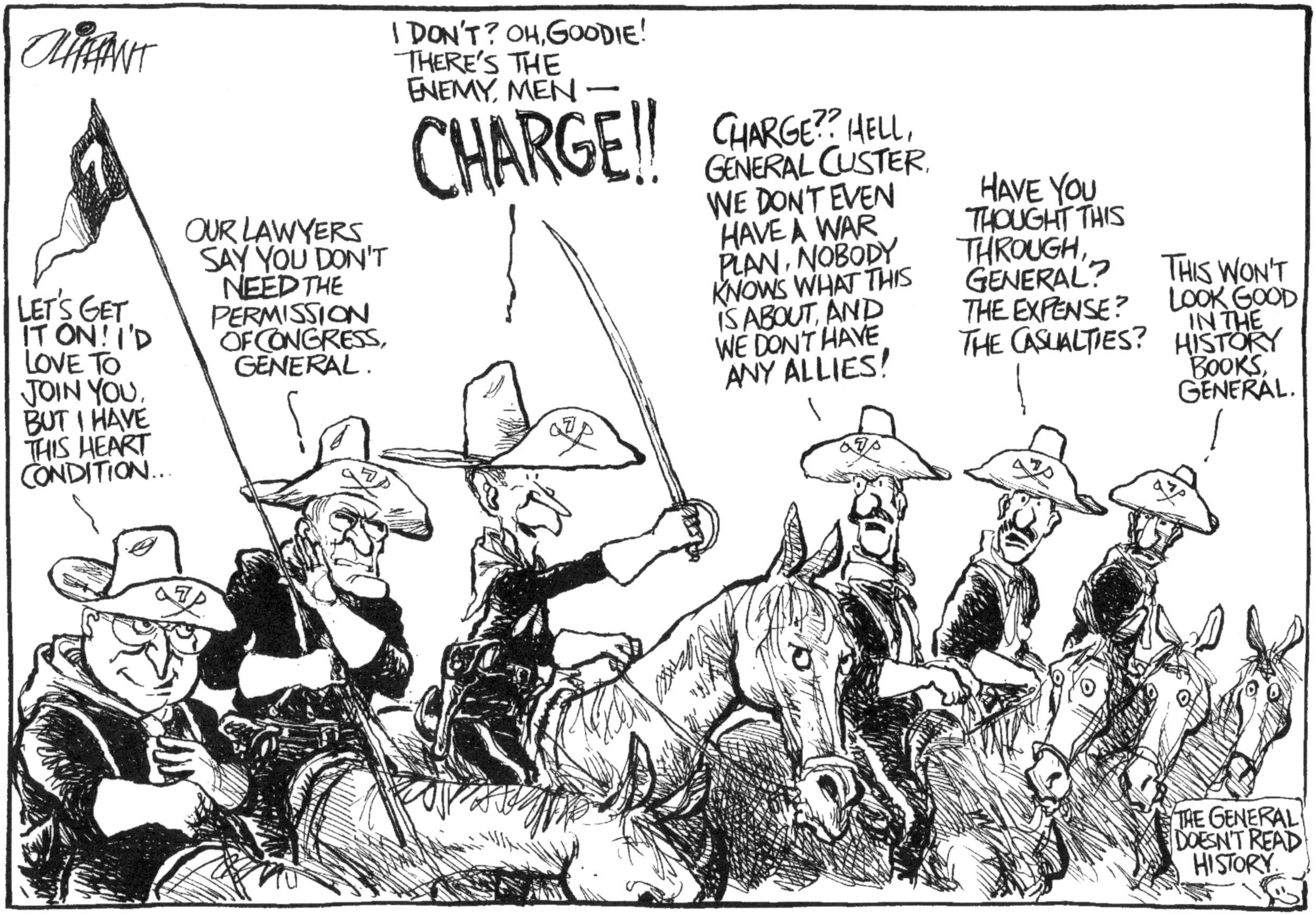
OLIPHANT
LET'S GET IT ON! I'D LOVE TO JOIN YOU, BUT I HAVE THIS HEART CONDITION...
OUR LAWYERS SAY YOU DON'T NEED THE PERMISSION OF CONGRESS, GENERAL.
I DON'T? OH, GOODIE! THERE'S THE ENEMY, MEN — CHARGE!!
CHARGE?? HELL, GENERAL CUSTER, WE DON'T EVEN HAVE A WAR PLAN, NOBODY KNOWS WHAT THIS IS ABOUT, AND WE DON'T HAVE ANY ALLIES!
HAVE YOU THOUGHT THIS THROUGH, GENERAL? THE EXPENSE? THE CASUALTIES?
THIS WON'T LOOK GOOD IN THE HISTORY BOOKS, GENERAL.
THE GENERAL DOESN'T READ HISTORY.

6.
Good Doggie!
October 7, 2002

The Democrats, true to form, performed their duties flawlessly.

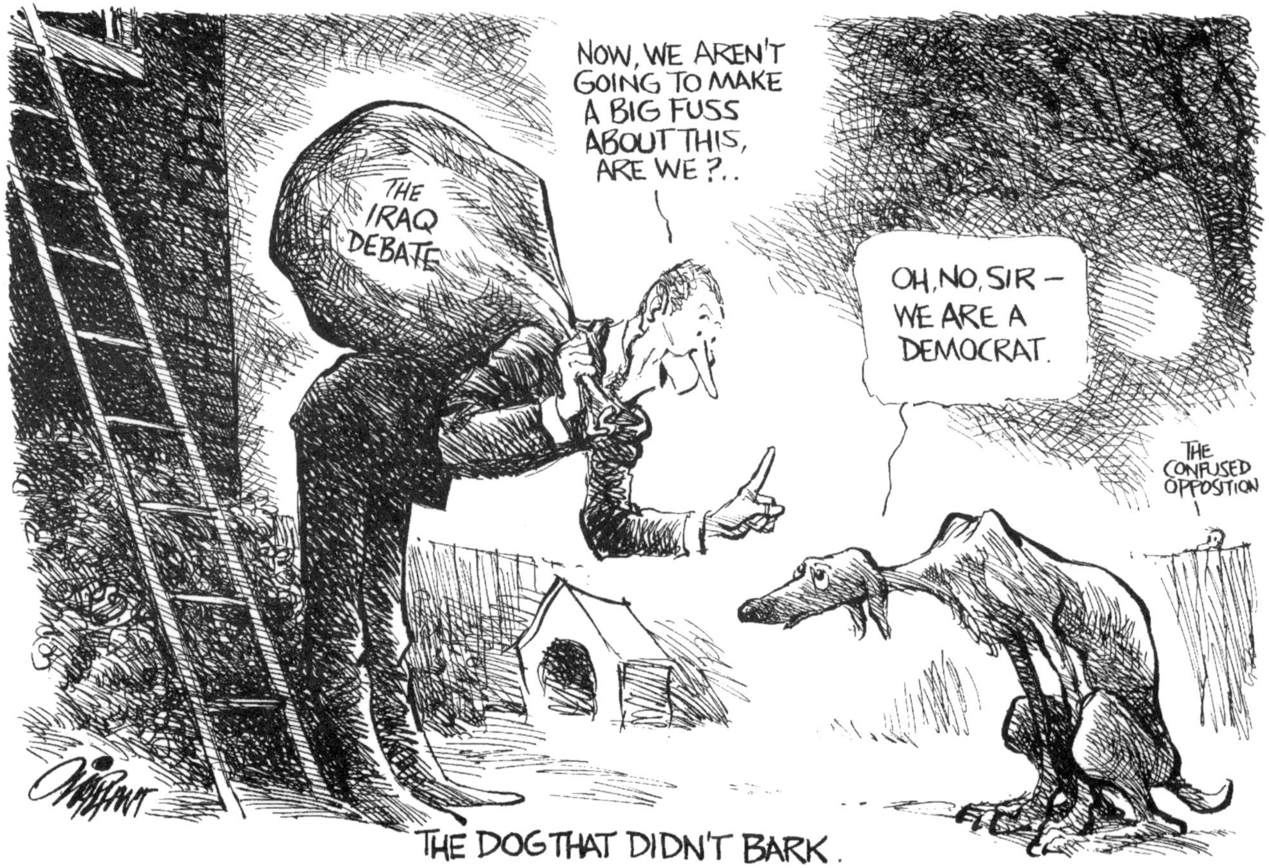
THE IRAQ DEBATE
NOW, WE AREN'T GOING TO MAKE A BIG FUSS ABOUT THIS, ARE WE ?..
OH, NO, SIR – WE ARE A DEMOCRAT.
THE CONFUSED OPPOSITION
THE DOG THAT DIDN'T BARK.

7.

And the Winner Is . . .

April 8, 2003

Why, Vice President Cheney's old company, Halliburton, no less.

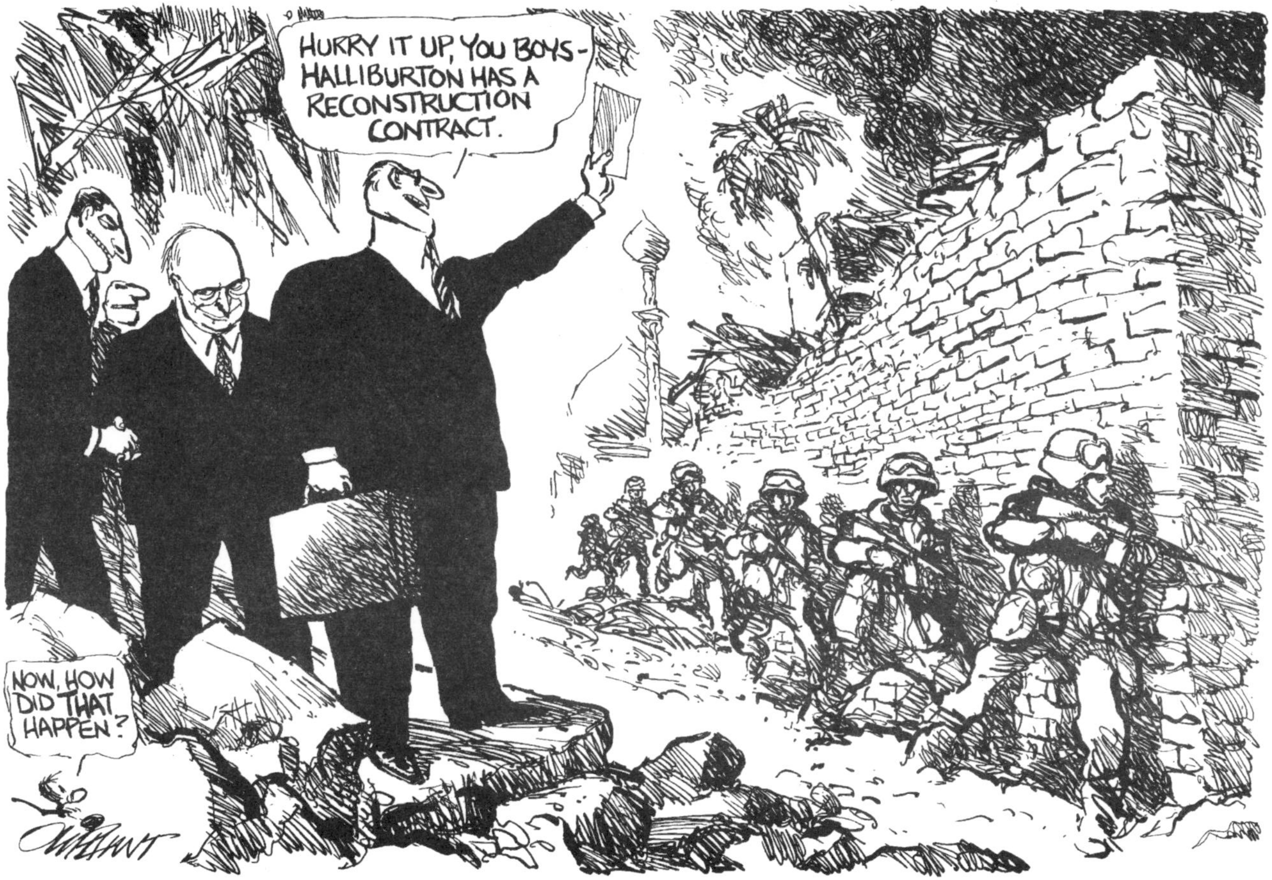
HURRY IT UP, YOU BOYS - HALLIBURTON HAS A RECONSTRUCTION CONTRACT.
NOW, HOW DID THAT HAPPEN?

8.
Right On, Mr. Blix
June 17, 2003

Chief U.N. weapons inspector Hans Blix searched Iraq fruitlessly for the weapons of mass destruction that Saddam Hussein reportedly possessed. Mr. Blix, in frustration, lashed out at "bastards in Washington" who he said consistently undermined his efforts and pressured his staff to tailor their reports to fit the Bush Administration's views and aims.

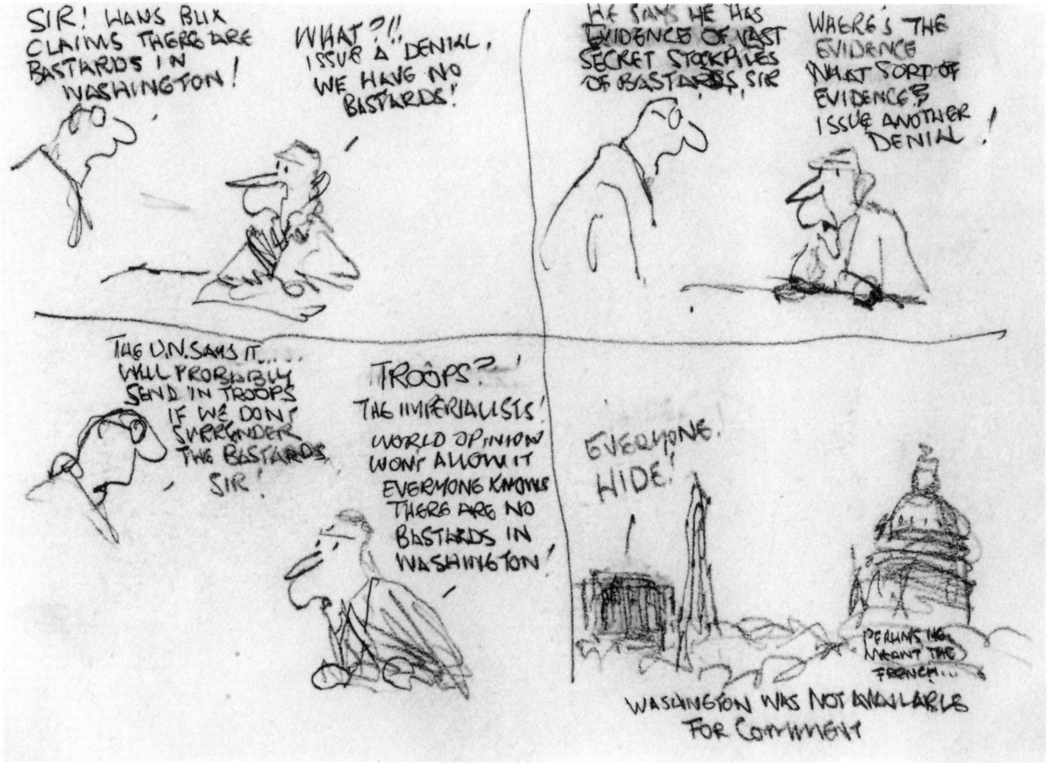
SIR! HANS BLIX CLAIMS THERE ARE BASTARDS IN WASHINGTON!
WHAT?!! ISSUE A DENIAL, WE HAVE NO BASTARDS!
HE SAYS HE HAS EVIDENCE OF VAST SECRET STOCKPILES OF BASTARDS, SIR
WHERE'S THE EVIDENCE WHAT SORT OF EVIDENCE? ISSUE ANOTHER DENIAL!
THE U.N. SAYS IT... WILL PROBABLY SEND IN TROOPS IF WE DON'T SURRENDER THE BASTARDS SIR!
TROOPS?! THE IMPERIALISTS! WORLD OPINION WON'T ALLOW IT EVERYONE KNOWS THERE ARE NO BASTARDS IN WASHINGTON!
EVERYONE HIDE!
PERHAPS HE MEANT THE FRENCH...
WASHINGTON WAS NOT AVAILABLE FOR COMMENT

Preliminary sketch for
Right On, Mr. Blix
Graphite on paper

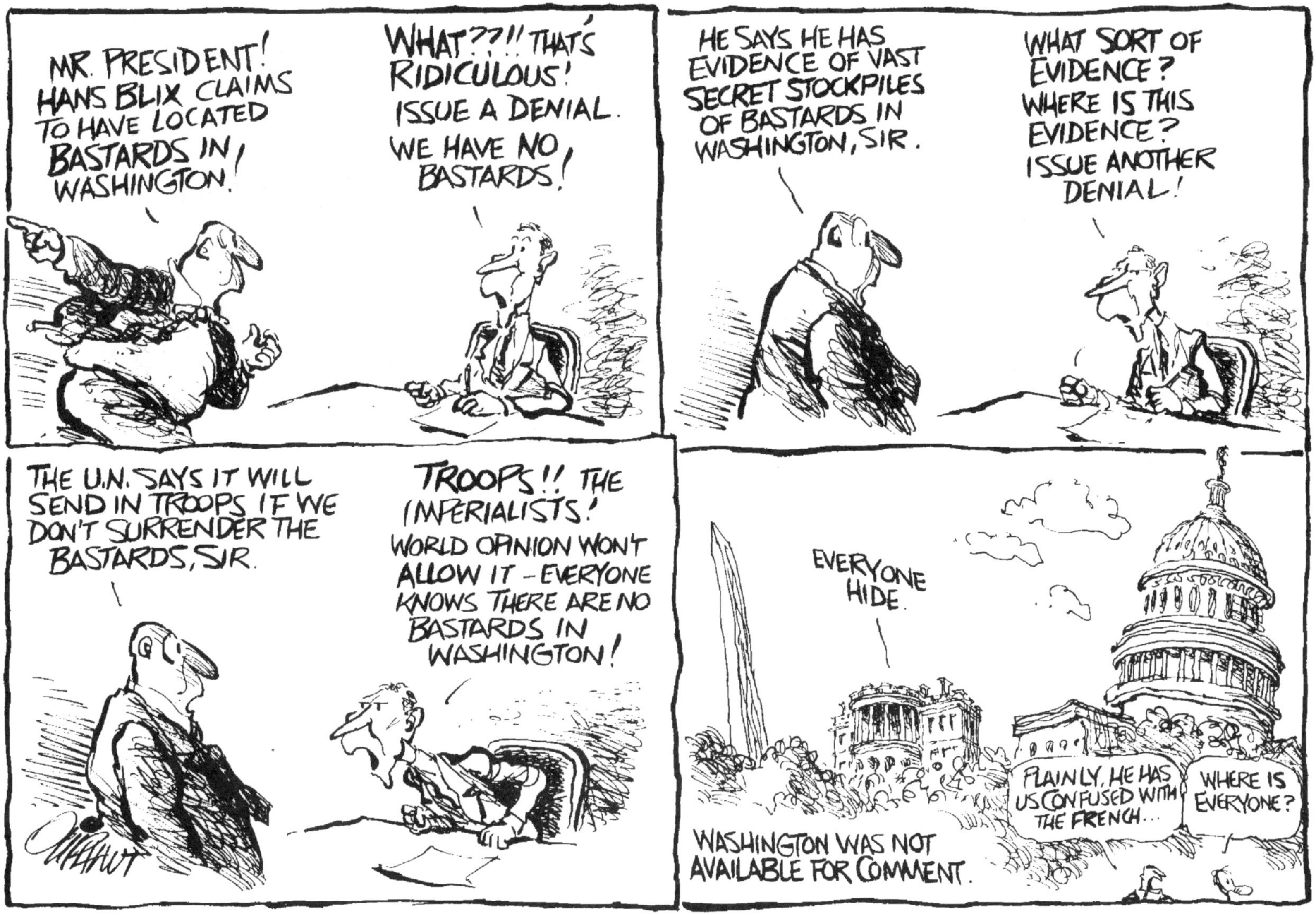
MR. PRESIDENT! HANS BLIX CLAIMS TO HAVE LOCATED BASTARDS IN WASHINGTON!
WHAT??!! THAT'S RIDICULOUS! ISSUE A DENIAL. WE HAVE NO BASTARDS!
HE SAYS HE HAS EVIDENCE OF VAST SECRET STOCKPILES OF BASTARDS IN WASHINGTON, SIR.
WHAT SORT OF EVIDENCE? WHERE IS THIS EVIDENCE? ISSUE ANOTHER DENIAL!
THE U.N. SAYS IT WILL SEND IN TROOPS IF WE DON'T SURRENDER THE BASTARDS, SIR.
TROOPS!! THE IMPERIALISTS! WORLD OPINION WON'T ALLOW IT - EVERYONE KNOWS THERE ARE NO BASTARDS IN WASHINGTON!
OLIPHANT
EVERYONE HIDE.
PLAINLY, HE HAS US CONFUSED WITH THE FRENCH...
WHERE IS EVERYONE?
WASHINGTON WAS NOT AVAILABLE FOR COMMENT.

9.

The Deprived

June 18, 2003

Kinder, gentler President Bush signed the Tax Relief Bill for the Rich.

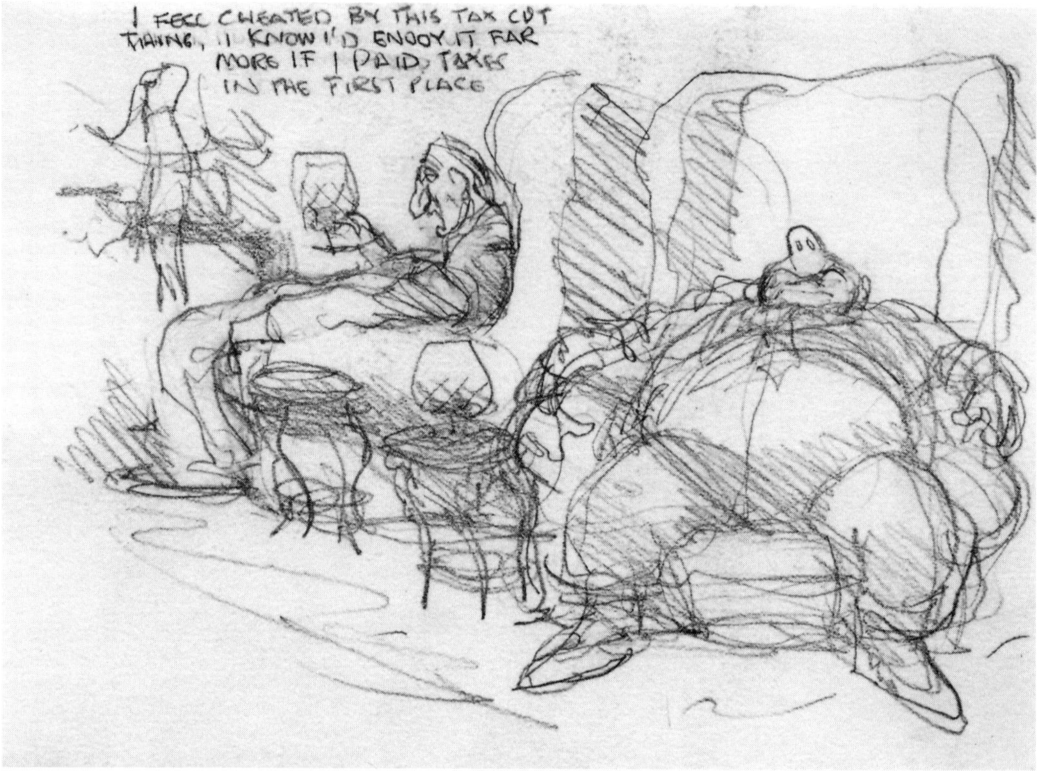
I FEEL CHEATED BY THIS TAX CUT THING, I KNOW I'D ENJOY IT FAR MORE IF I PAID TAXES IN THE FIRST PLACE

Preliminary sketch for
The Deprived
Graphite on paper

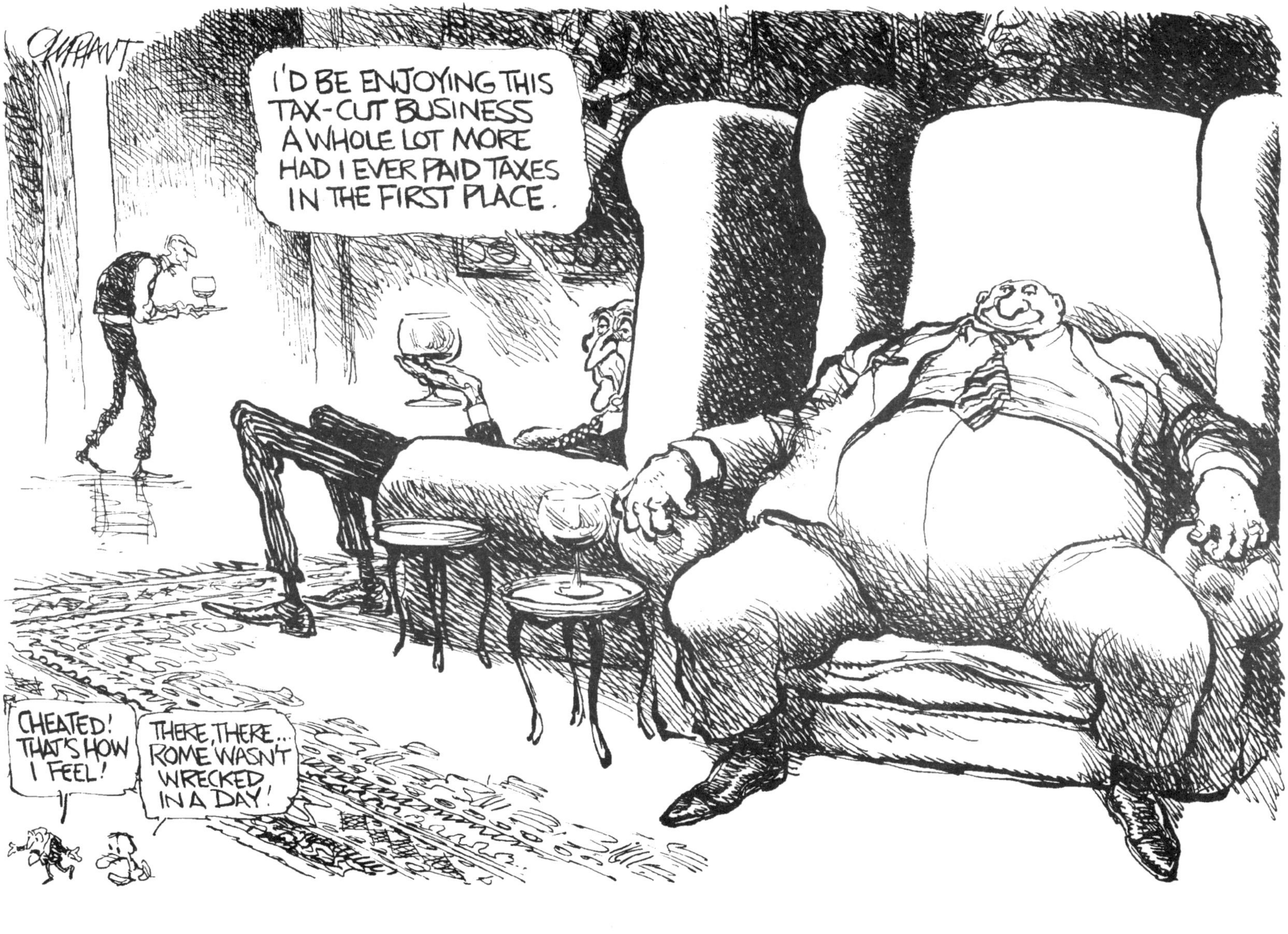
OLIPHANT
I'D BE ENJOYING THIS TAX-CUT BUSINESS A WHOLE LOT MORE HAD I EVER PAID TAXES IN THE FIRST PLACE.
CHEATED! THAT'S HOW I FEEL!
THERE, THERE... ROME WASN'T WRECKED IN A DAY!

10.
A Son to Be Proud Of
June 26, 2003

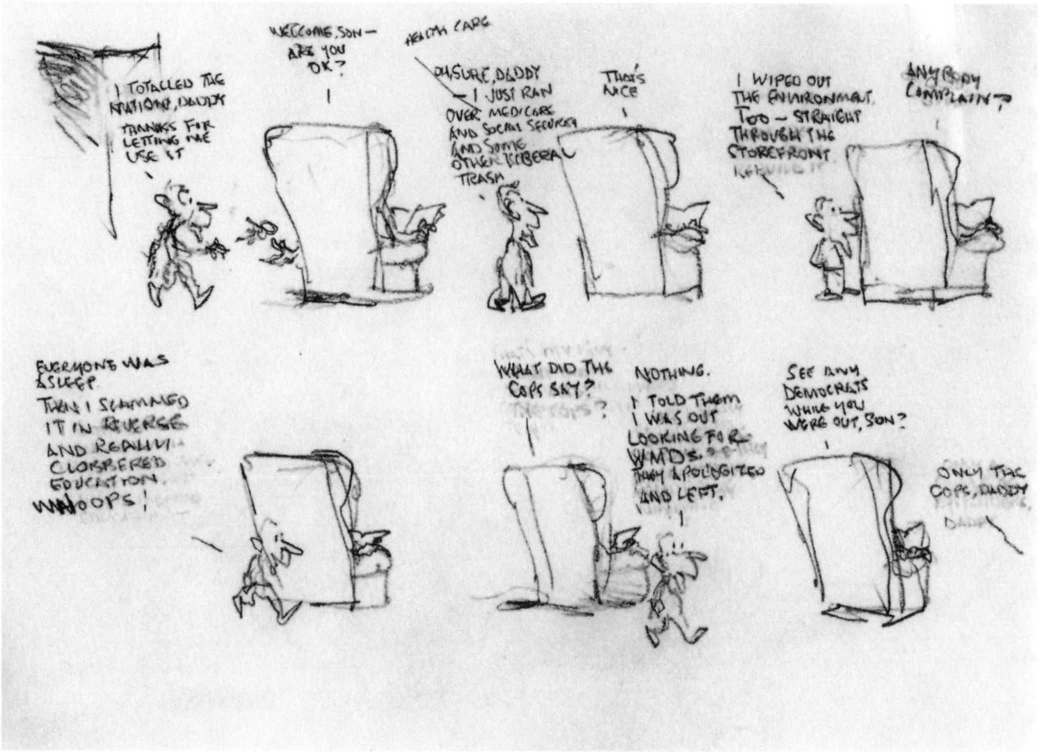
I TOTALLED THE NATION, DADDY
THANKS FOR LETTING ME USE IT
WELCOME, SON — ARE YOU OK?
HEALTH CARE
OH, SURE, DADDY — I JUST RAN OVER MEDICARE AND SOCIAL SECURITY AND SOME OTHER LIBERAL TRASH
THAT'S NICE
I WIPED OUT THE ENVIRONMENT, TOO — STRAIGHT THROUGH THE STOREFRONT
ANYBODY COMPLAIN?
EVERYONE WAS ASLEEP.
THEN I SLAMMED IT IN REVERSE AND REALLY CLOBBERED EDUCATION.
WHOOPS!
WHAT DID THE COPS SAY?
NOTHING.
I TOLD THEM I WAS OUT LOOKING FOR WMD'S.
THEY APOLOGIZED AND LEFT.
SEE ANY DEMOCRATS WHILE YOU WERE OUT, SON?
ONLY THE COPS, DADDY

Preliminary sketch for
A Son to Be Proud Of
Graphite on paper

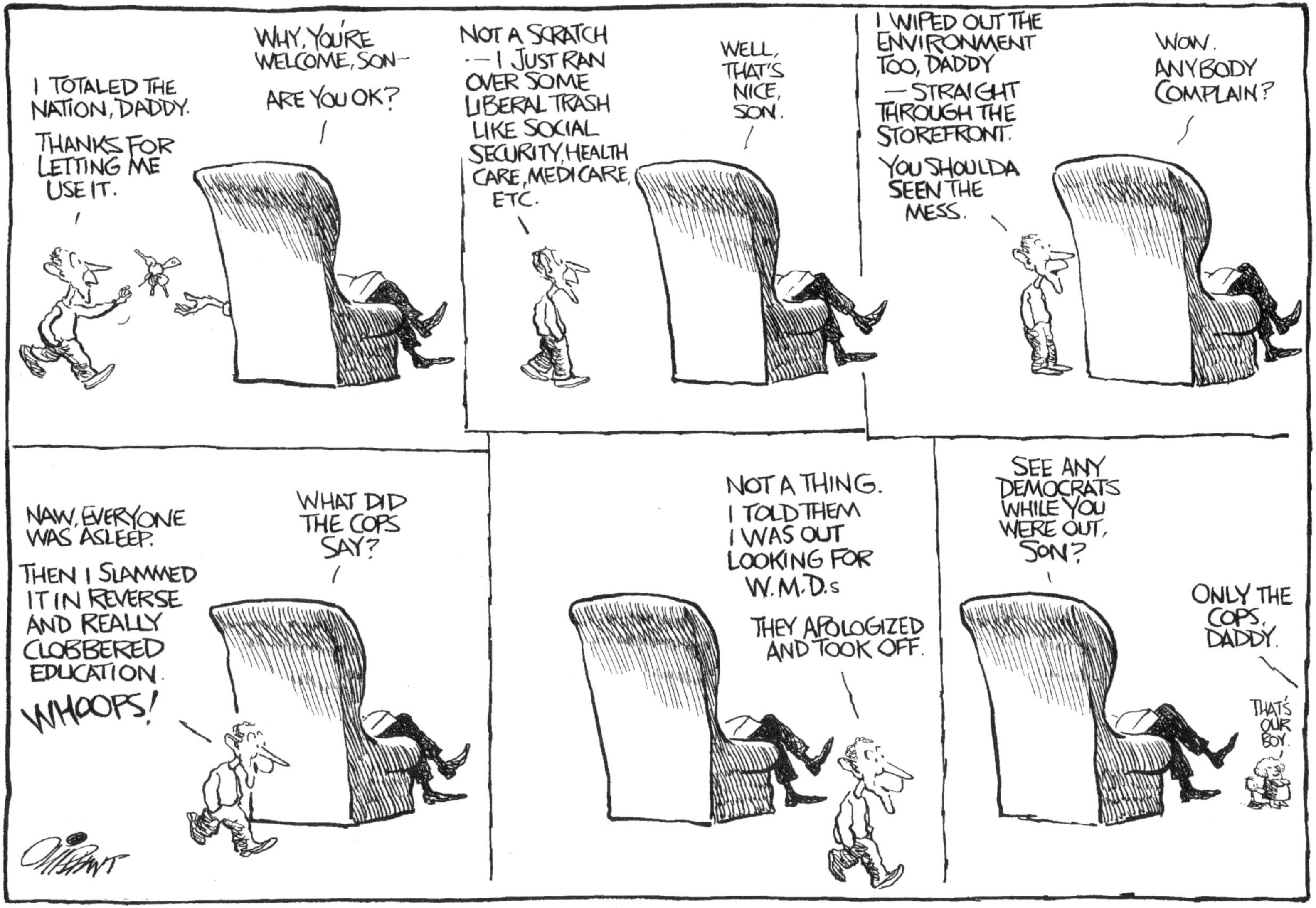
I TOTALED THE NATION, DADDY.
THANKS FOR LETTING ME USE IT.
WHY, YOU'RE WELCOME, SON—
ARE YOU OK?
NOT A SCRATCH — I JUST RAN OVER SOME LIBERAL TRASH LIKE SOCIAL SECURITY, HEALTH CARE, MEDICARE, ETC.
WELL, THAT'S NICE, SON.
I WIPED OUT THE ENVIRONMENT TOO, DADDY — STRAIGHT THROUGH THE STOREFRONT.
YOU SHOULDA SEEN THE MESS.
WOW. ANYBODY COMPLAIN?
NAW, EVERYONE WAS ASLEEP.
THEN I SLAMMED IT IN REVERSE AND REALLY CLOBBERED EDUCATION.
WHOOPS!
WHAT DID THE COPS SAY?
NOT A THING. I TOLD THEM I WAS OUT LOOKING FOR W.M.D.s
THEY APOLOGIZED AND TOOK OFF.
SEE ANY DEMOCRATS WHILE YOU WERE OUT, SON?
ONLY THE COPS, DADDY.
THAT'S OUR BOY.

11.
Take a Number
March 2, 2004

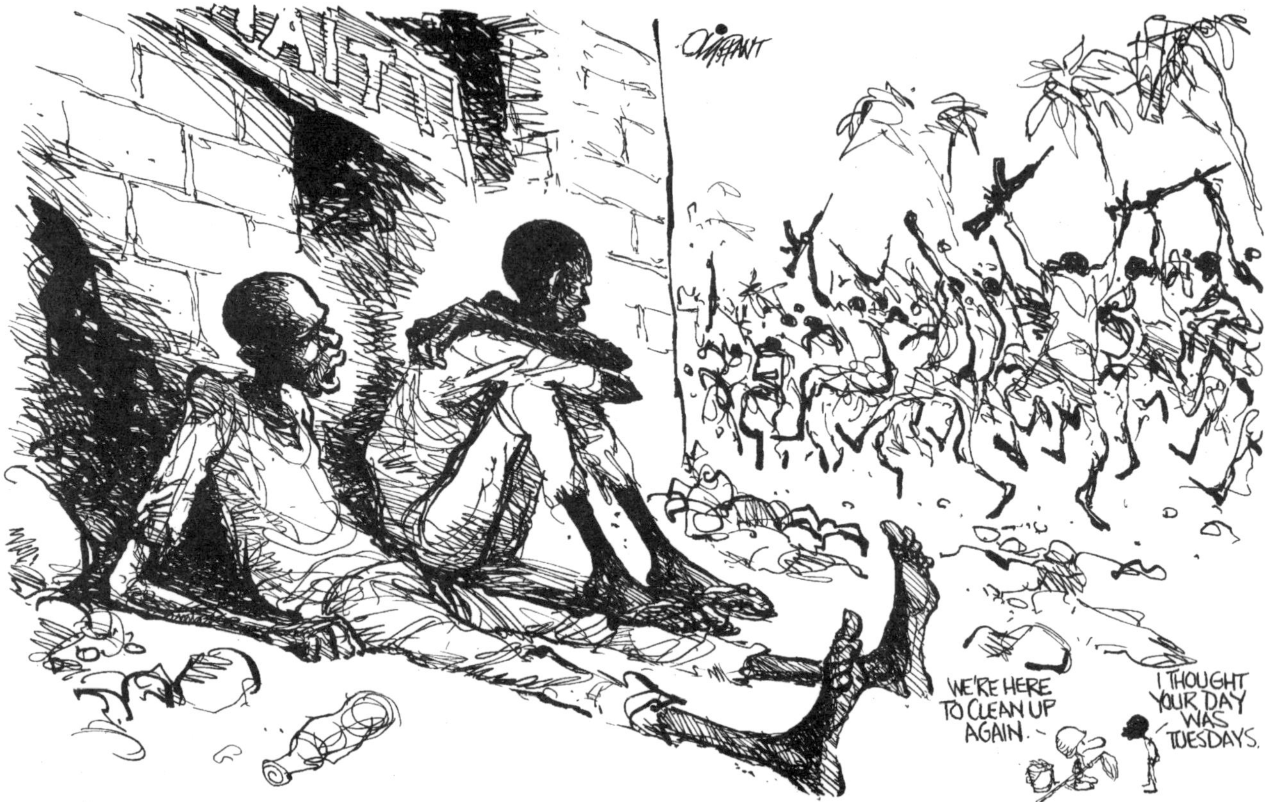
WE'RE HERE TO CLEAN UP AGAIN.
I THOUGHT YOUR DAY WAS TUESDAYS.

'WHO, I WONDER, WILL BE OUR NEXT U.S.-SANCTIONED, DEMOCRATICALLY ELECTED, PROGRESSIVE AND ENLIGHTENED BRUTAL OVERLORD...'

12.
Inspiration
May 24, 2004

A Bush State of the Union address in one compound word.

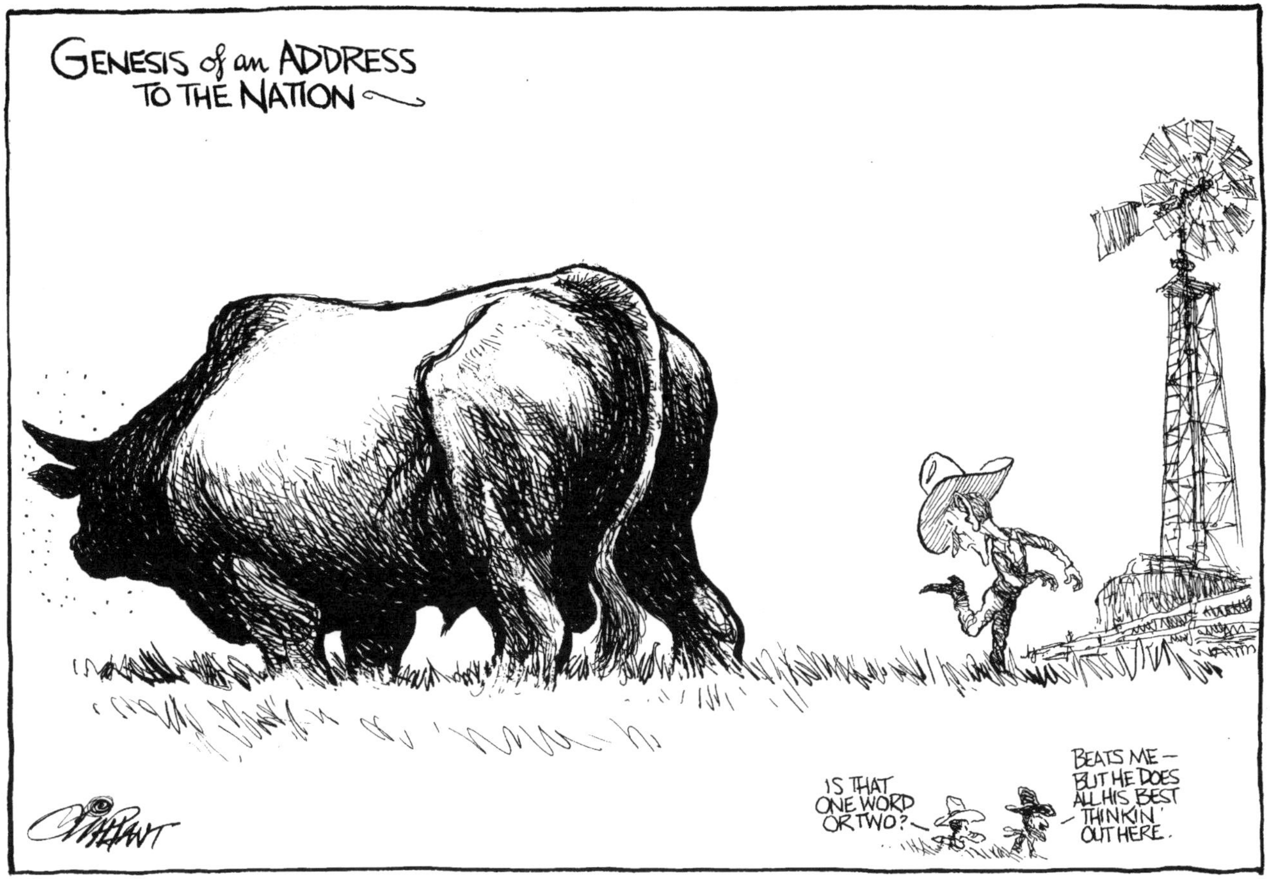
GENESIS of an ADDRESS TO THE NATION
IS THAT ONE WORD OR TWO?
BEATS ME — BUT HE DOES ALL HIS BEST THINKIN' OUT HERE.
OLIPHANT

13.
Say What?
May 17, 2004

Say What? . . . The Kerry campaign in full swing.

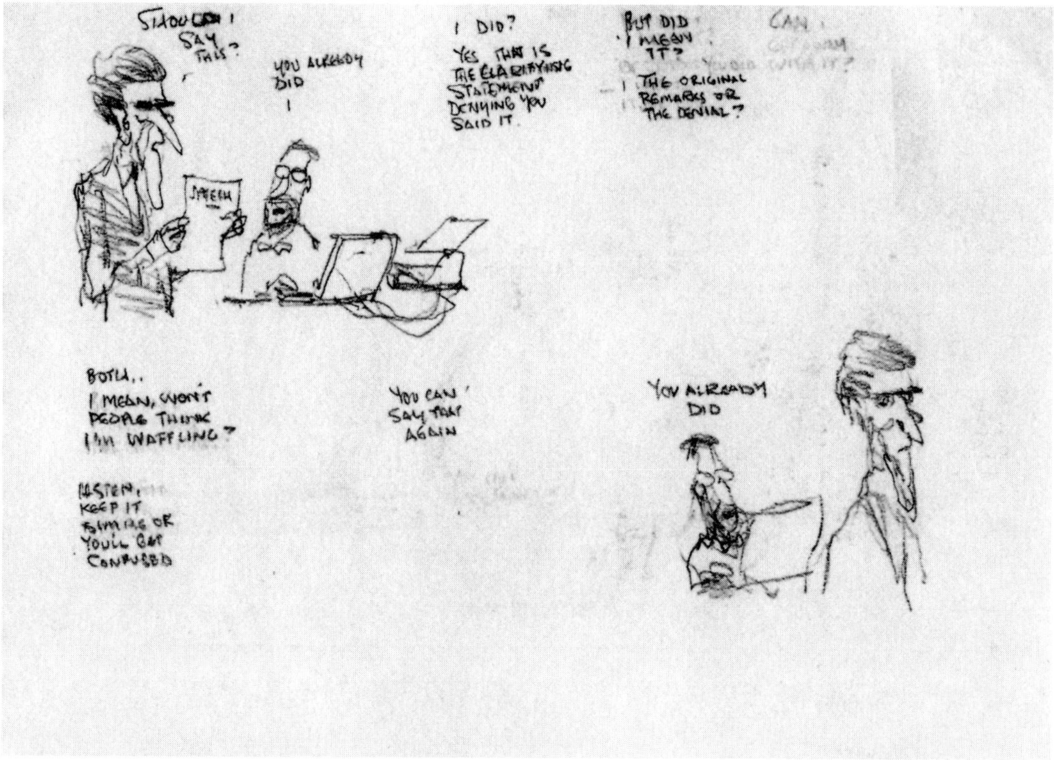
SAY THIS?
YOU ALREADY DID
I DID?
YES THAT IS THE CLARIFYING STATEMENT DENYING YOU SAID IT.
BUT DID I MEAN IT?
THE ORIGINAL REMARKS OR THE DENIAL?
BOTH..
I MEAN, WON'T PEOPLE THINK I'M WAFFLING?
YOU CAN SAY THAT AGAIN
YOU ALREADY DID
LISTEN, KEEP IT SIMPLE OR YOU'LL GET CONFUSED

Preliminary sketch for
Say What?
Graphite on paper

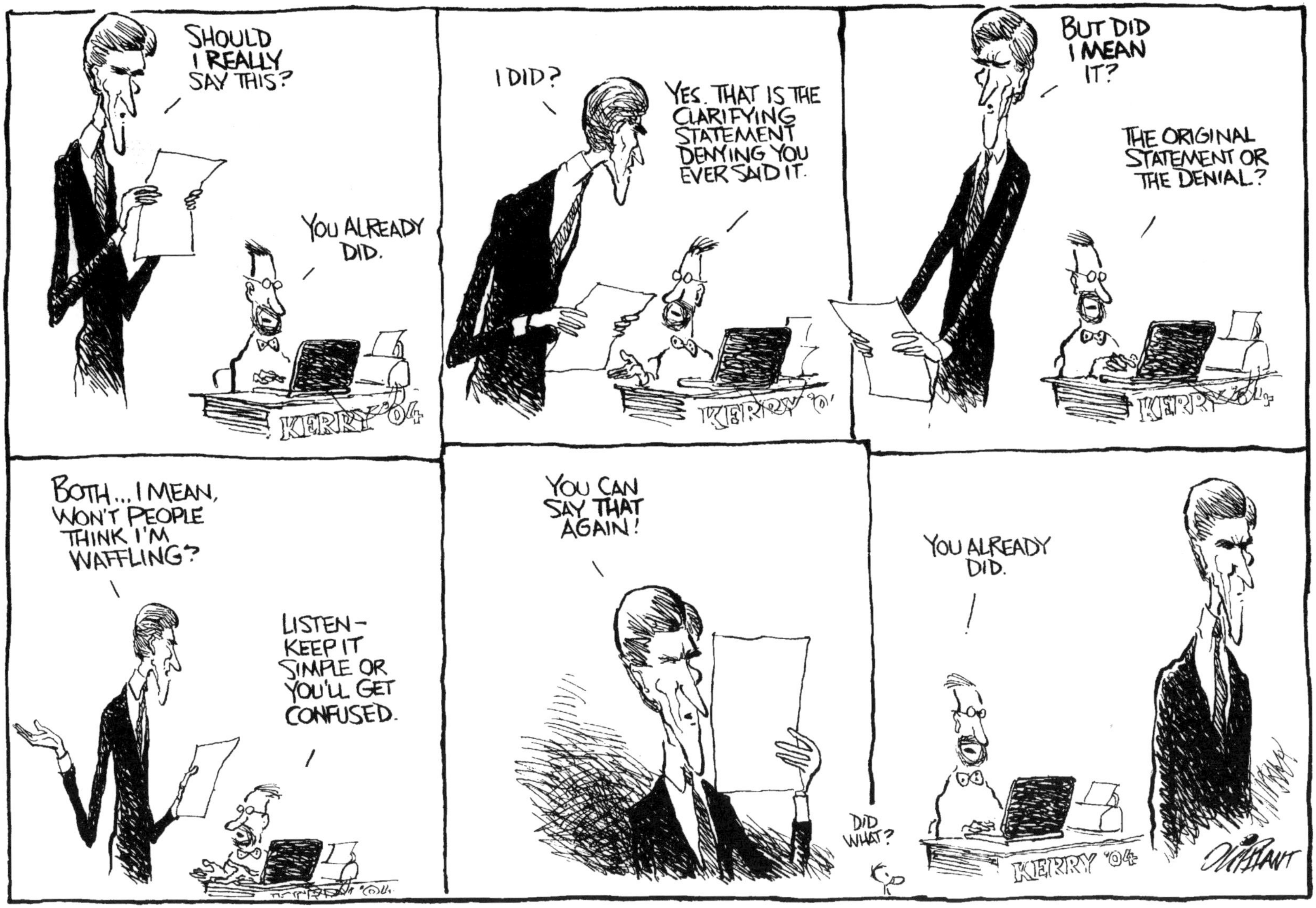
SHOULD I REALLY SAY THIS?
YOU ALREADY DID.
KERRY '04
I DID?
YES. THAT IS THE CLARIFYING STATEMENT DENYING YOU EVER SAID IT.
BUT DID I MEAN IT?
THE ORIGINAL STATEMENT OR THE DENIAL?
BOTH... I MEAN, WON'T PEOPLE THINK I'M WAFFLING?
LISTEN- KEEP IT SIMPLE OR YOU'LL GET CONFUSED.
YOU CAN SAY THAT AGAIN!
YOU ALREADY DID.
DID WHAT?
KERRY '04
OLIPHANT

14.
Last Role
June 7, 2004

Ronald Reagan leaves
the set.

Preliminary sketch for
Last Role
Graphite on paper

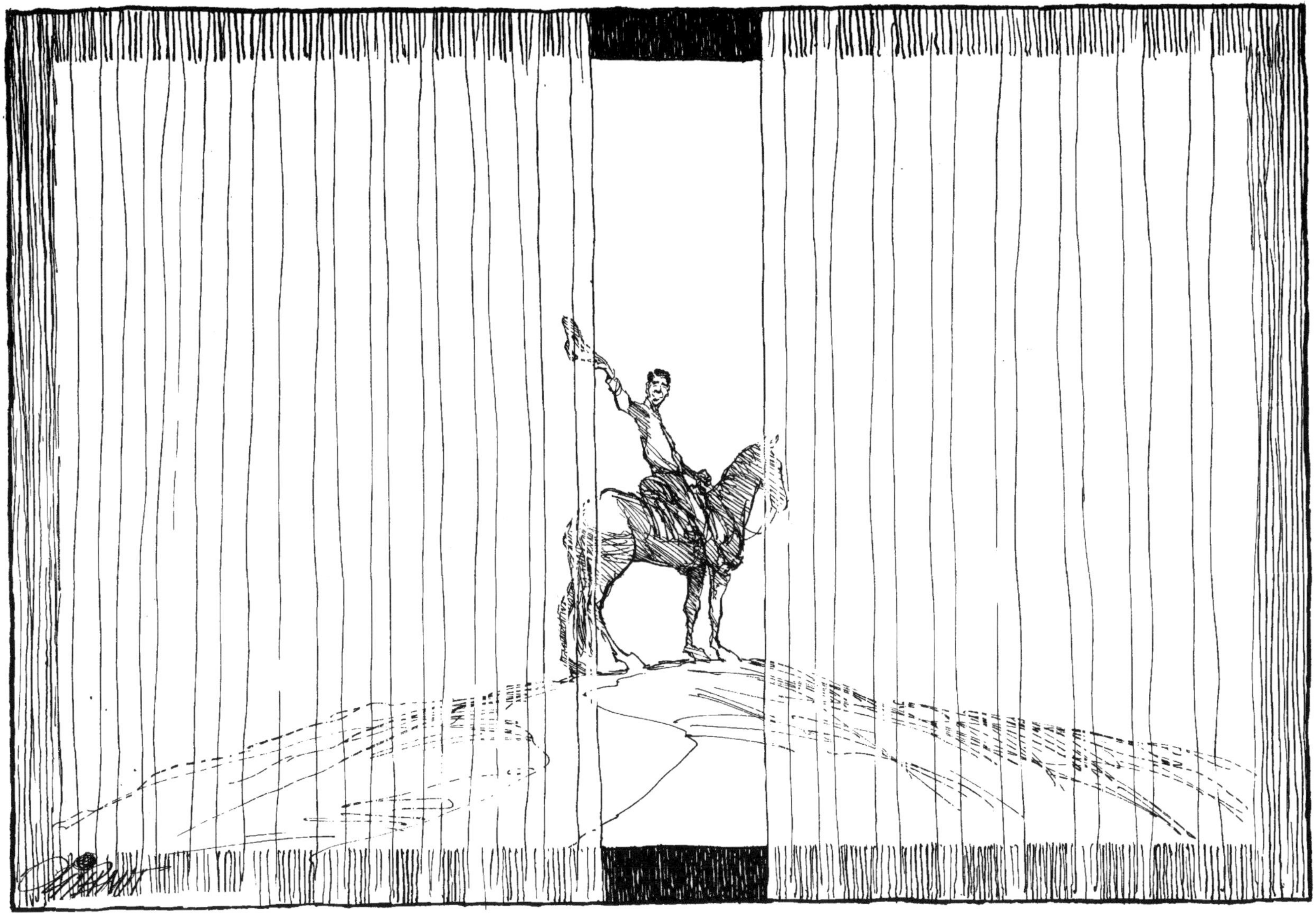

15.
The Eulogizer
June 8, 2004

At his funeral service, Ronald Reagan was eulogized by George W. Bush, who, among other things, became noted for his opposition to stem cell research, that same research which could aid in finding a cure for the affliction that was a contributory factor in the death of Mr. Reagan. Irony is everywhere.

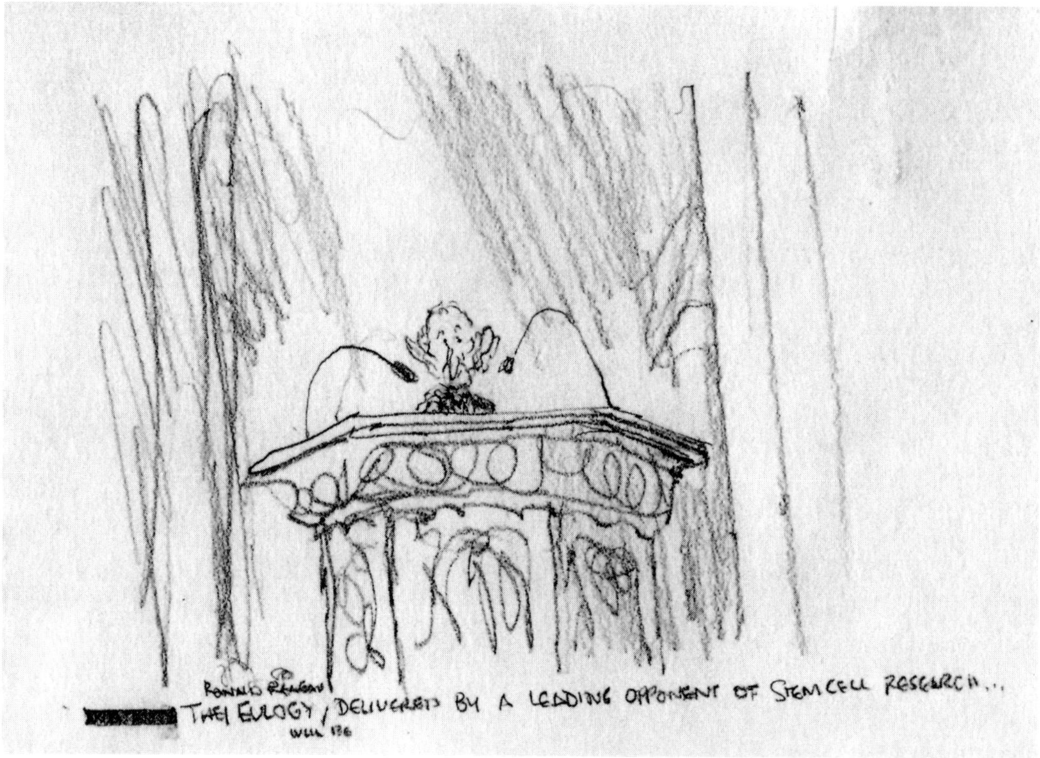
RONALD REAGAN
[redacted] THE EULOGY / DELIVERED BY A LEADING OPPONENT OF STEM CELL RESEARCH...
WILL BE

Preliminary sketch for
The Eulogizer
Graphite on paper

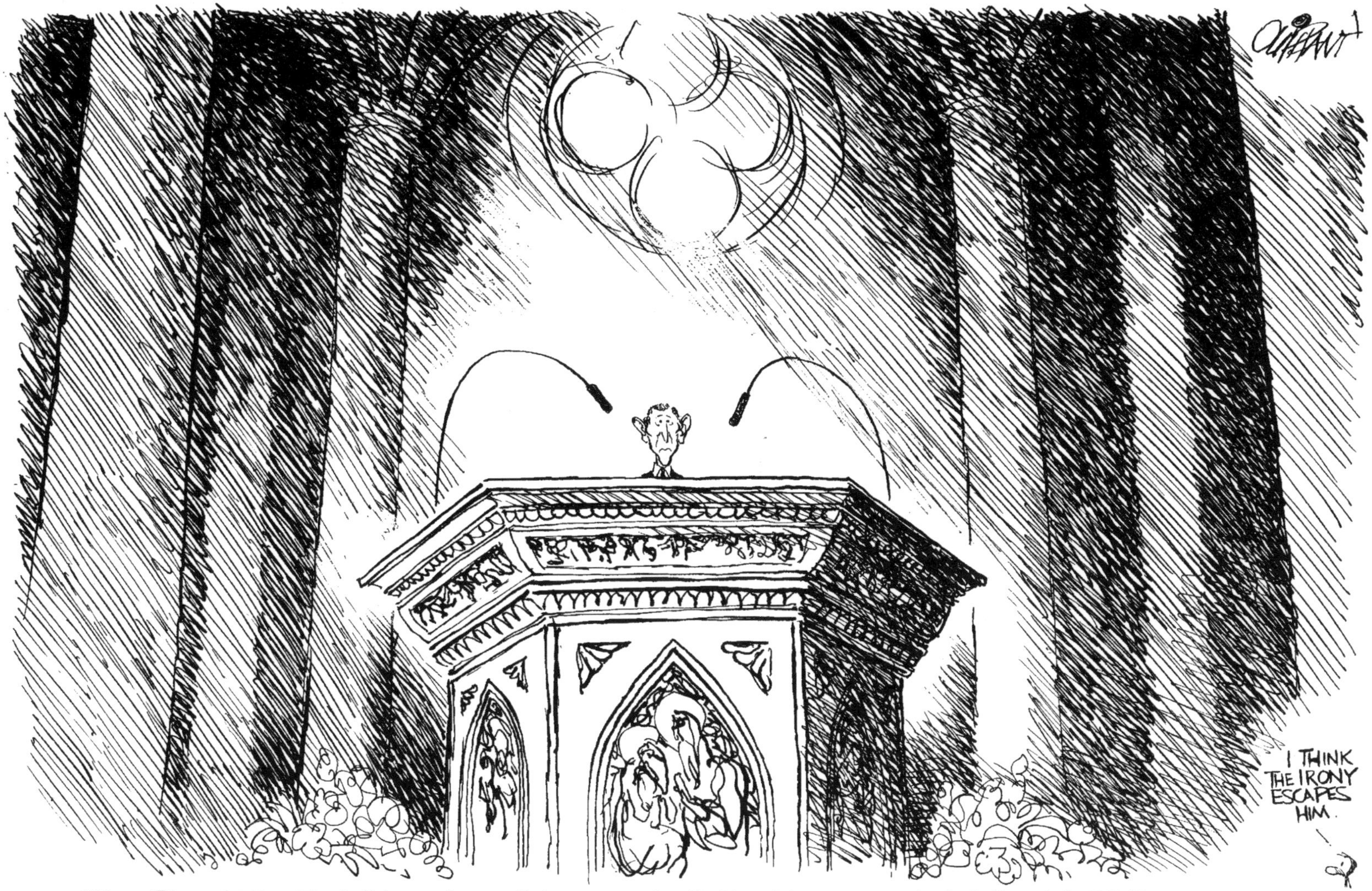
OLIPHANT
I THINK THE IRONY ESCAPES HIM.

THE RONALD REAGAN EULOGY WILL BE DELIVERED BY A LEADING OPPONENT OF STEM CELL RESEARCH.

16.
Legacies
June 15, 2004

Legacies: who gave us what.

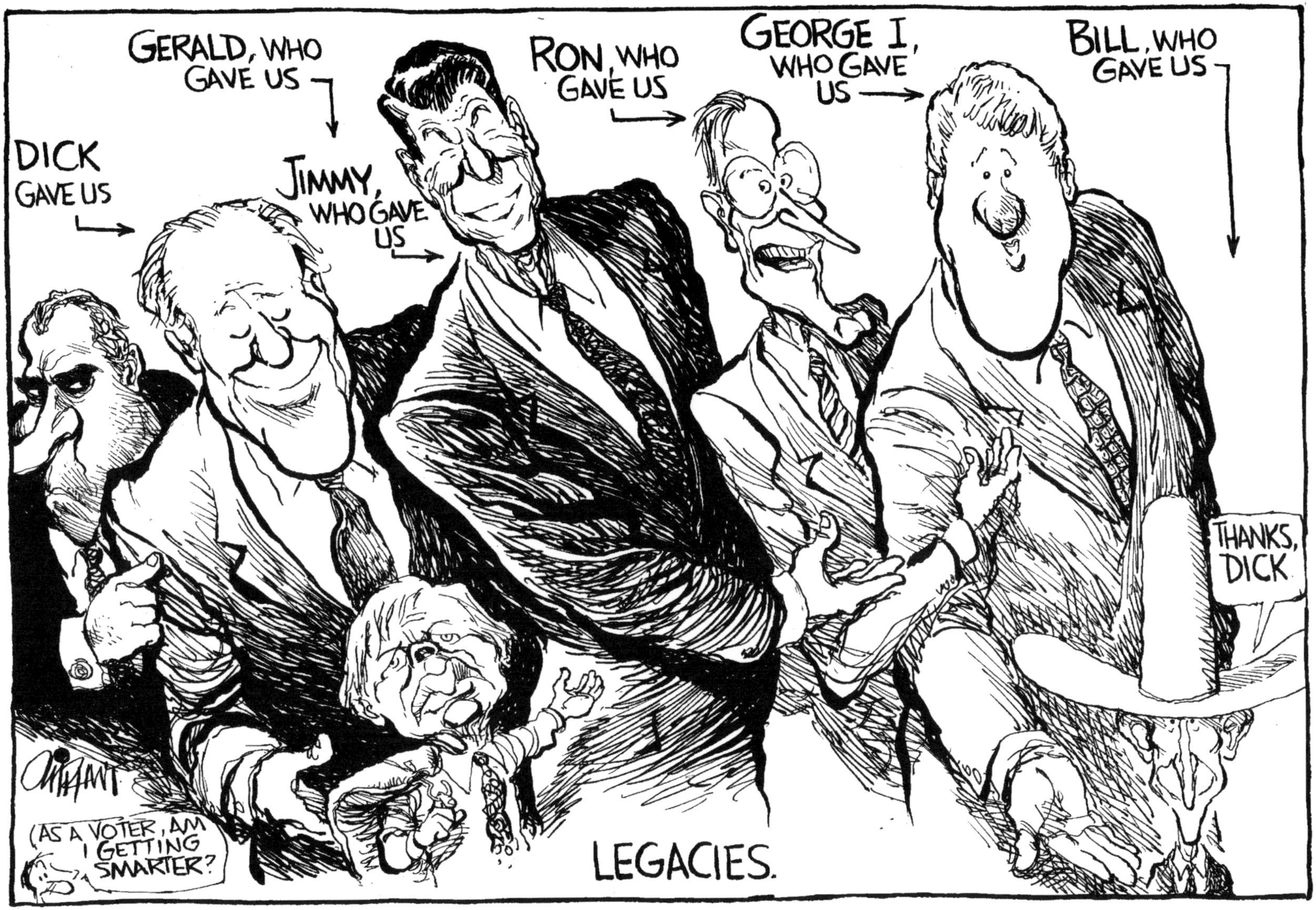
DICK GAVE US
GERALD, WHO GAVE US
JIMMY, WHO GAVE US
RON, WHO GAVE US
GEORGE I, WHO GAVE US
BILL, WHO GAVE US
THANKS, DICK
(AS A VOTER, AM I GETTING SMARTER?
LEGACIES.

17.
Easy
June 22, 2004

Officially sanctioned torture, we were told, had been used in the U.S. military interrogation of terror suspects at Abu Ghraib Prison. Defense Secretary Rumsfeld saw nothing particularly troubling in that.

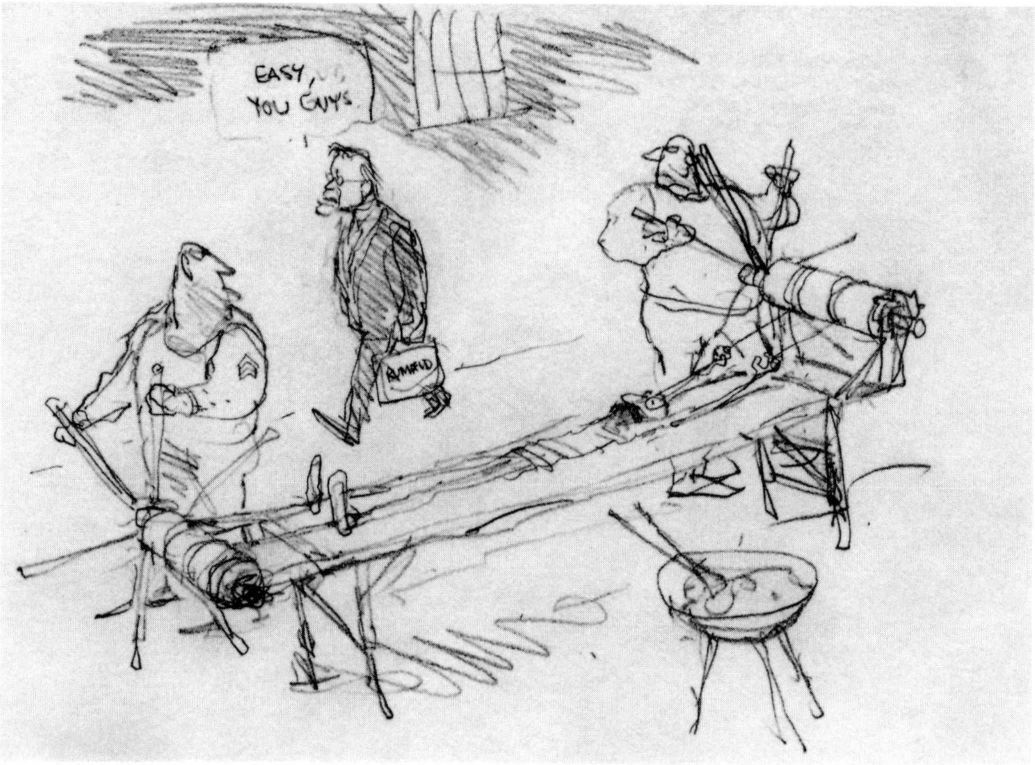
EASY,
YOU GUYS
RUMSFELD

Preliminary sketch for
Easy
Graphite on paper

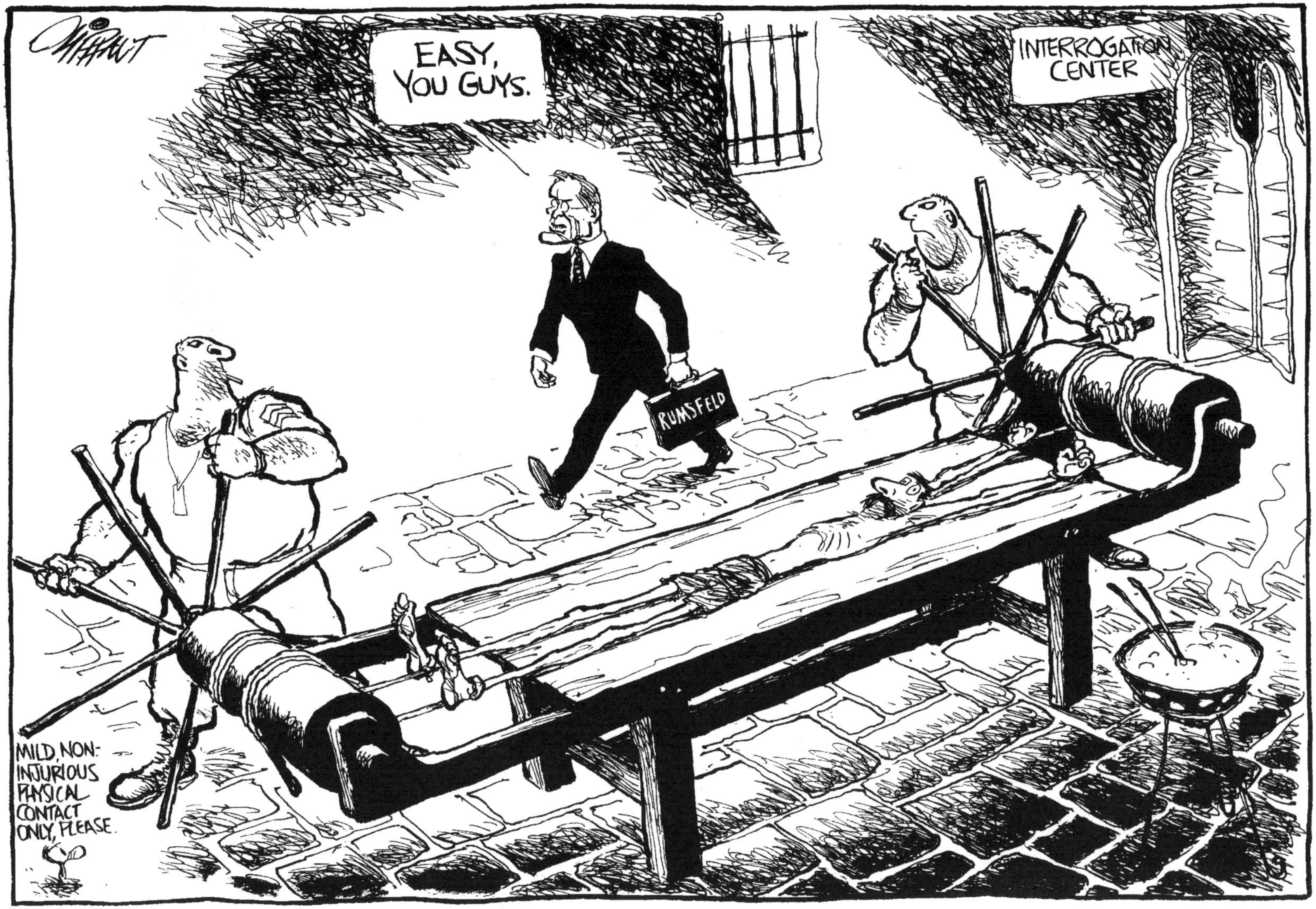
EASY, YOU GUYS.
INTERROGATION CENTER
RUMSFELD
MILD, NON-INJURIOUS PHYSICAL CONTACT ONLY, PLEASE.

18.
Rhymes with Duck
June 28, 2004

Rhymes with Duck: not quite the sort of invitation or exhortation we expected to hear from a Vice President, but it did speak volumes about Administration attitudes.

YEAH, I TOLD LEAHY TO GO FUCK HIMSELF. SURE I DID. SO, WHAT OF IT? AND WHAT'S MORE, AMERICA, –
FROM ME AN' GEORGE, AMERICA. YOU CAN ALL GO FUCK YOURSELVES, EVERY ONE OF YOU.

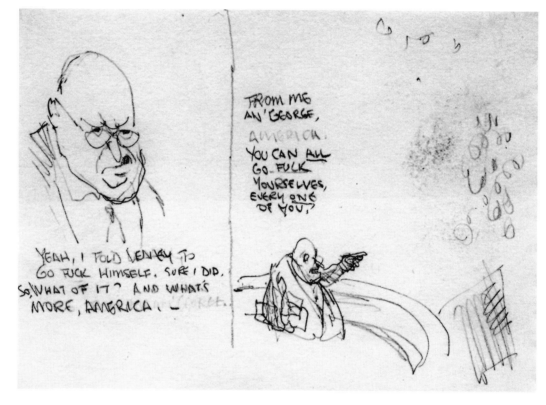

Preliminary sketch for
Rhymes with Duck
Graphite on paper

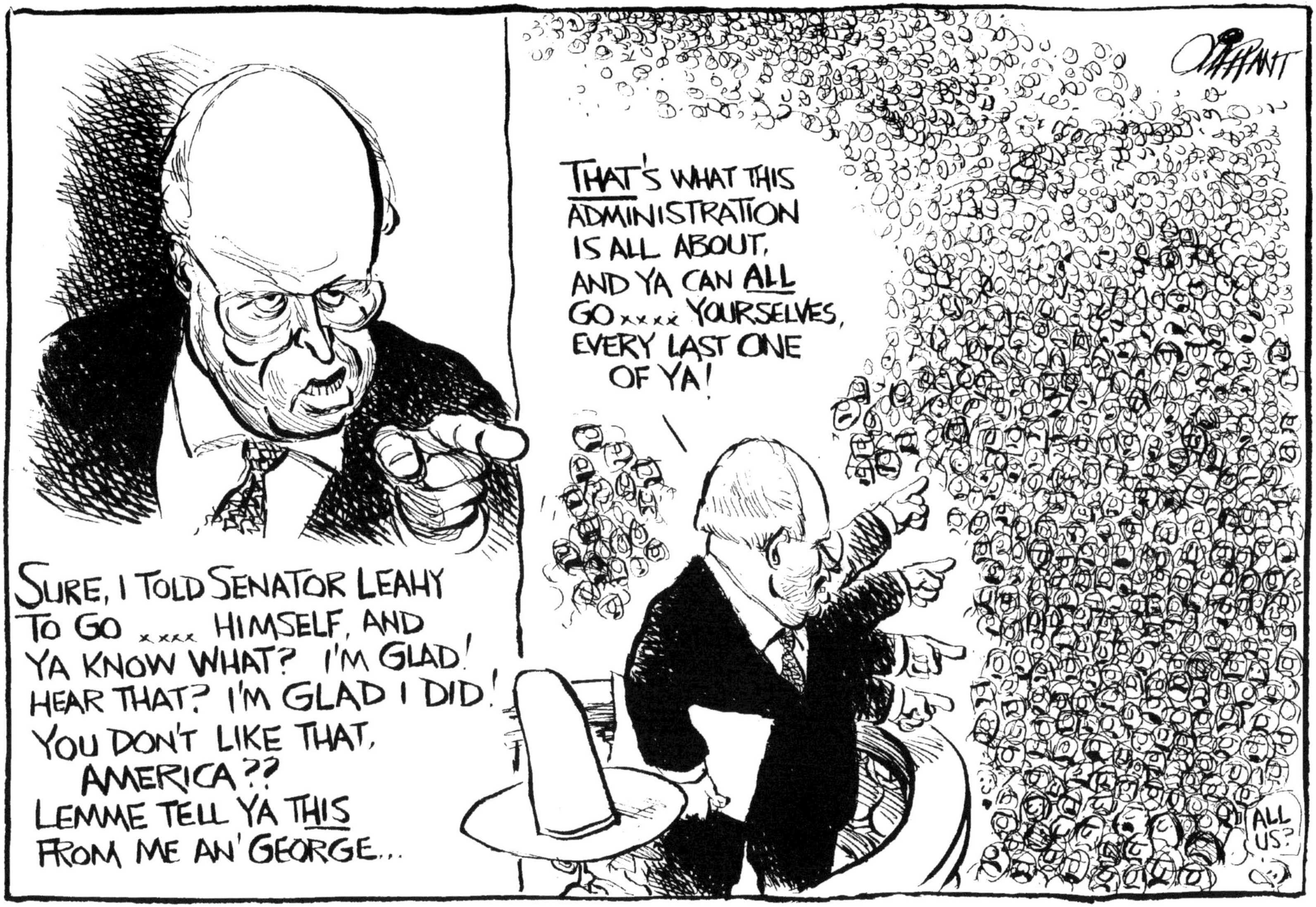
SURE, I TOLD SENATOR LEAHY TO GO xxxx HIMSELF, AND YA KNOW WHAT? I'M GLAD! HEAR THAT? I'M GLAD I DID! YOU DON'T LIKE THAT, AMERICA?? LEMME TELL YA THIS FROM ME AN' GEORGE...
THAT'S WHAT THIS ADMINISTRATION IS ALL ABOUT, AND YA CAN ALL GO xxxx YOURSELVES, EVERY LAST ONE OF YA!
ALL US?

19.
The Vows of Poverty
July 8, 2004

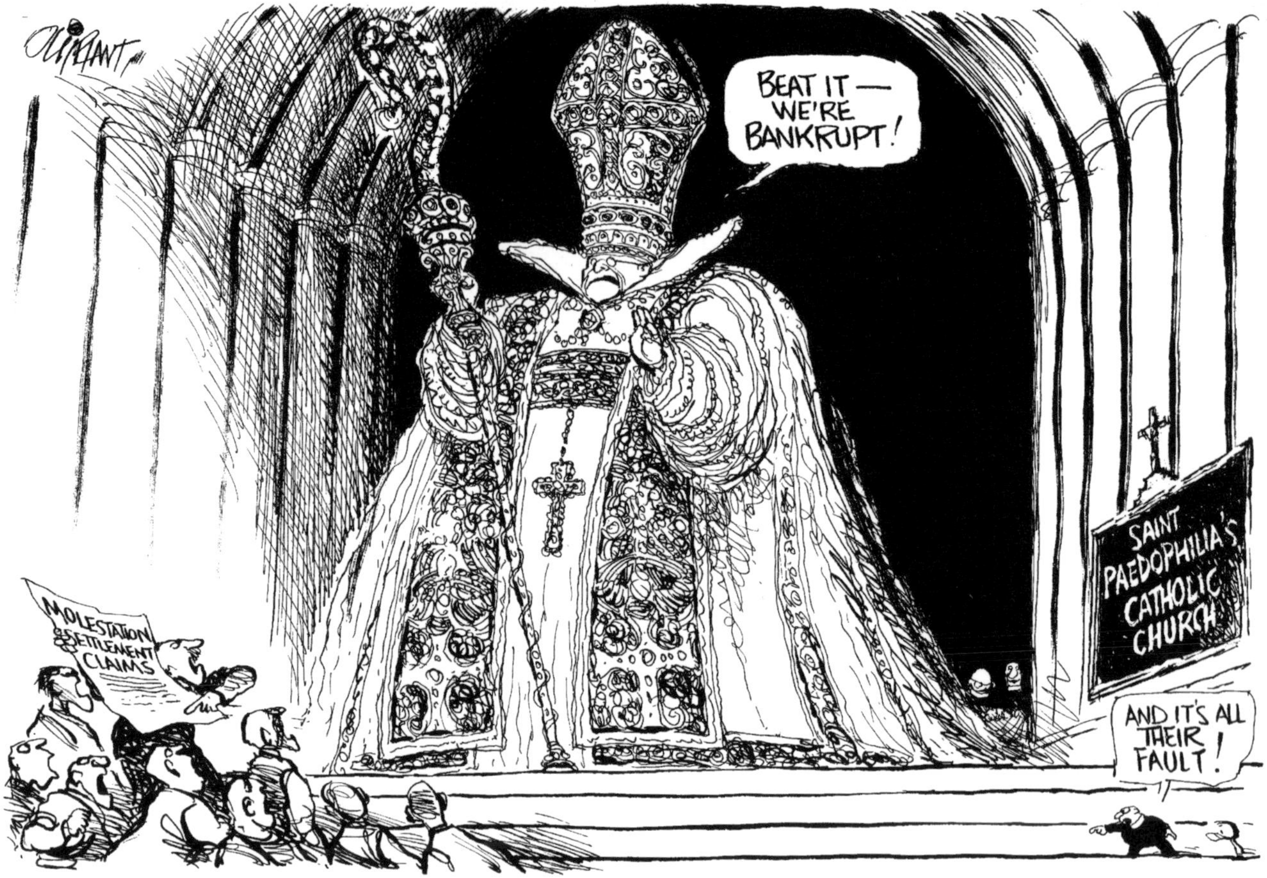

BEAT IT — WE'RE BANKRUPT!
MOLESTATION SETTLEMENT CLAIMS
SAINT PAEDOPHILIA'S CATHOLIC CHURCH
AND IT'S ALL THEIR FAULT!

20.
Pietà
July 12, 2004

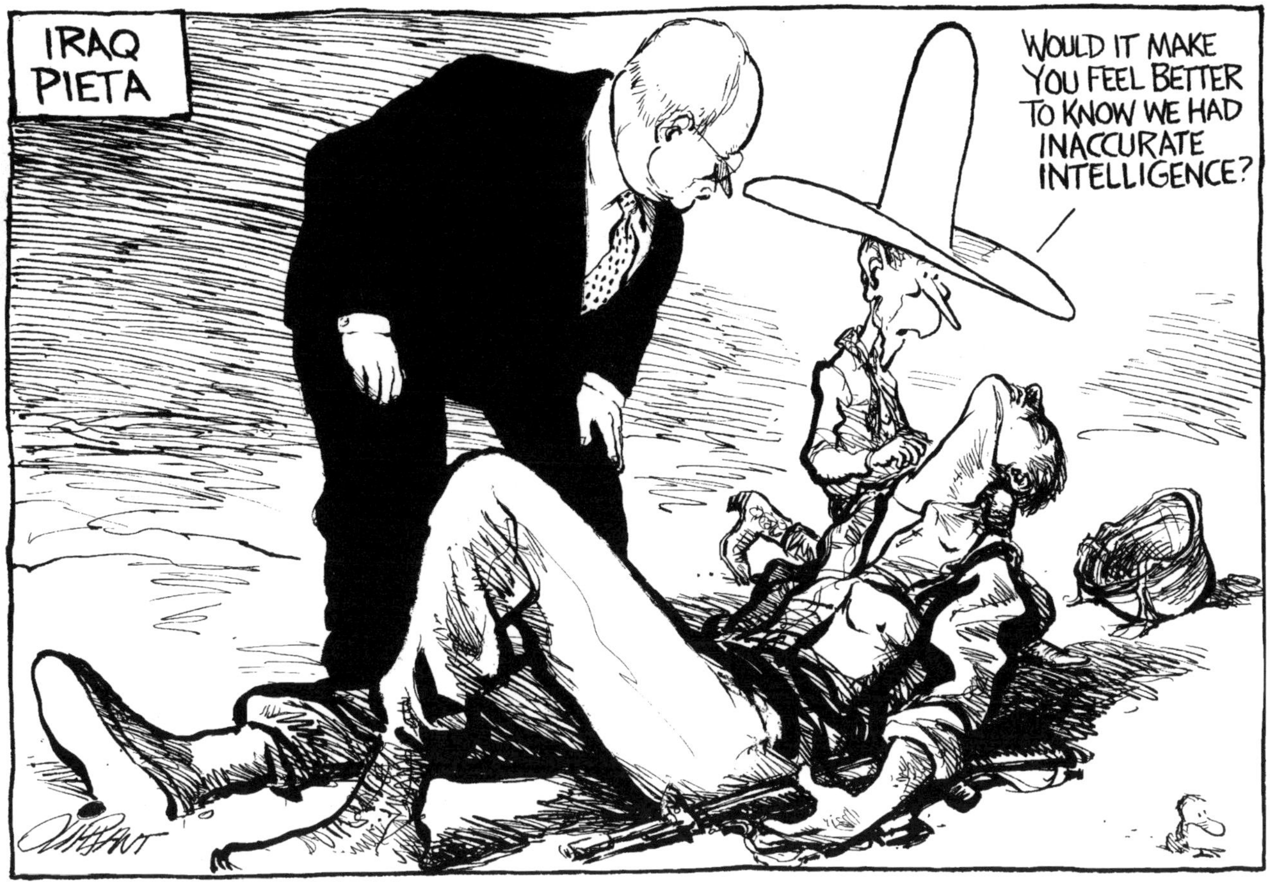
IRAQ
PIETA
WOULD IT MAKE
YOU FEEL BETTER
TO KNOW WE HAD
INACCURATE
INTELLIGENCE?

21.
Apocalypse
August 11, 2004

Horse-mounted Arab Janjaweed militias were committing widespread genocidal atrocities against black villagers and displacing hundreds of thousands of people from their homes in Sudan.

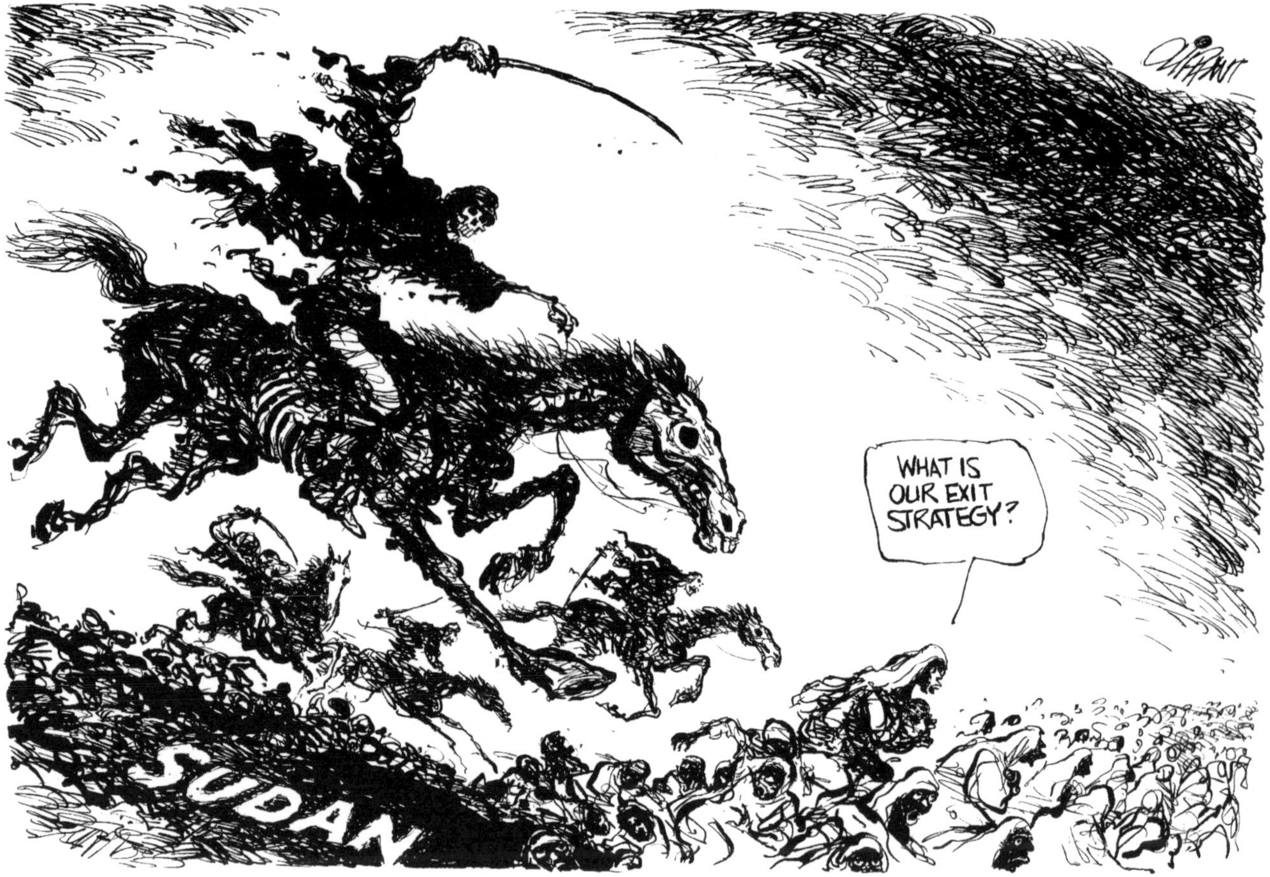
WHAT IS OUR EXIT STRATEGY?
SUDAN

22.
The Leaderer
November 3, 2004

The Great Leaderer.

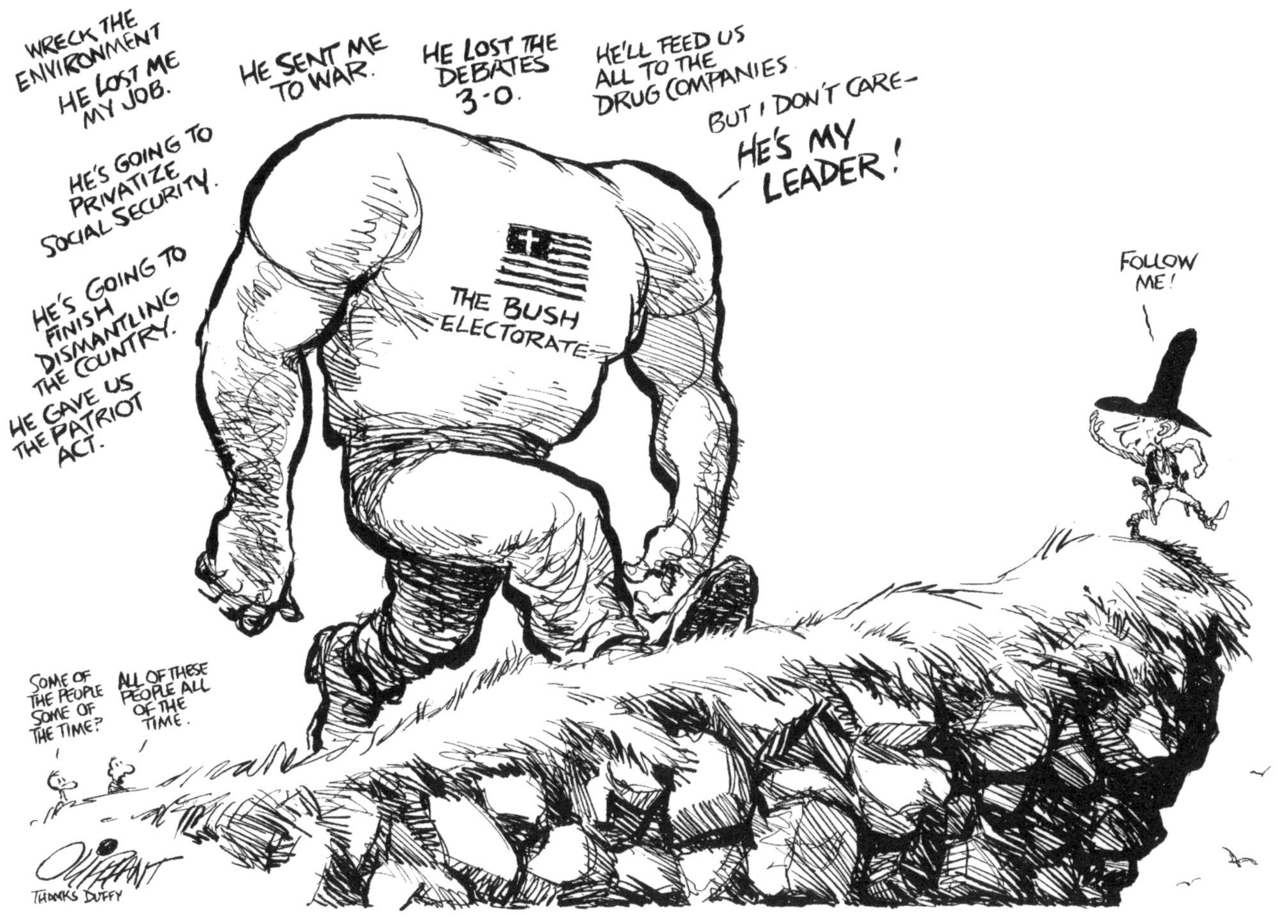
WRECK THE ENVIRONMENT
HE LOST ME MY JOB.
HE SENT ME TO WAR.
HE LOST THE DEBATES 3-0.
HE'LL FEED US ALL TO THE DRUG COMPANIES.
HE'S GOING TO PRIVATIZE SOCIAL SECURITY.
HE'S GOING TO FINISH DISMANTLING THE COUNTRY.
HE GAVE US THE PATRIOT ACT.
BUT I DON'T CARE- HE'S MY LEADER!
THE BUSH ELECTORATE
FOLLOW ME!
SOME OF THE PEOPLE SOME OF THE TIME?
ALL OF THESE PEOPLE ALL OF THE TIME.
OLIPHANT
THANKS DUFFY

23.
Medals, Medals, Medals
December 15, 2004

Medals, medals, and more medals.

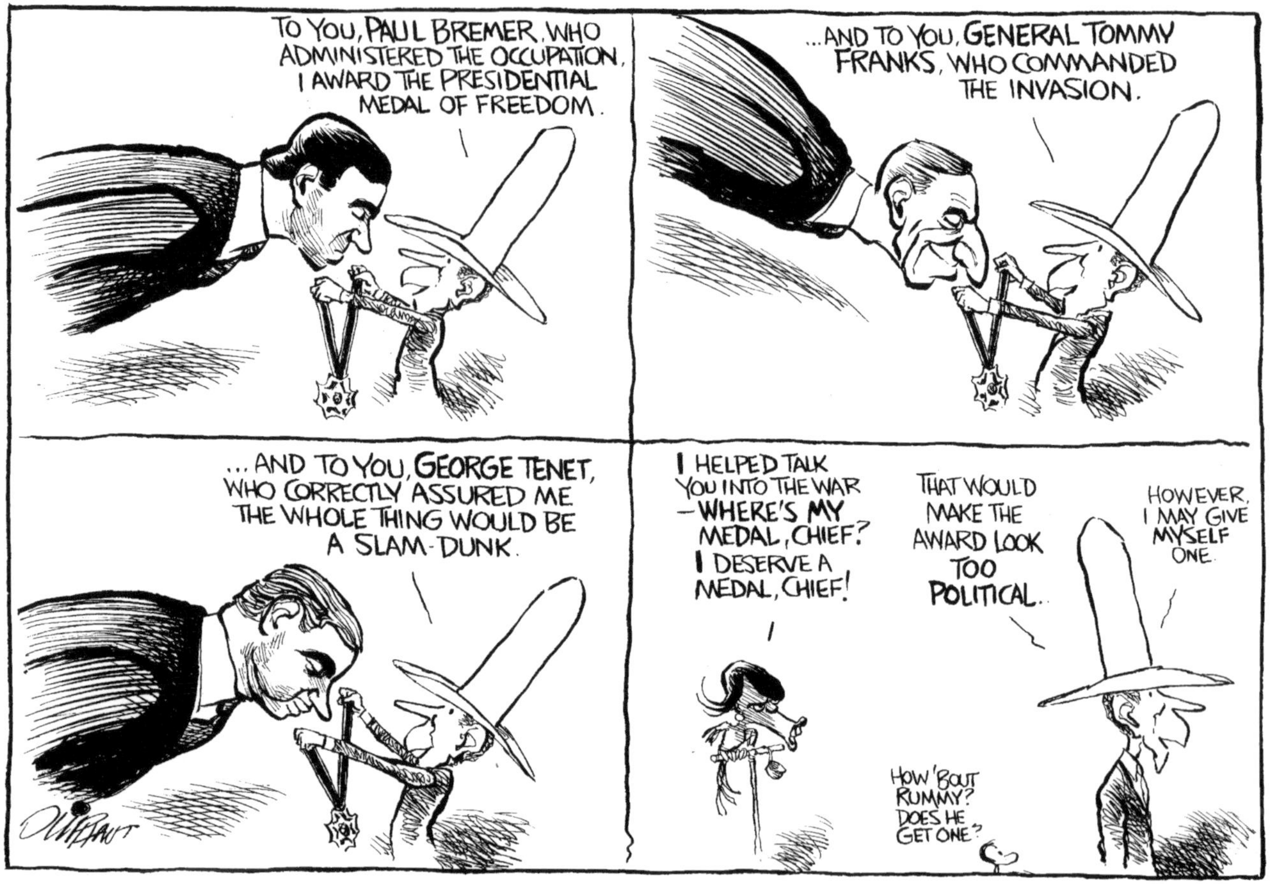

TO YOU, PAUL BREMER, WHO ADMINISTERED THE OCCUPATION, I AWARD THE PRESIDENTIAL MEDAL OF FREEDOM.
...AND TO YOU, GENERAL TOMMY FRANKS, WHO COMMANDED THE INVASION.
...AND TO YOU, GEORGE TENET, WHO CORRECTLY ASSURED ME THE WHOLE THING WOULD BE A SLAM-DUNK.
I HELPED TALK YOU INTO THE WAR —WHERE'S MY MEDAL, CHIEF? I DESERVE A MEDAL, CHIEF!
THAT WOULD MAKE THE AWARD LOOK TOO POLITICAL..
HOWEVER, I MAY GIVE MYSELF ONE.
HOW 'BOUT RUMMY? DOES HE GET ONE?
OLIPHANT

24.
Tsunami Aid
January 3, 2005

On December 26, 2005, a disastrous tidal wave caused by an undersea earthquake struck coastal Thailand. The Bush Administration dragged its feet in offering adequate aid to the survivors.

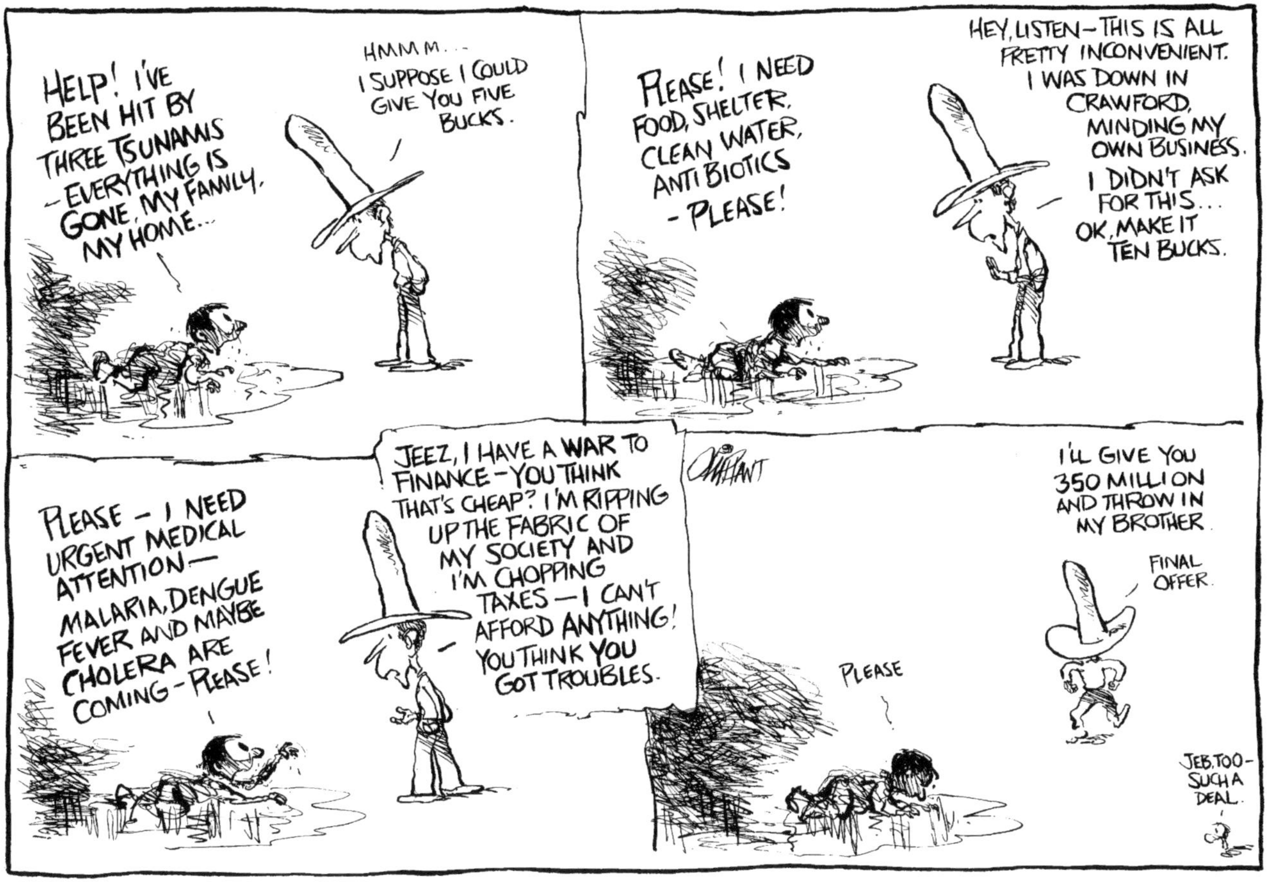
HELP! I'VE BEEN HIT BY THREE TSUNAMIS —EVERYTHING IS GONE, MY FAMILY, MY HOME...
HMMM... I SUPPOSE I COULD GIVE YOU FIVE BUCKS.
PLEASE! I NEED FOOD, SHELTER, CLEAN WATER, ANTI BIOTICS - PLEASE!
HEY, LISTEN—THIS IS ALL PRETTY INCONVENIENT. I WAS DOWN IN CRAWFORD, MINDING MY OWN BUSINESS. I DIDN'T ASK FOR THIS... OK, MAKE IT TEN BUCKS.
PLEASE — I NEED URGENT MEDICAL ATTENTION— MALARIA, DENGUE FEVER AND MAYBE CHOLERA ARE COMING - PLEASE!
JEEZ, I HAVE A WAR TO FINANCE—YOU THINK THAT'S CHEAP? I'M RIPPING UP THE FABRIC OF MY SOCIETY AND I'M CHOPPING TAXES—I CAN'T AFFORD ANYTHING! YOU THINK YOU GOT TROUBLES.
OLIPHANT
I'LL GIVE YOU 350 MILLION AND THROW IN MY BROTHER.
FINAL OFFER.
PLEASE
JEB, TOO- SUCH A DEAL.

25.

Explain It Again . . . Slowly

January 12, 2005

Explain it again . . . slowly.
Then go home—
whatever you're selling
they don't want.

IN A DEMOCRACY THE MAJORITY RULES. SO, WHAT WILL HAPPEN IF YOU WIN THE ELECTION, MR. SHIITE?
SHIITE
JAN 30
I KILL HIM
SUNNIS
IN YOUR DREAMS MAJORITY DOG — I KILL YOU FIRST,
JAN 30
DEAR ME. UM BUT WHAT IF MR SUNNI WINS, MR SHIITE?
JAN 30
I KILL HIM.
NO NO NO — SEE, IN A DEMOCRACY...
YOU NEVER GET TO THE POLLS, SWINE!
JAN 30

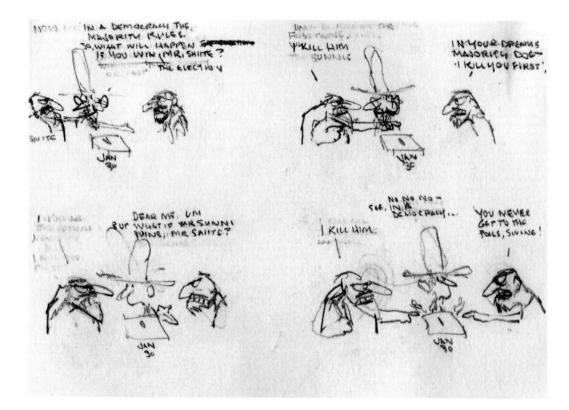

Preliminary sketch for
Explain It Again . . . Slowly
Graphite on paper

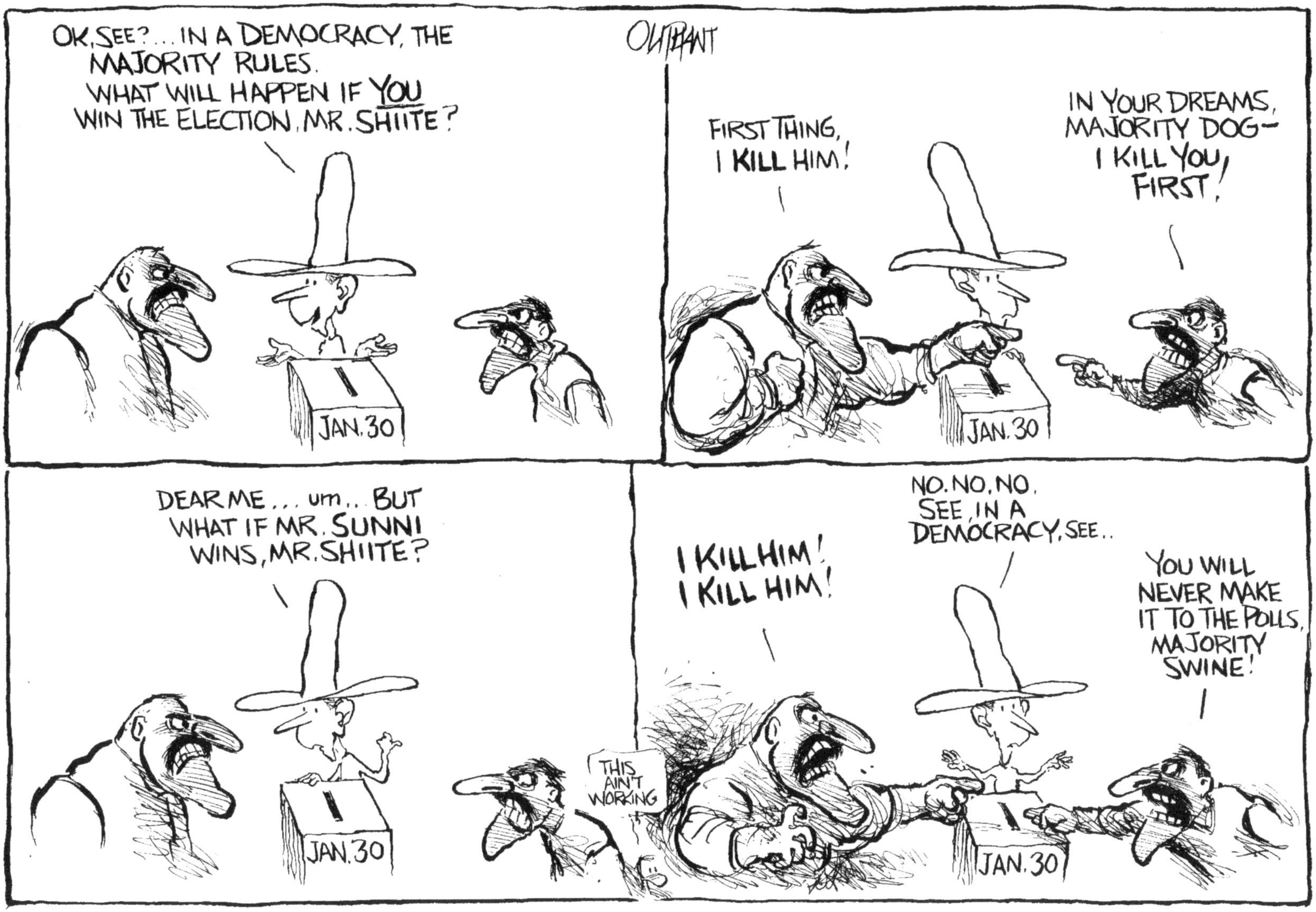
OK, SEE?... IN A DEMOCRACY, THE MAJORITY RULES. WHAT WILL HAPPEN IF YOU WIN THE ELECTION, MR. SHIITE?
OLIPHANT
JAN. 30
FIRST THING, I KILL HIM!
IN YOUR DREAMS, MAJORITY DOG— I KILL YOU, FIRST!
JAN. 30
DEAR ME... um... BUT WHAT IF MR. SUNNI WINS, MR. SHIITE?
JAN. 30
THIS AIN'T WORKING
NO. NO. NO. SEE, IN A DEMOCRACY, SEE..
I KILL HIM! I KILL HIM!
YOU WILL NEVER MAKE IT TO THE POLLS, MAJORITY SWINE!
JAN. 30

26.
Here Comes Democracy
January 31, 2005

Like it or not, here comes democracy.

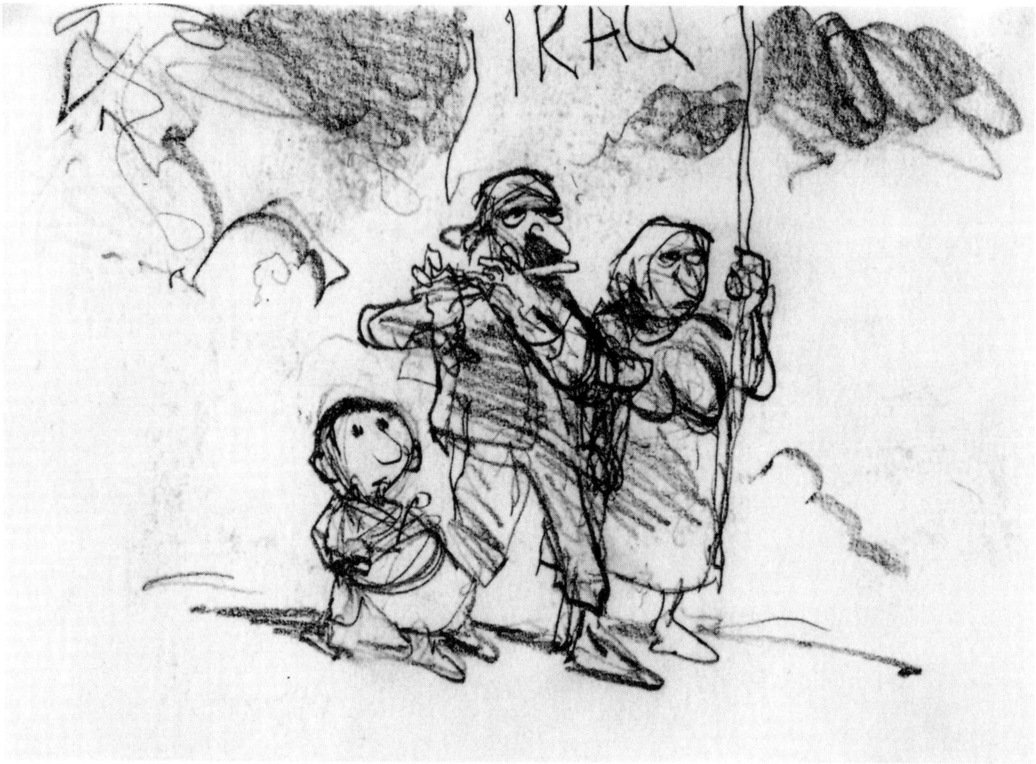
IRAQ

Preliminary sketch for
Here Comes Democracy
Graphite on paper

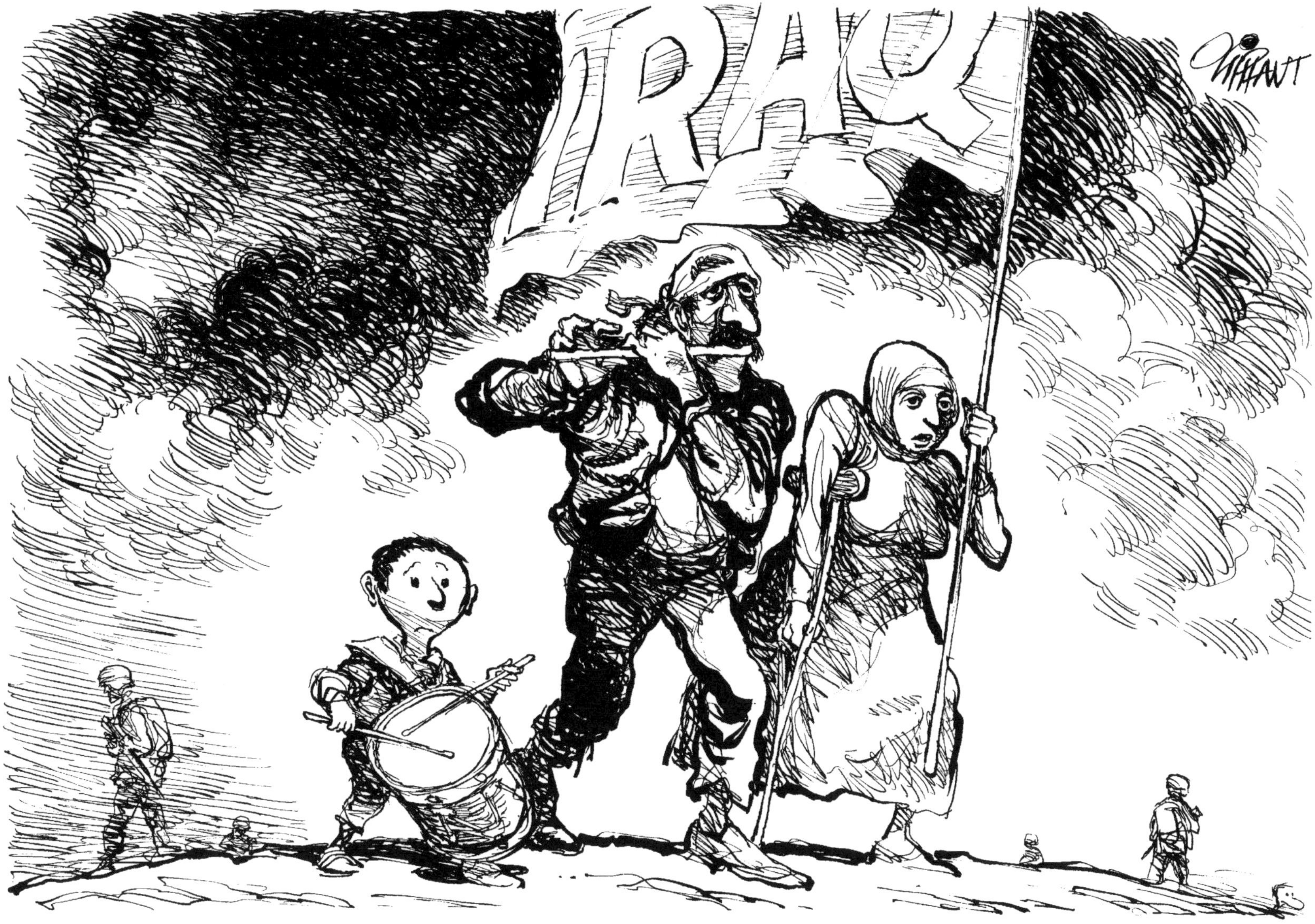
IRAQ

27.
Brain Check
March 29, 2005

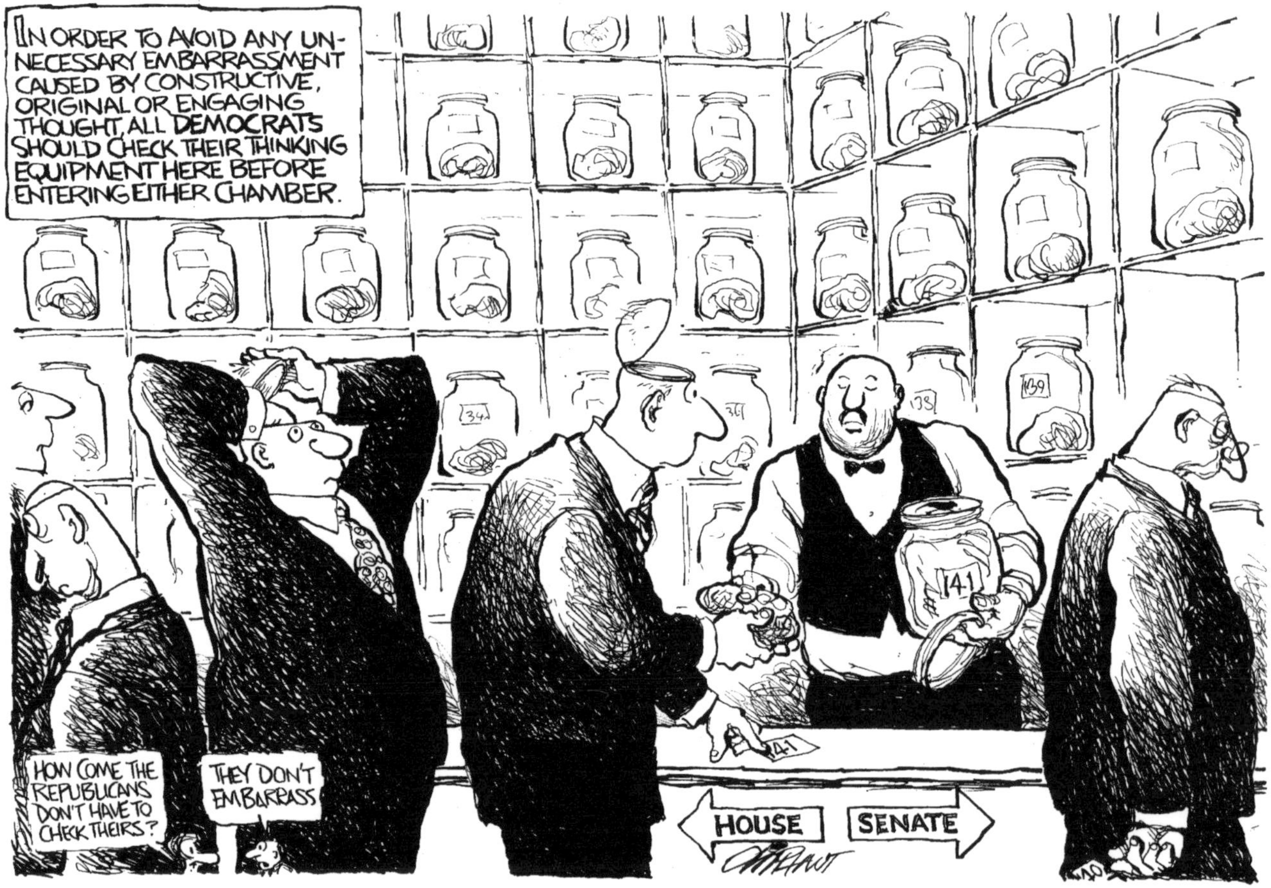

28.
The Education President
April 5, 2005

The Education President (aka The Educaterer).

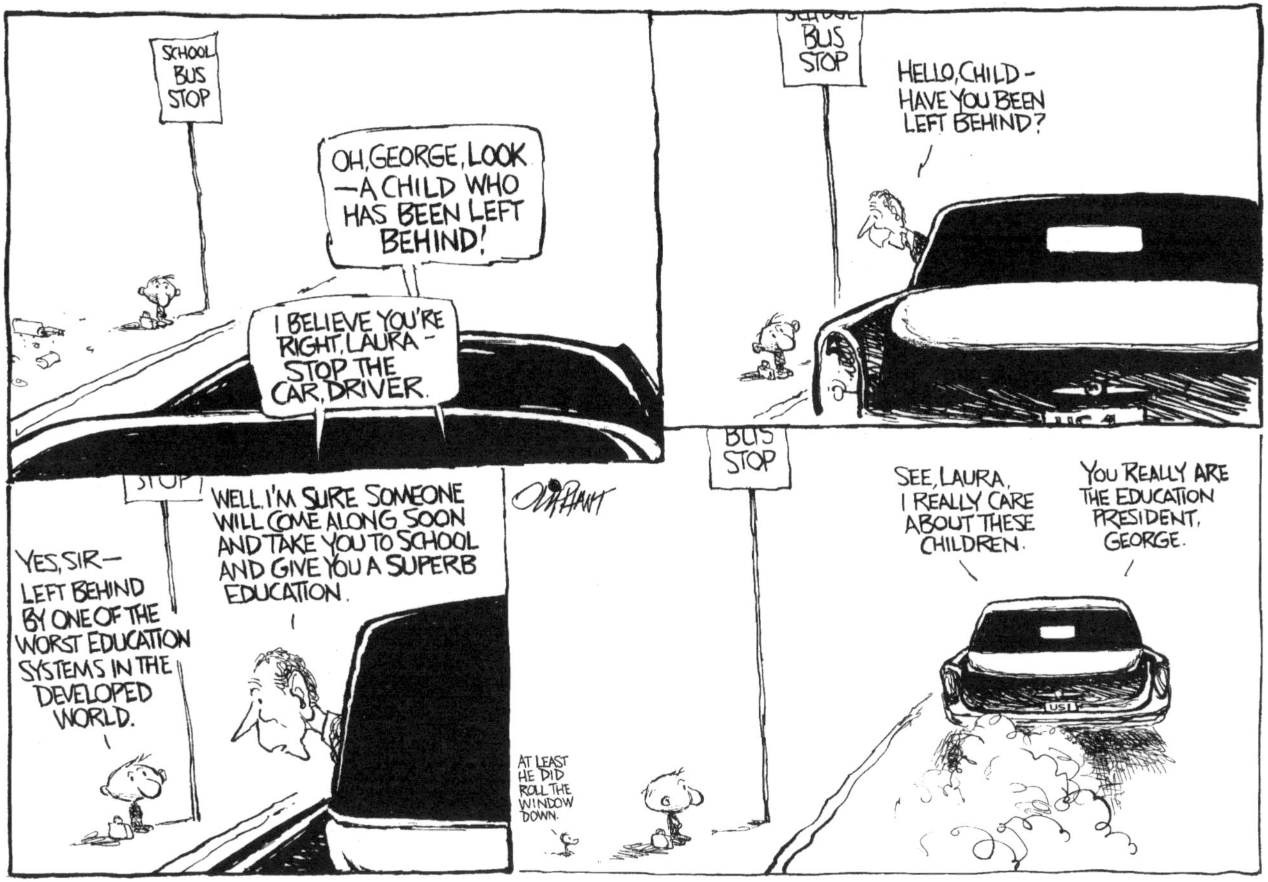
SCHOOL BUS STOP
OH, GEORGE, LOOK —A CHILD WHO HAS BEEN LEFT BEHIND!
I BELIEVE YOU'RE RIGHT, LAURA - STOP THE CAR, DRIVER.
BUS STOP
HELLO, CHILD - HAVE YOU BEEN LEFT BEHIND?
YES, SIR— LEFT BEHIND BY ONE OF THE WORST EDUCATION SYSTEMS IN THE DEVELOPED WORLD.
WELL, I'M SURE SOMEONE WILL COME ALONG SOON AND TAKE YOU TO SCHOOL AND GIVE YOU A SUPERB EDUCATION.
BUS STOP
SEE, LAURA, I REALLY CARE ABOUT THESE CHILDREN.
YOU REALLY ARE THE EDUCATION PRESIDENT, GEORGE.
AT LEAST HE DID ROLL THE WINDOW DOWN.

29.

No! No! Not the Woods!

April 26, 2005

Dear Ann Landers: President Bush invited Saudi crown prince Abdullah to his ranch in Crawford, Texas, where, the Associated Press told us, the pair greeted each other with a warm embrace and a kiss on both cheeks. They then went walking off hand in hand through a field of bluebonnets. Should we be alarmed about this? Signed, Confused.

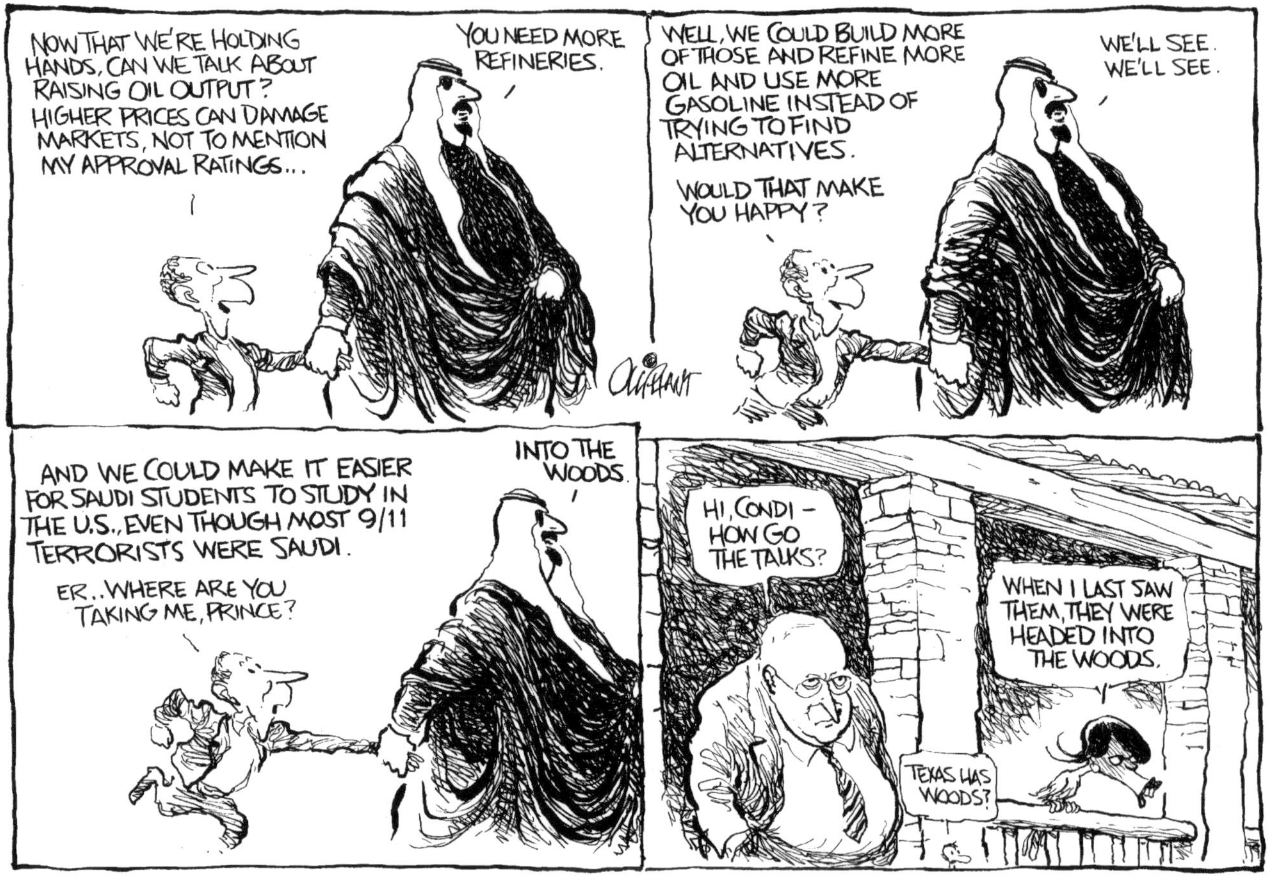

NOW THAT WE'RE HOLDING HANDS, CAN WE TALK ABOUT RAISING OIL OUTPUT? HIGHER PRICES CAN DAMAGE MARKETS, NOT TO MENTION MY APPROVAL RATINGS...
YOU NEED MORE REFINERIES.
WELL, WE COULD BUILD MORE OF THOSE AND REFINE MORE OIL AND USE MORE GASOLINE INSTEAD OF TRYING TO FIND ALTERNATIVES.
WOULD THAT MAKE YOU HAPPY?
WE'LL SEE. WE'LL SEE.
AND WE COULD MAKE IT EASIER FOR SAUDI STUDENTS TO STUDY IN THE U.S., EVEN THOUGH MOST 9/11 TERRORISTS WERE SAUDI.
ER.. WHERE ARE YOU TAKING ME, PRINCE?
INTO THE WOODS.
HI, CONDI - HOW GO THE TALKS?
WHEN I LAST SAW THEM, THEY WERE HEADED INTO THE WOODS.
TEXAS HAS WOODS?

30.
Spear Carriers
May 9, 2005

The loyal and fawning press. Semper Fidelis.

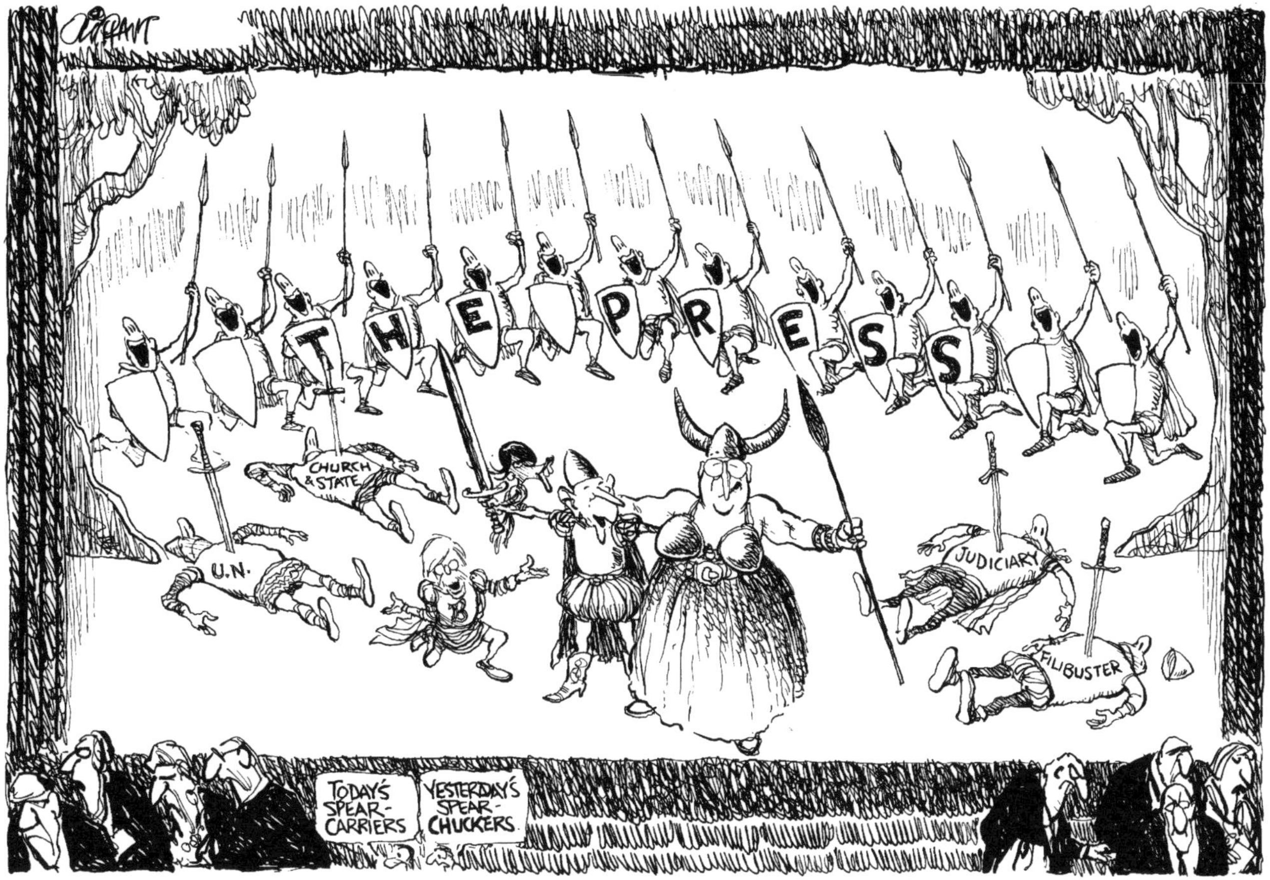

THE PRESS
CHURCH & STATE
U.N.
JUDICIARY
FILIBUSTER
TODAY'S SPEAR-CARRIERS
YESTERDAY'S SPEAR-CHUCKERS

31.
Democratize!
June 21, 2005

Oh, shut up. Or at least take a time out, pretty Polly.

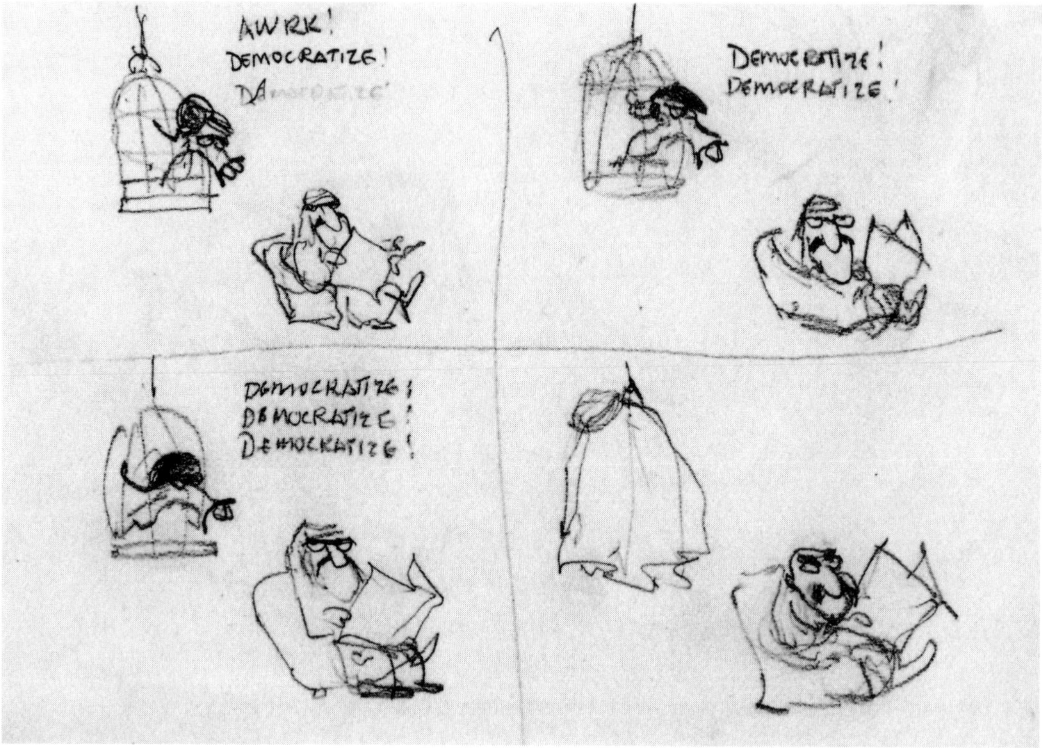
AWRK!
DEMOCRATIZE!
DEMOCRATIZE!
DEMOCRATIZE!
DEMOCRATIZE!
DEMOCRATIZE!
DEMOCRATIZE!

81.
Preliminary sketch for
Democratize!
Graphite on paper
2005

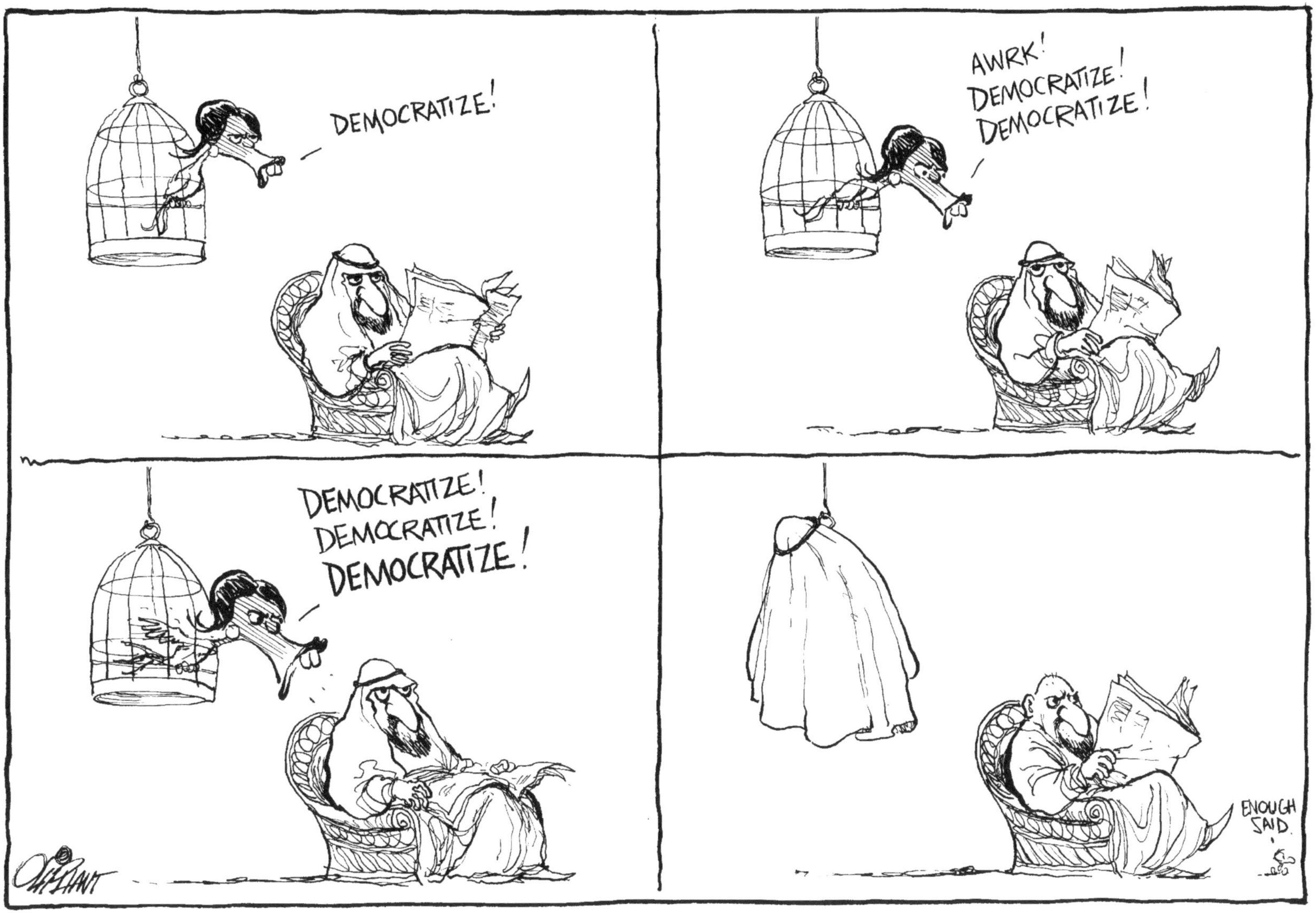
DEMOCRATIZE!
AWRK! DEMOCRATIZE! DEMOCRATIZE!
DEMOCRATIZE! DEMOCRATIZE! DEMOCRATIZE!
ENOUGH SAID.

32.
Comparative Greatness
July 5, 2005

Justice Sandra Day O'Connor, the greatly admired swing vote on the U.S. Supreme Court, retired. Bush saw this as a chance to slip by with his sorry nominee for attorney general, the lamentable Alberto Gonzales.

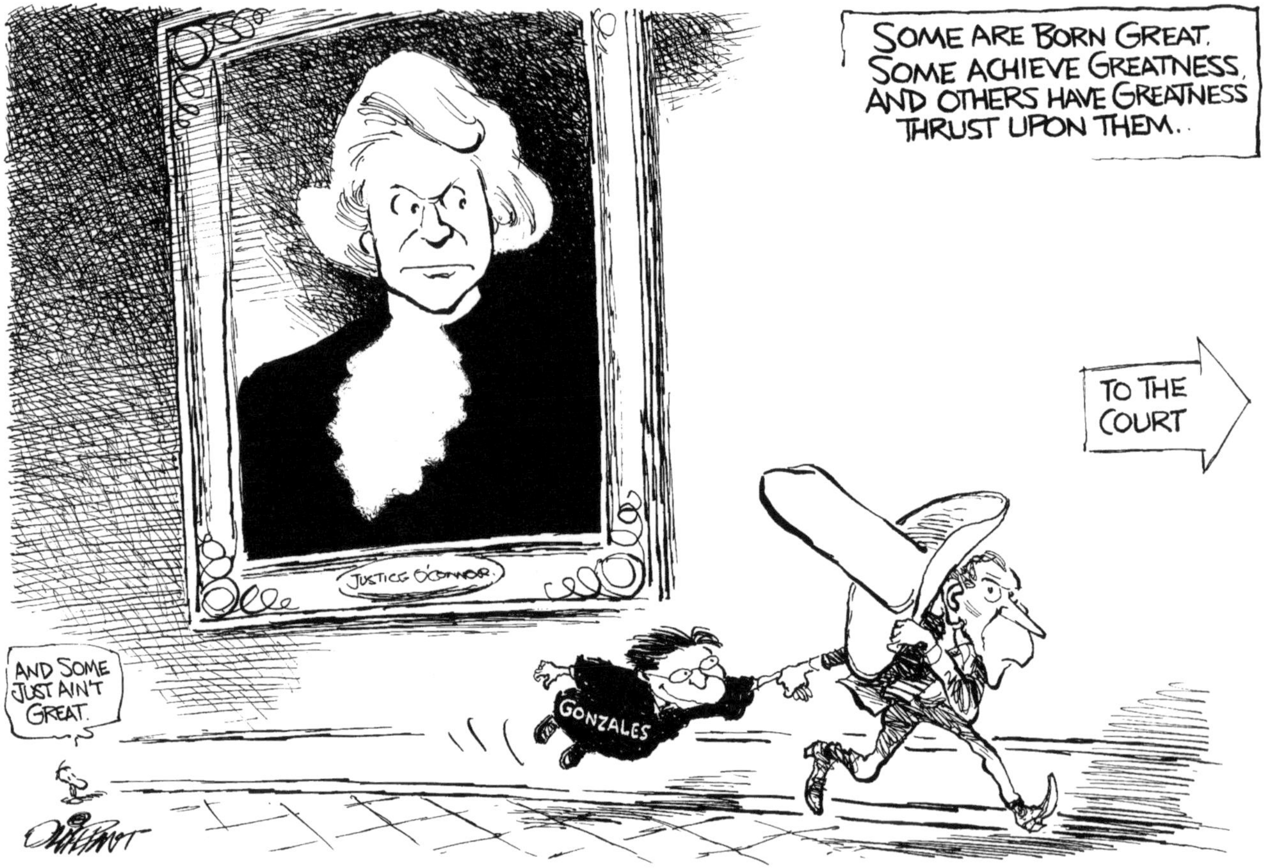
SOME ARE BORN GREAT, SOME ACHIEVE GREATNESS, AND OTHERS HAVE GREATNESS THRUST UPON THEM..
JUSTICE O'CONNOR
TO THE COURT
AND SOME JUST AIN'T GREAT.
GONZALES

33.

On the Road

August 23, 2005

There are those who believe that the world is only a couple of thousand years old. There are those who think it is flat. These kind folks reject all thought of Darwin's theory. They believe in something called Intelligent Design, which is supposed to reconcile both theories into one cohesive coherence. (George falls off his bike a lot, hence the training wheels.)

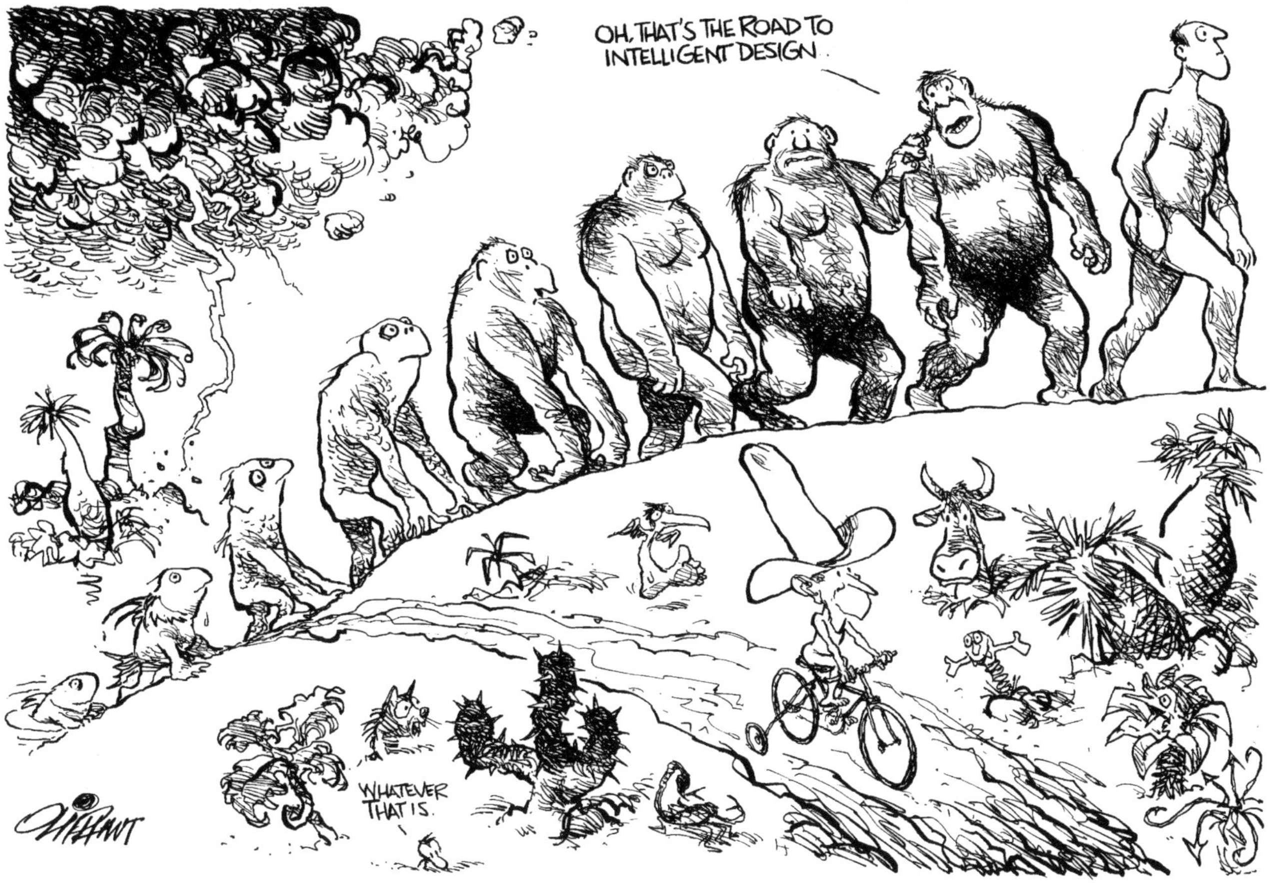
OH, THAT'S THE ROAD TO INTELLIGENT DESIGN.
WHATEVER THAT IS.

34.
The Perils of Overwork
September 5, 2005

Hurricane Katrina struck the Louisiana coast, destroyed the levees, and flooded New Orleans. Late for work as usual, George dashed to the rescue.

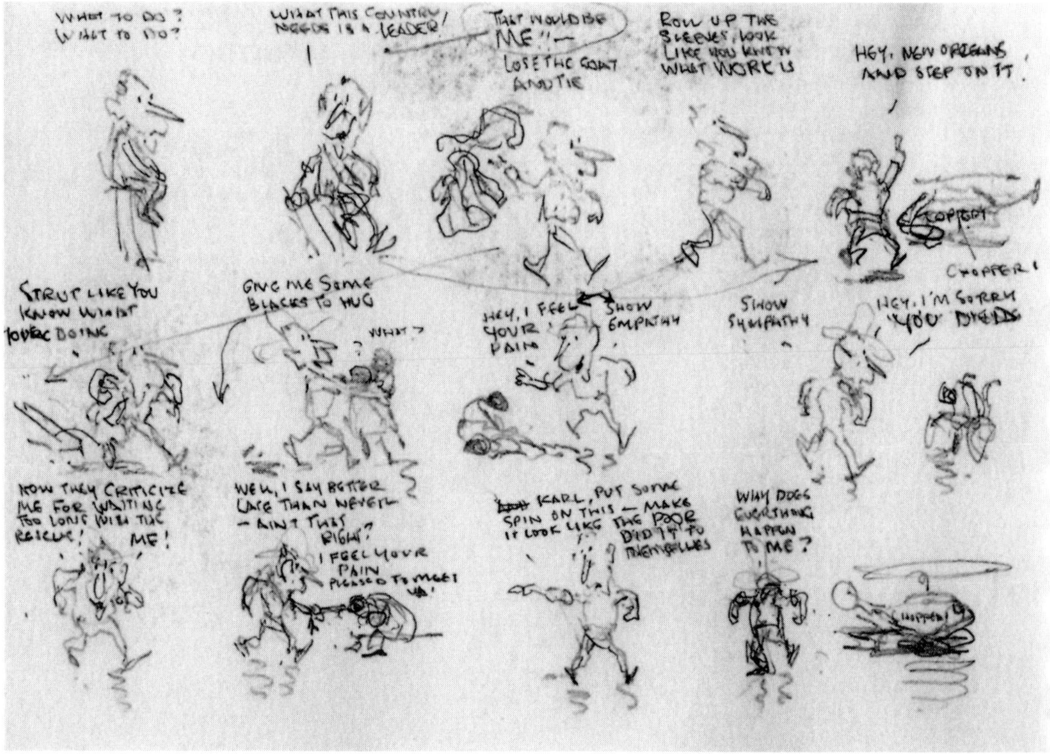
WHAT TO DO? WHAT TO DO?
WHAT THIS COUNTRY NEEDS IS A LEADER!
THAT WOULD BE ME!!—
LOSE THE COAT AND TIE
ROLL UP THE SLEEVES, LOOK LIKE YOU KNOW WHAT WORK IS
HEY, NEW ORLEANS, AND STEP ON IT.
CHOPPER!
STRUT LIKE YOU KNOW WHAT YOU'RE DOING
GIVE ME SOME BLACKS TO HUG
WHAT?
HEY, I FEEL YOUR PAIN
SHOW EMPATHY
SHOW SYMPATHY
NOW THEY CRITICIZE ME FOR WAITING TOO LONG WITH THE RESCUE!
ME!
WELL, I SAY BETTER LATE THAN NEVER — AIN'T THIS RIGHT?
I FEEL YOUR PAIN
PLEASED TO MEET YA!
KARL, PUT SOME SPIN ON THIS — MAKE IT LOOK LIKE THE POOR DID IT TO THEMSELVES
WHY DOES EVERYTHING HAPPEN TO ME?

Preliminary sketch for
The Perils of Overwork
Graphite on paper

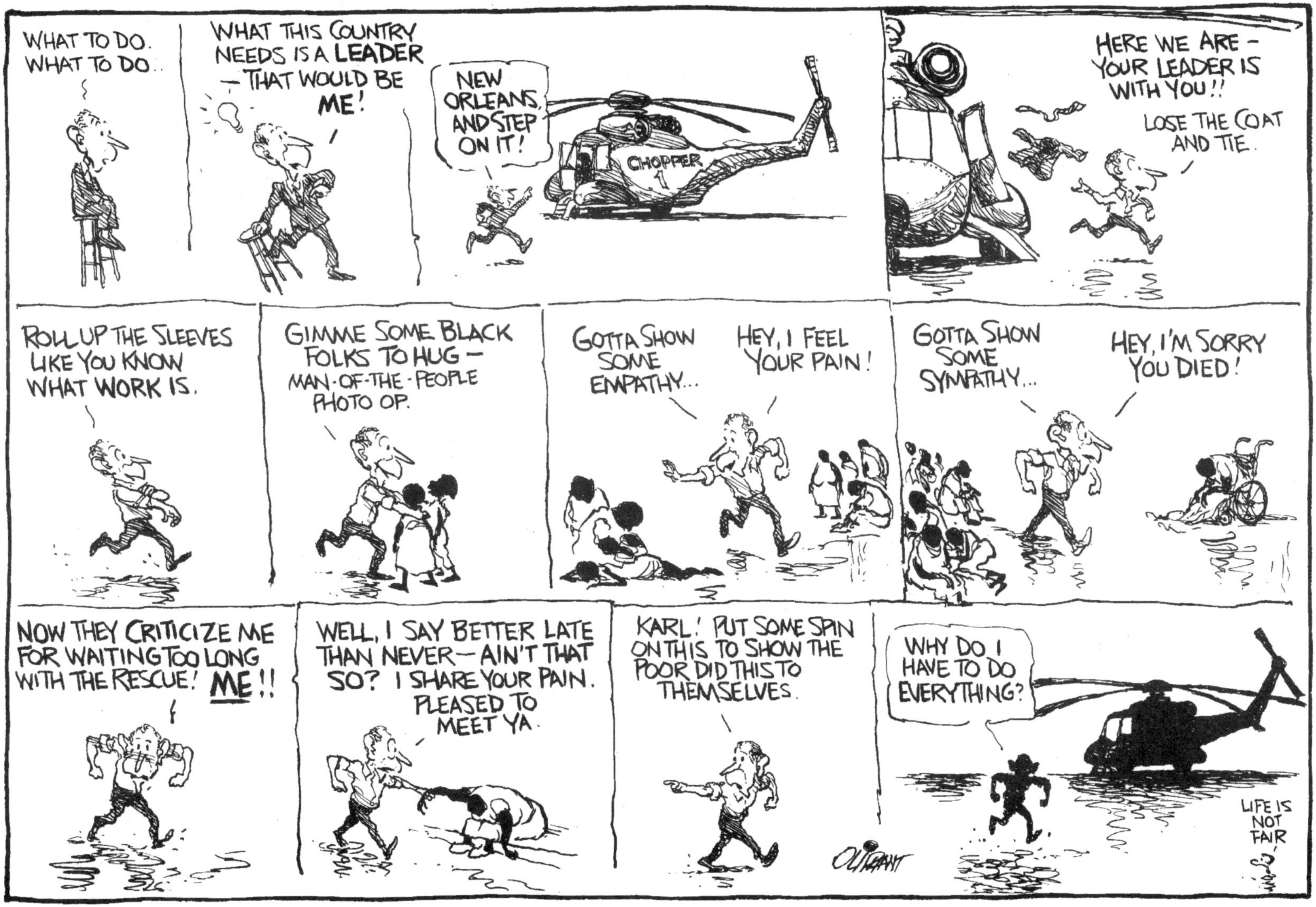
WHAT TO DO. WHAT TO DO..
WHAT THIS COUNTRY NEEDS IS A LEADER — THAT WOULD BE ME!
NEW ORLEANS, AND STEP ON IT!
CHOPPER 1
HERE WE ARE — YOUR LEADER IS WITH YOU!!
LOSE THE COAT AND TIE.
ROLL UP THE SLEEVES LIKE YOU KNOW WHAT WORK IS.
GIMME SOME BLACK FOLKS TO HUG — MAN-OF-THE-PEOPLE PHOTO OP.
GOTTA SHOW SOME EMPATHY...
HEY, I FEEL YOUR PAIN!
GOTTA SHOW SOME SYMPATHY...
HEY, I'M SORRY YOU DIED!
NOW THEY CRITICIZE ME FOR WAITING TOO LONG WITH THE RESCUE! ME!!
WELL, I SAY BETTER LATE THAN NEVER — AIN'T THAT SO? I SHARE YOUR PAIN.
PLEASED TO MEET YA.
KARL! PUT SOME SPIN ON THIS TO SHOW THE POOR DID THIS TO THEMSELVES.
OLIPHANT
WHY DO I HAVE TO DO EVERYTHING?
LIFE IS NOT FAIR!

35.
Ship of Fools
September 9, 2005

The Royal Tour of the New Orleans wreckage. At this time, Barbara Bush, the Royal Mother, issued her famous statement referring to the wretched victims huddling under horrendous conditions in the sports stadium: "So many of the people in the arena here, you know, were underprivileged anyway, so this (she chuckles) is working very well for them."

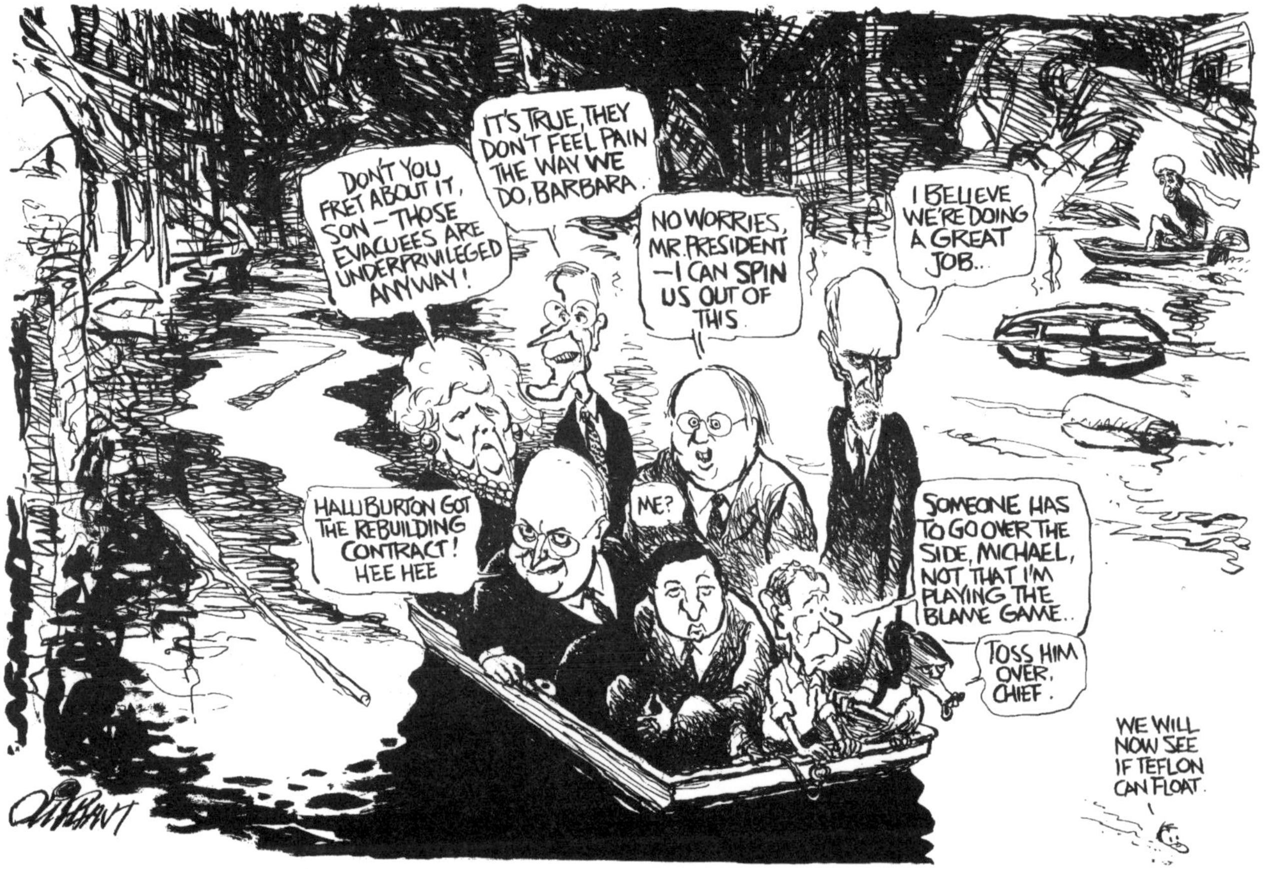
DON'T YOU FRET ABOUT IT, SON – THOSE EVACUEES ARE UNDERPRIVILEGED ANYWAY!
IT'S TRUE, THEY DON'T FEEL PAIN THE WAY WE DO, BARBARA.
NO WORRIES, MR. PRESIDENT —I CAN SPIN US OUT OF THIS.
I BELIEVE WE'RE DOING A GREAT JOB..
HALLIBURTON GOT THE REBUILDING CONTRACT! HEE HEE
ME?
SOMEONE HAS TO GO OVER THE SIDE, MICHAEL, NOT THAT I'M PLAYING THE BLAME GAME..
TOSS HIM OVER, CHIEF.
WE WILL NOW SEE IF TEFLON CAN FLOAT.
OLIPHANT

36.
The Responsibility of the Irresponsible
September 14, 2005

The Responsibility of the Irresponsible: Noblesse Oblige.

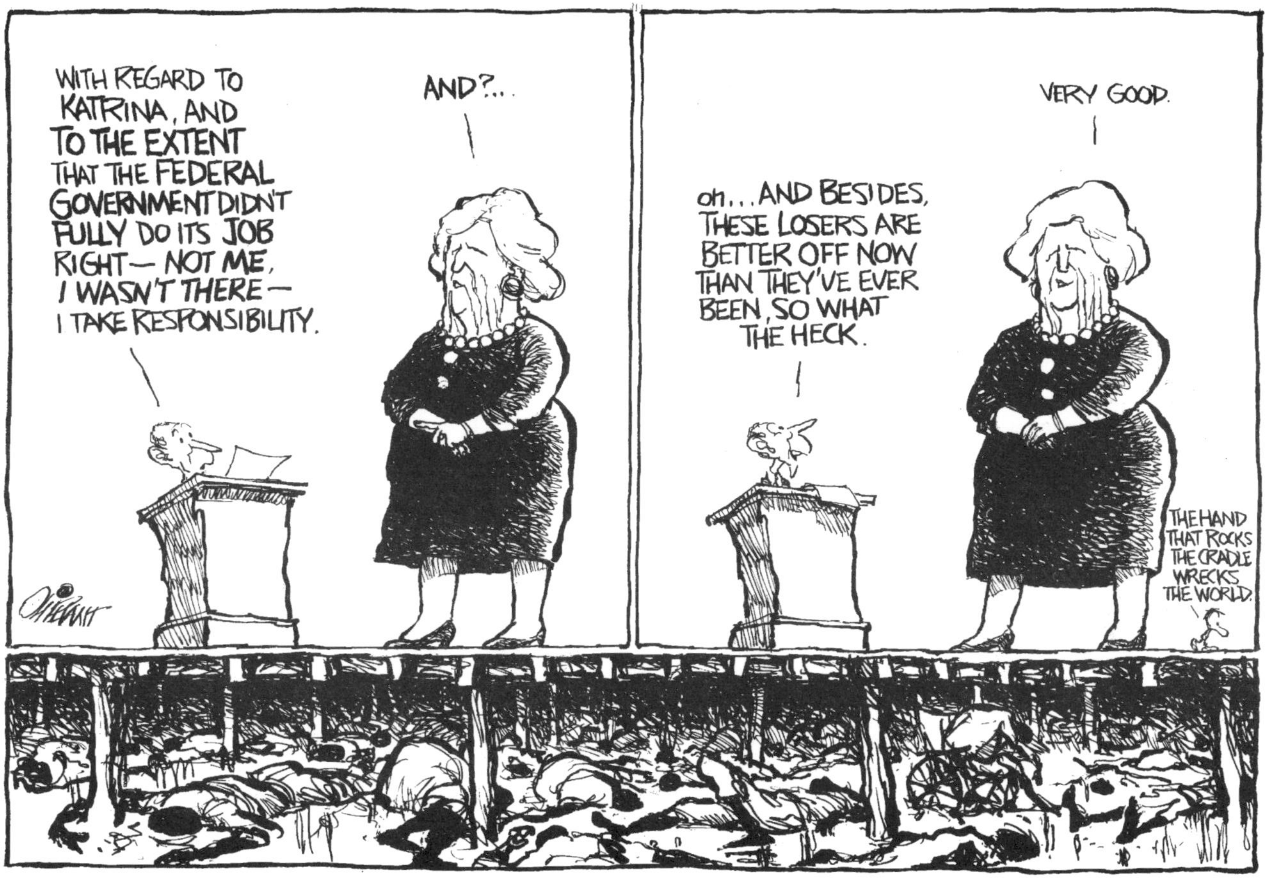
WITH REGARD TO KATRINA, AND TO THE EXTENT THAT THE FEDERAL GOVERNMENT DIDN'T FULLY DO ITS JOB RIGHT— NOT ME, I WASN'T THERE— I TAKE RESPONSIBILITY.
AND?...
OH... AND BESIDES, THESE LOSERS ARE BETTER OFF NOW THAN THEY'VE EVER BEEN, SO WHAT THE HECK.
VERY GOOD.
THE HAND THAT ROCKS THE CRADLE WRECKS THE WORLD.

37.
The Righted
October 11, 2005

White House Counsel and close Bush crony Harriet Miers was George's choice to replace Sandra Day O'Connor on the U.S. Supreme Court. Both right and left challenged the nomination, the right wanting a more clear record of her opposition to abortion and other things dear to their hearts, the left wanting more proof of her basic qualifications.

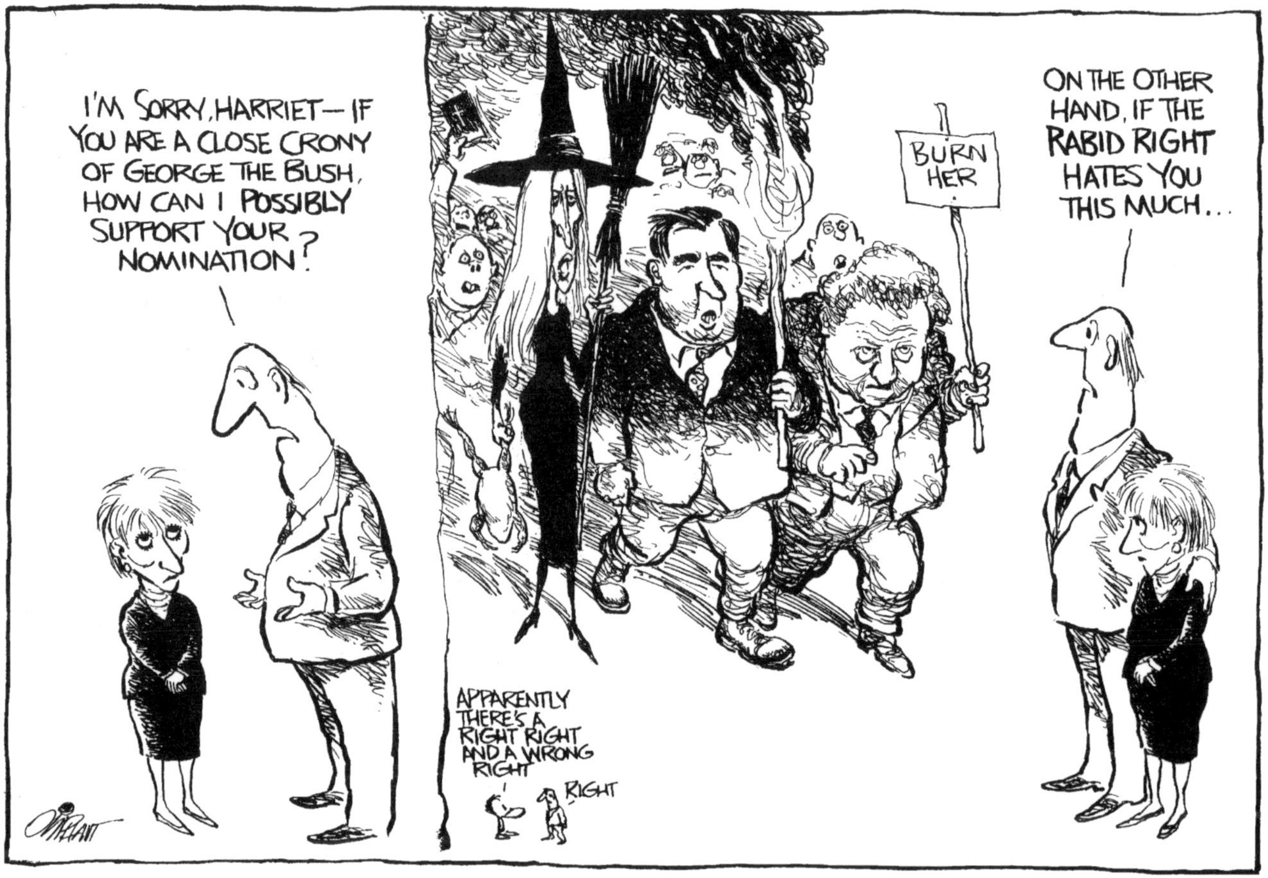
I'M SORRY, HARRIET— IF YOU ARE A CLOSE CRONY OF GEORGE THE BUSH, HOW CAN I POSSIBLY SUPPORT YOUR NOMINATION?
BURN HER
ON THE OTHER HAND, IF THE RABID RIGHT HATES YOU THIS MUCH...
APPARENTLY THERE'S A RIGHT RIGHT AND A WRONG RIGHT
RIGHT

38.
A Study in Pliancy
October 17, 2005

Harriet Miers, no slouch when it came to obsequiousness, hung on to her nomination to become a Supreme. The impasse was later resolved when she withdrew.

THE PRESIDENT WOULD BE BOTH ASHAMED & AFRAID TO BRING FORWARD FOR THE MOST DISTINGUISHED or LUCRATIVE STATIONS, CANDIDATES WHO HAD NO OTHER MERIT THAN THAT of COMING FROM THE SAME STATE TO WHICH HE PARTICULARLY BELONGED, OR OF BEING IN SOME WAY or OTHER PERSONALLY ALLIED TO HIM, or of POSSESSING THE NECESSARY INSIGNIFICANCE or PLIANCY TO RENDER THEM THE OBSEQUIOUS INSTRUMENTS of HIS PLEASURE.

Alexander Hamilton *in the Federalist Papers.*

HA! THEY FORGET, HARRIET, THAT I HAVE NO SHAME!

OH, I AGREE, SIR, YOU ARE THE MOST SHAMELESSEST PERSON I HAVE EVER HAD THE PLEASURE AND THE HONOR OF SERVING, SIR.

AND TOO DUMB TO BE AFRAID

39.
Dominatrix
December 8, 2005

Dominatrix and Secretary of State.

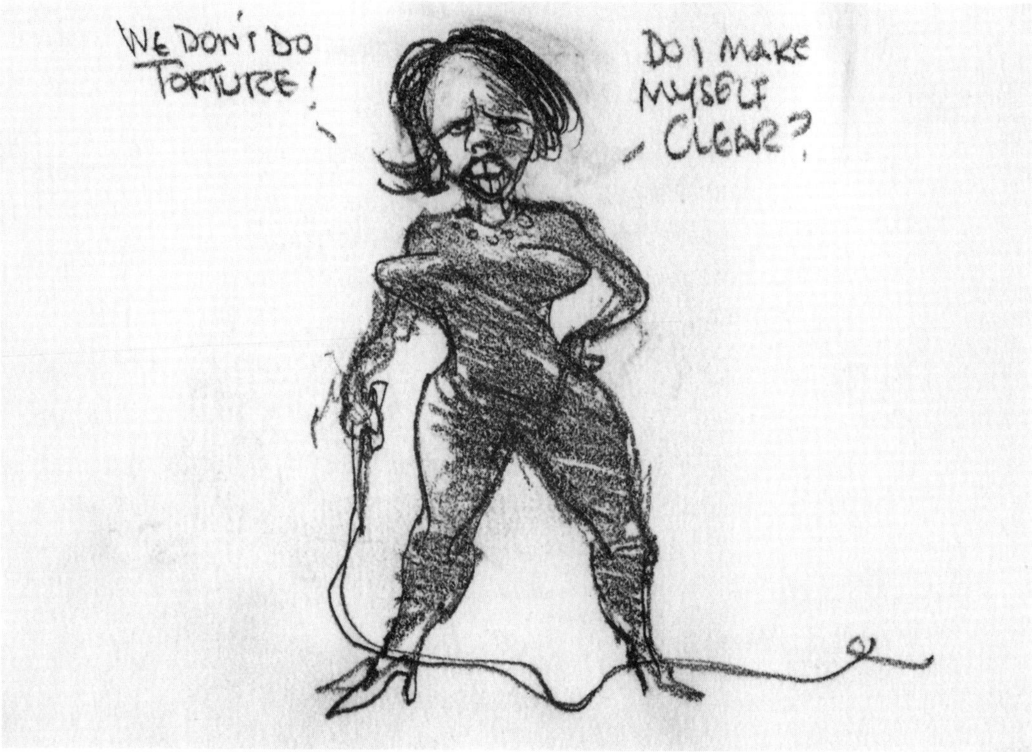
WE DON'T DO TORTURE!
DO I MAKE MYSELF CLEAR?

Preliminary sketch for
Dominatrix
Graphite on paper

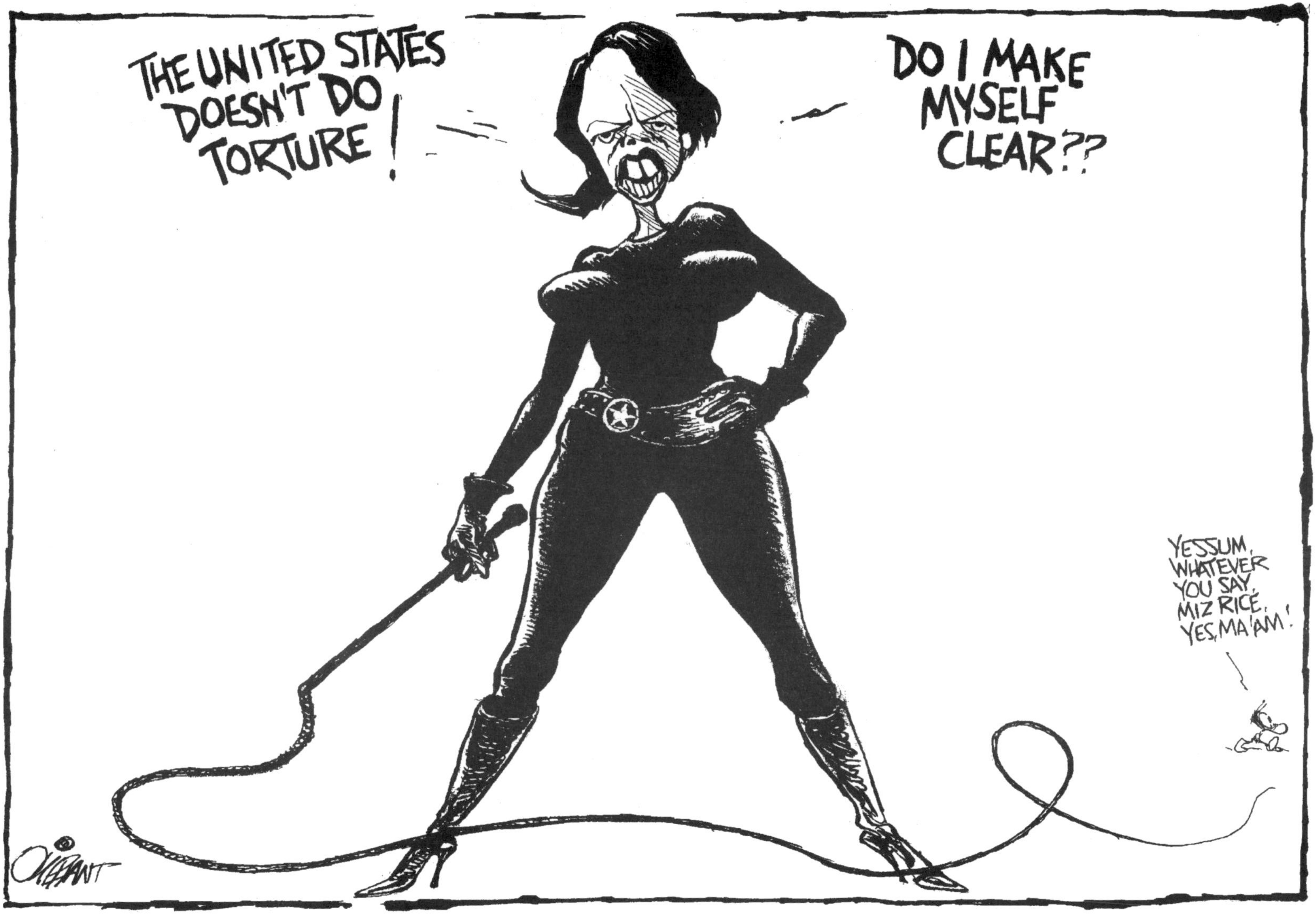
THE UNITED STATES DOESN'T DO TORTURE!
DO I MAKE MYSELF CLEAR??
YESSUM, WHATEVER YOU SAY, MIZ RICE, YES, MA'AM!
OLIPHANT

40.
Poor Devil
December 27, 2005

And we thought there were
laws against usury.

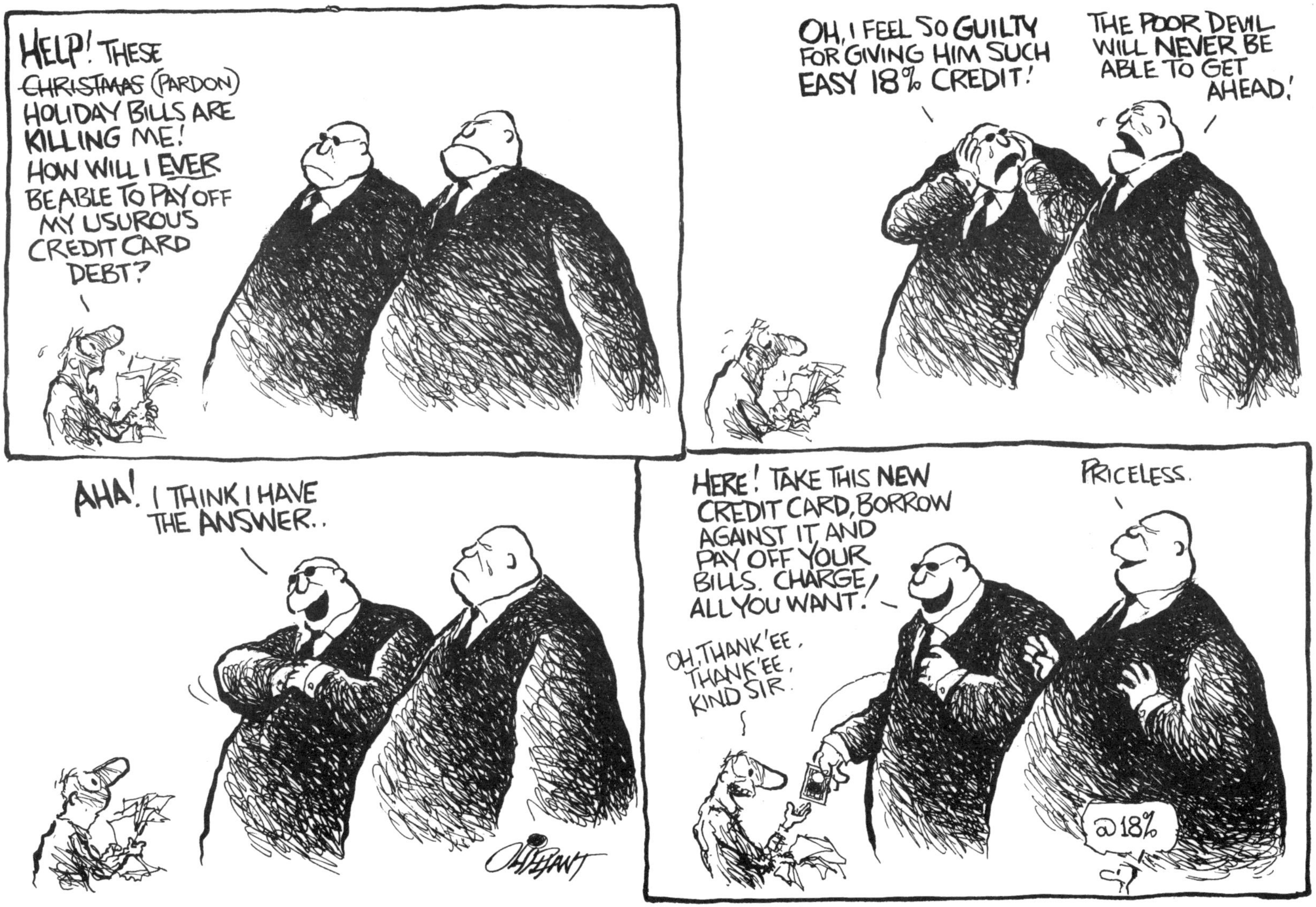
HELP! THESE CHRISTMAS (PARDON) HOLIDAY BILLS ARE KILLING ME! HOW WILL I EVER BE ABLE TO PAY OFF MY USUROUS CREDIT CARD DEBT?
OH, I FEEL SO GUILTY FOR GIVING HIM SUCH EASY 18% CREDIT!
THE POOR DEVIL WILL NEVER BE ABLE TO GET AHEAD!
AHA! I THINK I HAVE THE ANSWER..
HERE! TAKE THIS NEW CREDIT CARD, BORROW AGAINST IT, AND PAY OFF YOUR BILLS. CHARGE ALL YOU WANT!
PRICELESS.
OH, THANK'EE, THANK'EE, KIND SIR.
@18%
OLIPHANT

41.

You Have to Believe

December 26, 2005

The Patriot Act, grasping for greater authority to monitor for possible terrorism activity, was due to be reauthorized by Congress, and President Bush was allowing the NSA to wiretap international phone calls without a warrant.

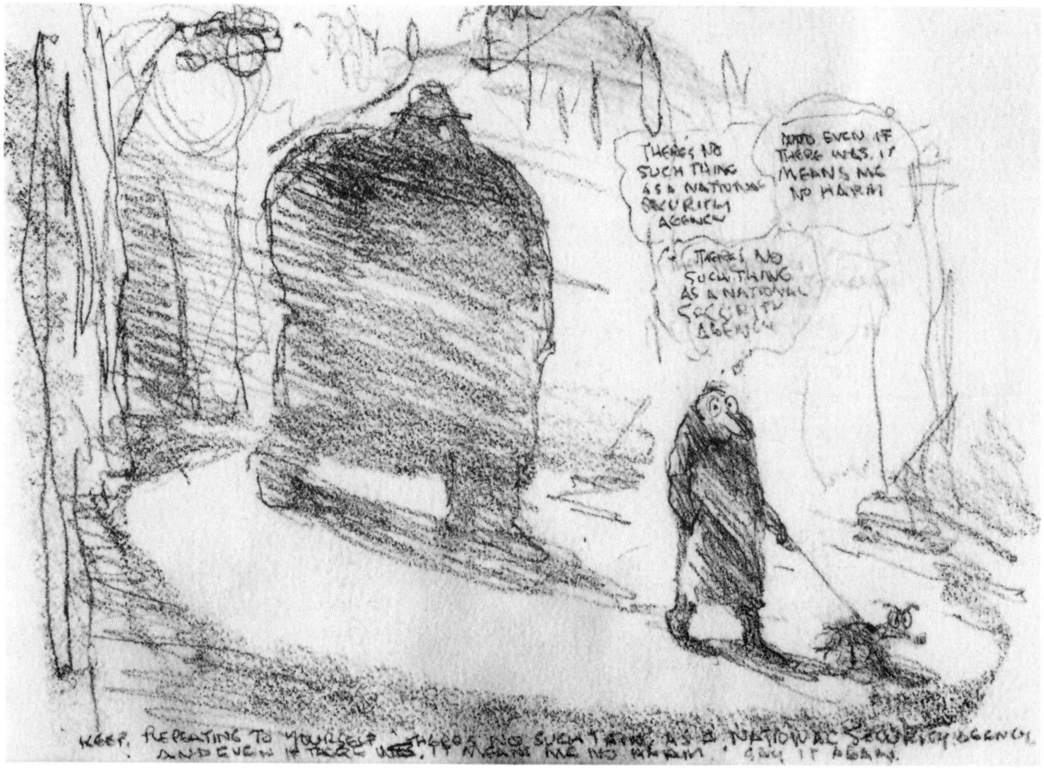
THERES NO SUCH THING AS A NATIONAL SECURITY AGENCY
AND EVEN IF THERE WAS, IT MEANS ME NO HARM
THERES NO SUCH THING AS A NATIONAL SECURITY AGENCY

Preliminary sketch for
You Have to Believe
Graphite on paper

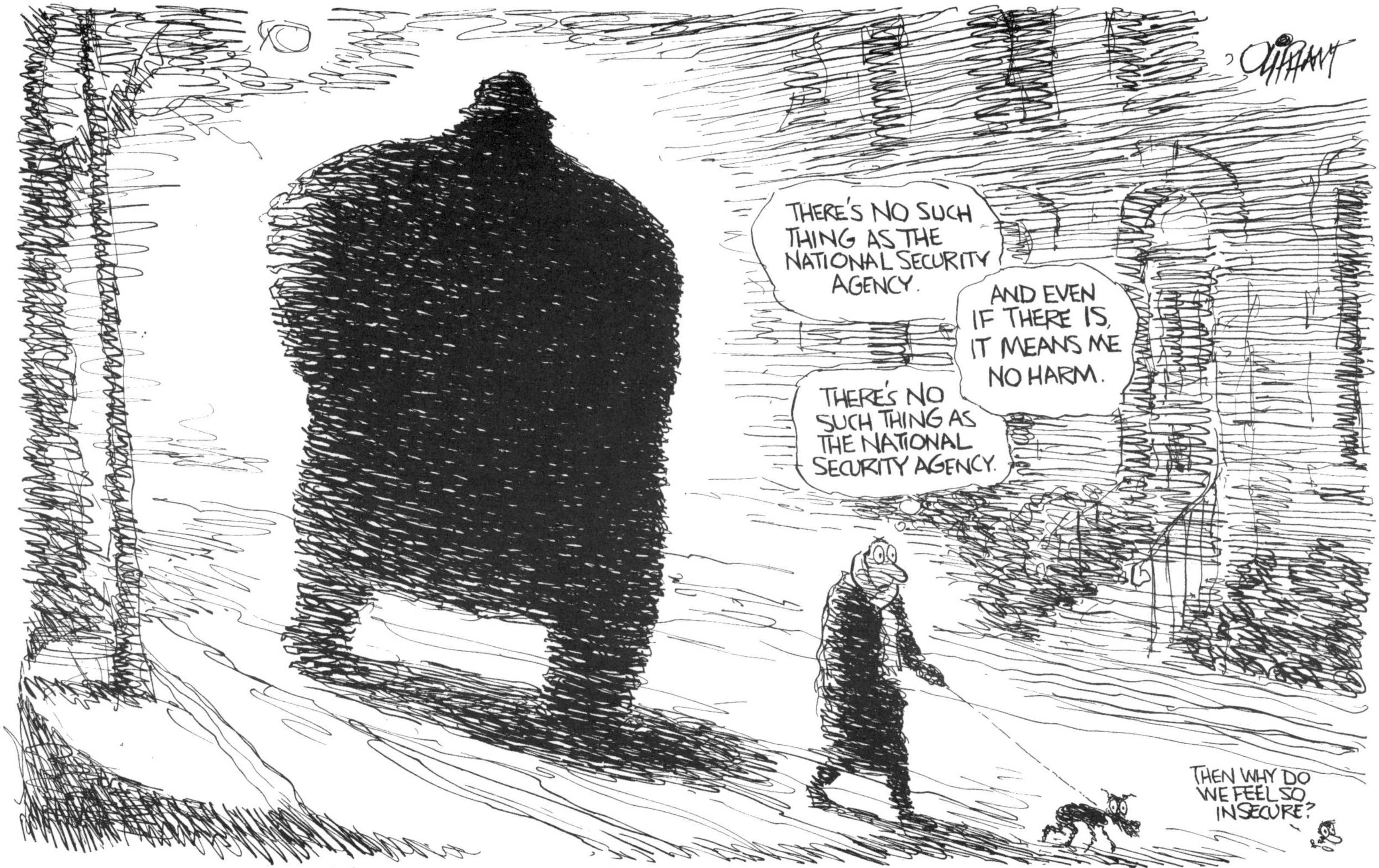
OLIPHANT
THERE'S NO SUCH THING AS THE NATIONAL SECURITY AGENCY.
AND EVEN IF THERE IS, IT MEANS ME NO HARM.
THERE'S NO SUCH THING AS THE NATIONAL SECURITY AGENCY.
THEN WHY DO WE FEEL SO INSECURE?

KEEP REPEATING TO YOURSELF: 'THERE'S NO SUCH THING AS THE NATIONAL SECURITY AGENCY, AND EVEN IF THERE IS, IT MEANS ME NO HARM.' NOW SAY IT AGAIN...

42.
Hunter
February 15, 2006

Vice President Cheney,
on a quail hunt in Texas,
accidentally shot his hunting
companion, a seventy-eight-
year-old lawyer, in the face.
He made no haste to report
the incident; it was, after
all, just a casual shooting
between friends.

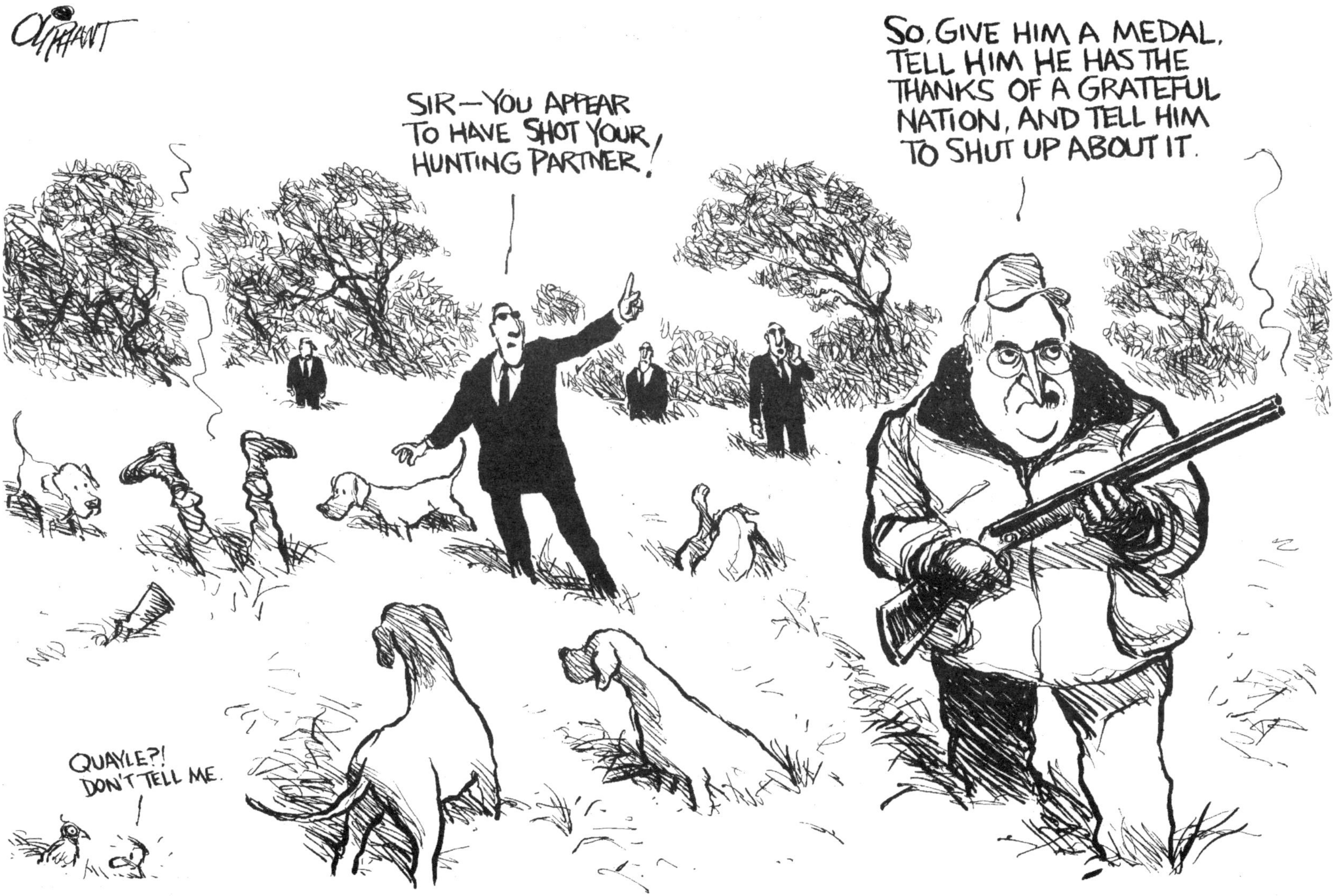
OLIPHANT
SIR—YOU APPEAR TO HAVE SHOT YOUR HUNTING PARTNER!
SO, GIVE HIM A MEDAL, TELL HIM HE HAS THE THANKS OF A GRATEFUL NATION, AND TELL HIM TO SHUT UP ABOUT IT.
QUAYLE?! DON'T TELL ME.

43.
Medicare Explained
March 16, 2006

"Take that, you #&+ **^!!!" they explained.

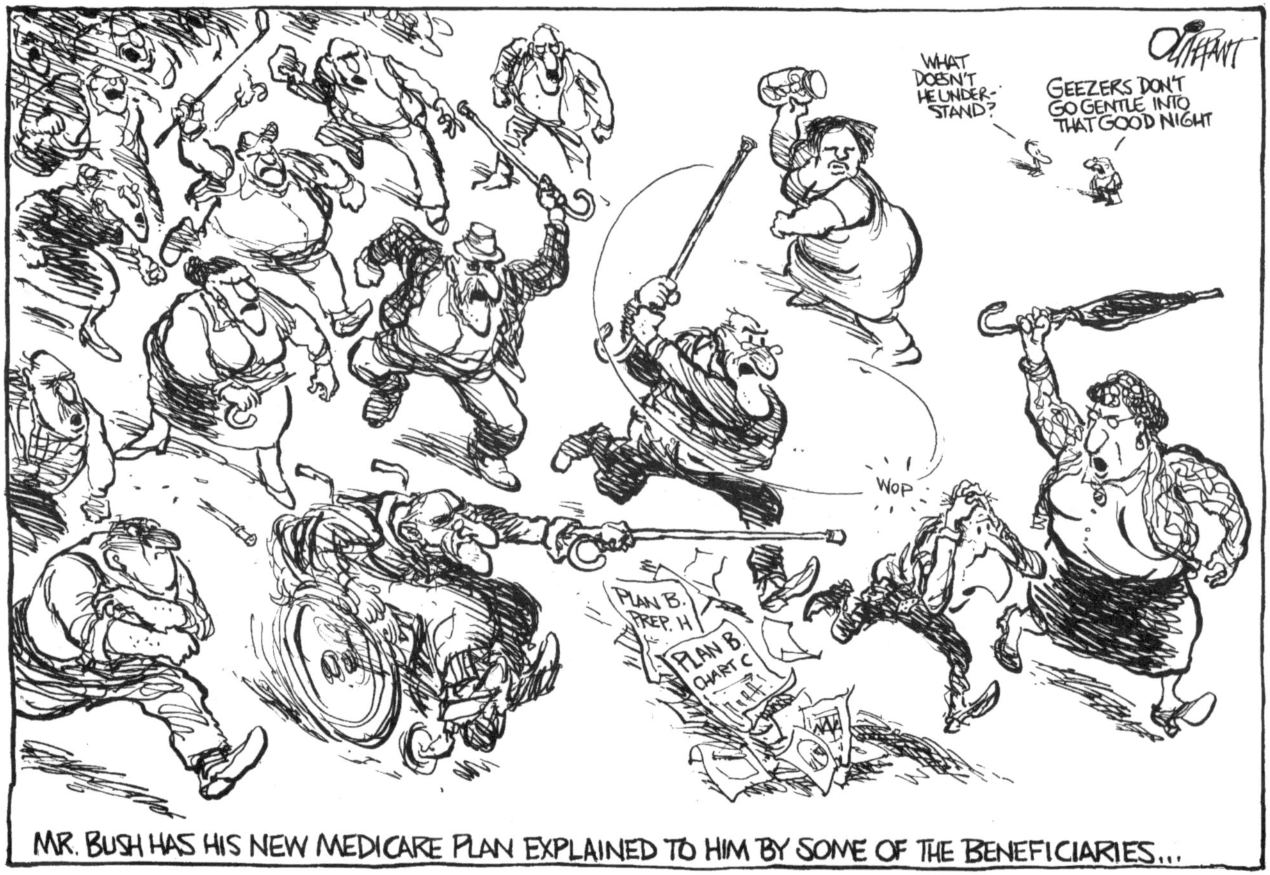
WHAT DOESN'T HE UNDER-STAND?
GEEZERS DON'T GO GENTLE INTO THAT GOOD NIGHT
WOP
PLAN B. PREP. H
PLAN B. CHART C
MR. BUSH HAS HIS NEW MEDICARE PLAN EXPLAINED TO HIM BY SOME OF THE BENEFICIARIES...

44.
Third Anniversary
March 20, 2006

Celebrating three years of Mission Accomplished in Iraq.

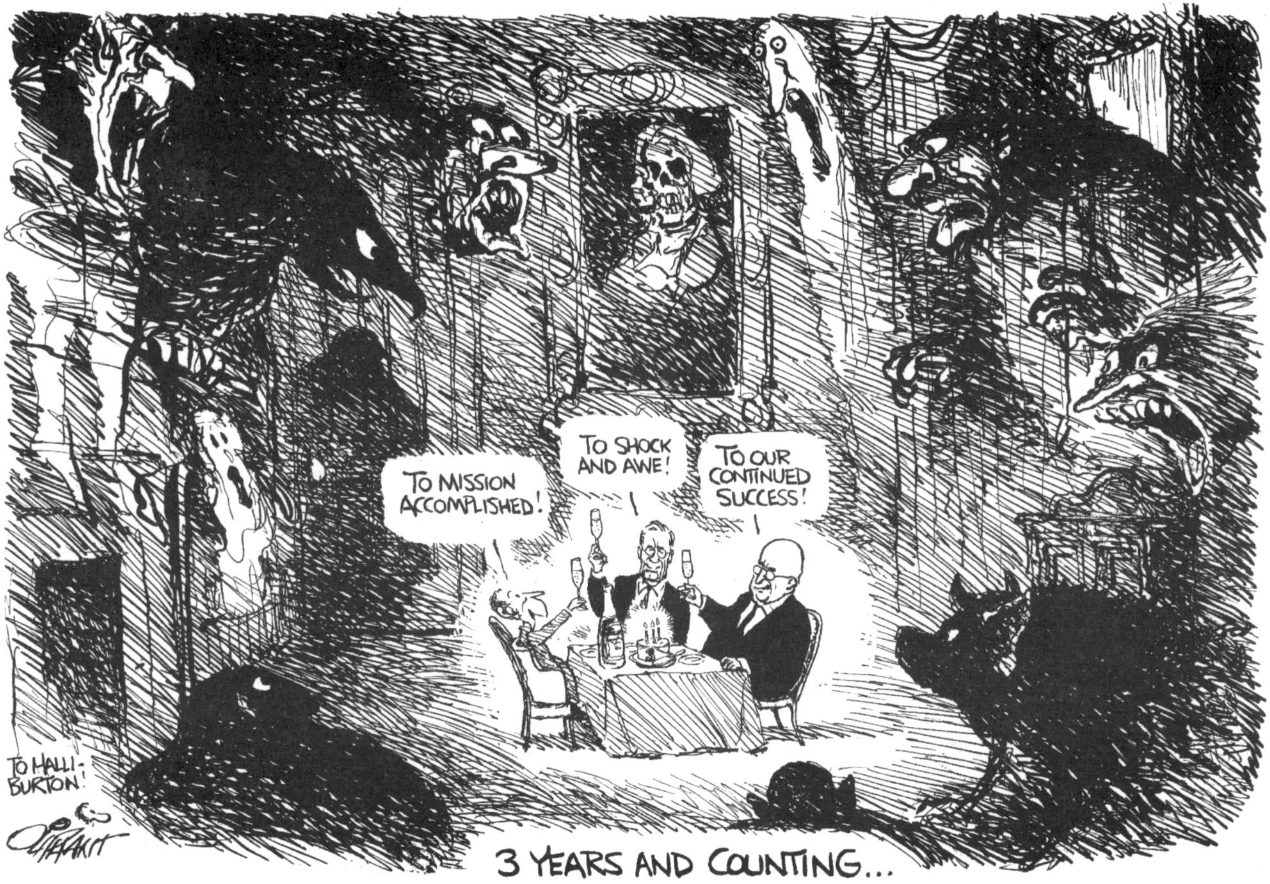
TO MISSION ACCOMPLISHED!
TO SHOCK AND AWE!
TO OUR CONTINUED SUCCESS!
TO HALLI-BURTON!
3 YEARS AND COUNTING...

45.
The Great Wall
March 29, 2006

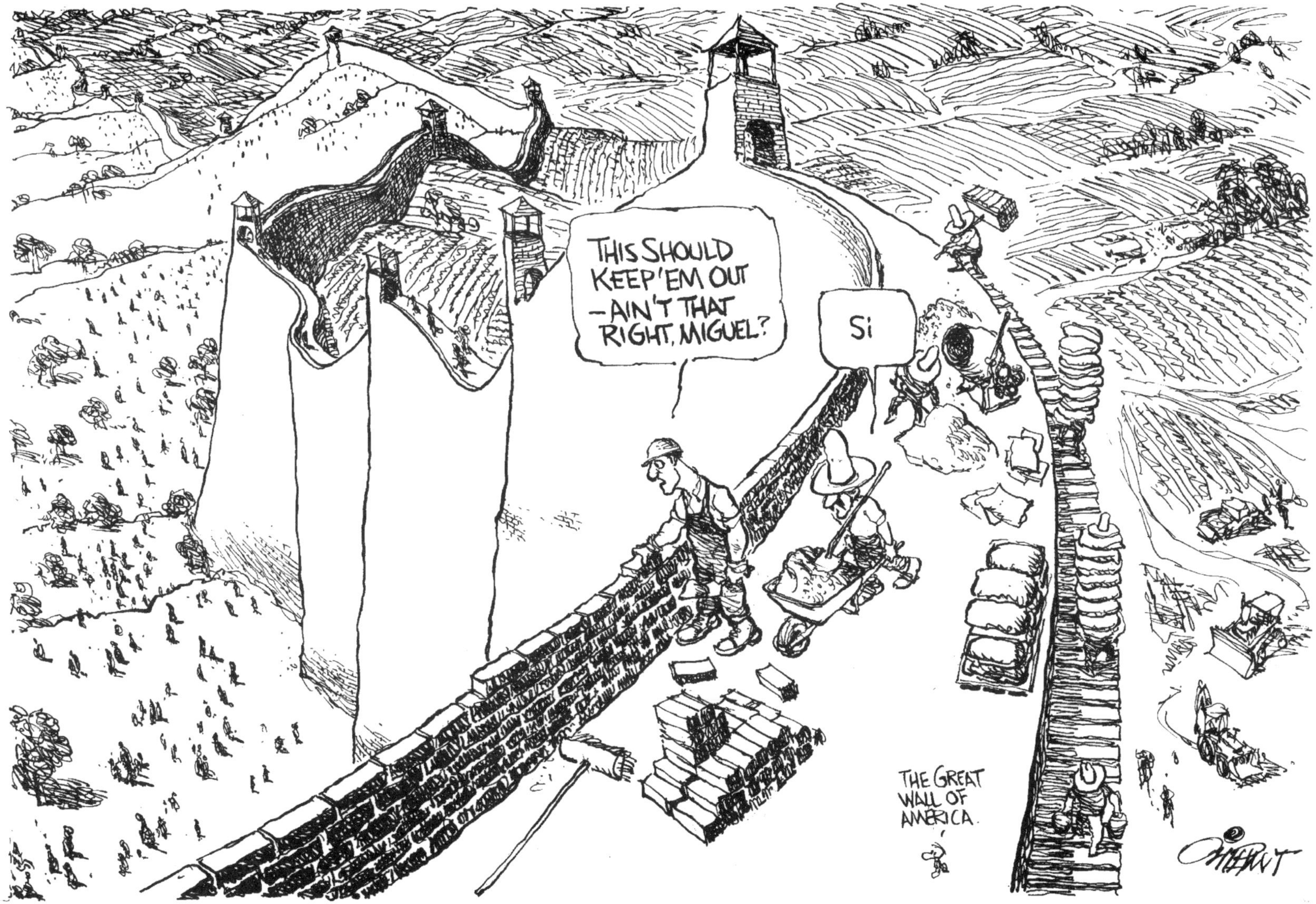
THIS SHOULD KEEP'EM OUT
-AIN'T THAT RIGHT, MIGUEL?
Si
THE GREAT WALL OF AMERICA

46.
Lucky All Round
March 22, 2006

GOLLY, MR. LBJ – THIS IRAQ WAR IS DESTROYING MY PRESIDENCY (SUCH AS IT IS).
Y'ALL ARE TOO YOUNG TO REMEMBER, LI'L FELLER...
BUT VIETNAM FINALLY CAUSED ME TO UTTER THE FOLLOWIN' WORDS...
"AH WILL NOT SEEK, NOR WILL AH ACCEPT, MY PARTY'S NOMINATION FOR PRESIDENT OF THE UNITED STATES."
BUT IN MY TIME AH DID GET A LOT OF USEFUL LEGISLATION THROUGH THE CONGRESS...
WHICH IS MORE'N Y'ALL CAN SAY FOR Y'SELF, LIL FELLER!
BUT I'M LUCKY, MR. LBJ – I CAN'T RUN AGAIN, ANYWAY!!
THE COUNTRY'S GOOD FORTUNE, LIL FELLER.
NOTE THE SIMILARITY OF THE TWO?
ONLY IN THE WARS AND THE EARS
OLIPHANT

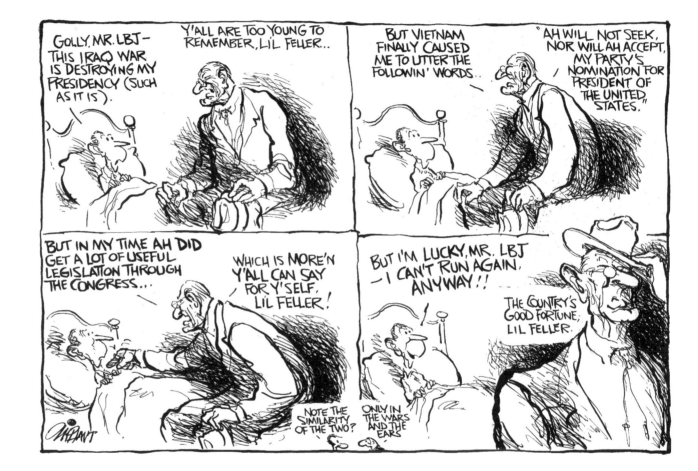

47.

Don't Hit on Her

May 1, 2006

The brilliant Republican plan was to offer voters $100 gasoline rebate checks to offset the pain of high pump prices. Don't feel insulted—hit him again for the rest of us.

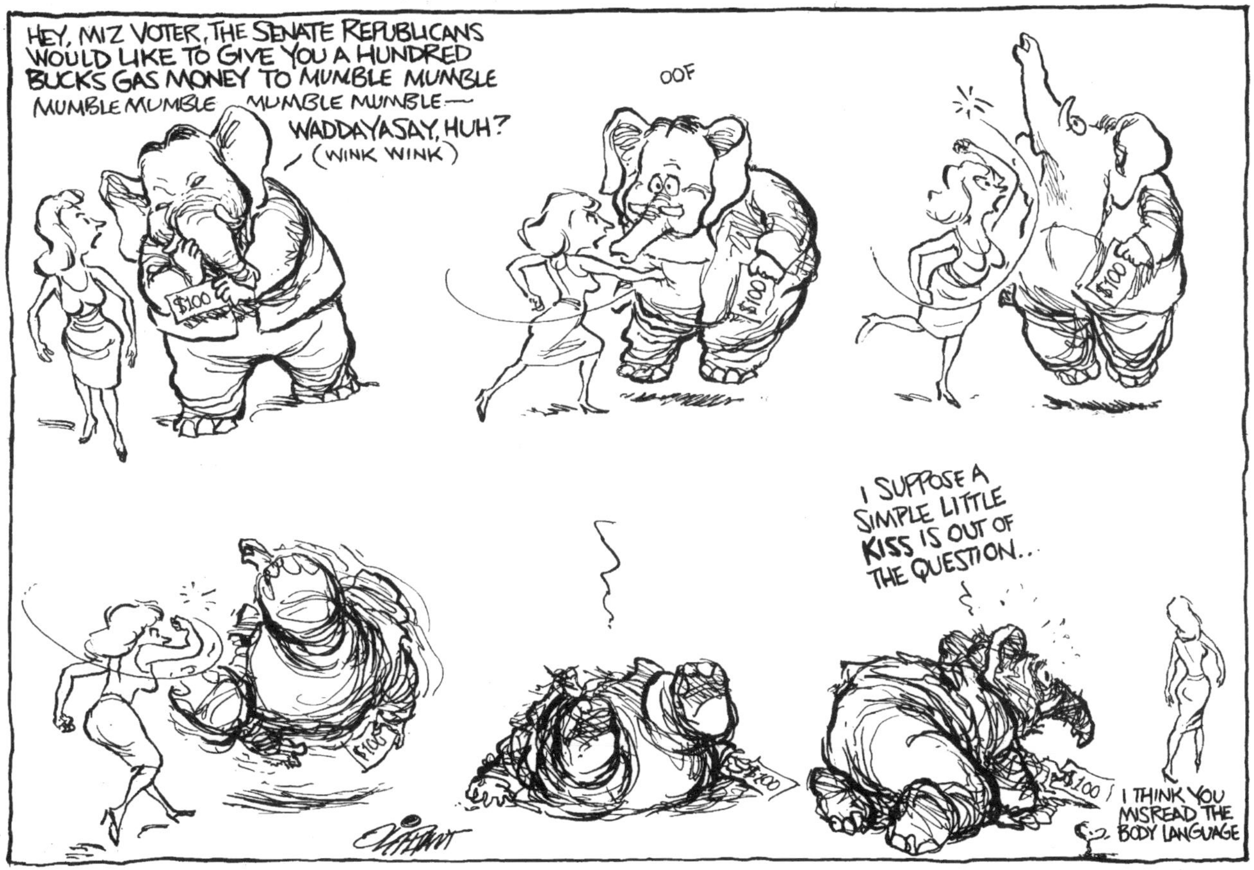
HEY, MIZ VOTER, THE SENATE REPUBLICANS WOULD LIKE TO GIVE YOU A HUNDRED BUCKS GAS MONEY TO MUMBLE MUMBLE MUMBLE MUMBLE MUMBLE MUMBLE—
WADDAYASAY, HUH?
(WINK WINK)
$100
OOF
$100
$100
$100
I SUPPOSE A SIMPLE LITTLE KISS IS OUT OF THE QUESTION...
$100
I THINK YOU MISREAD THE BODY LANGUAGE

48.
Transition
May 3, 2006

Pump pain solved.

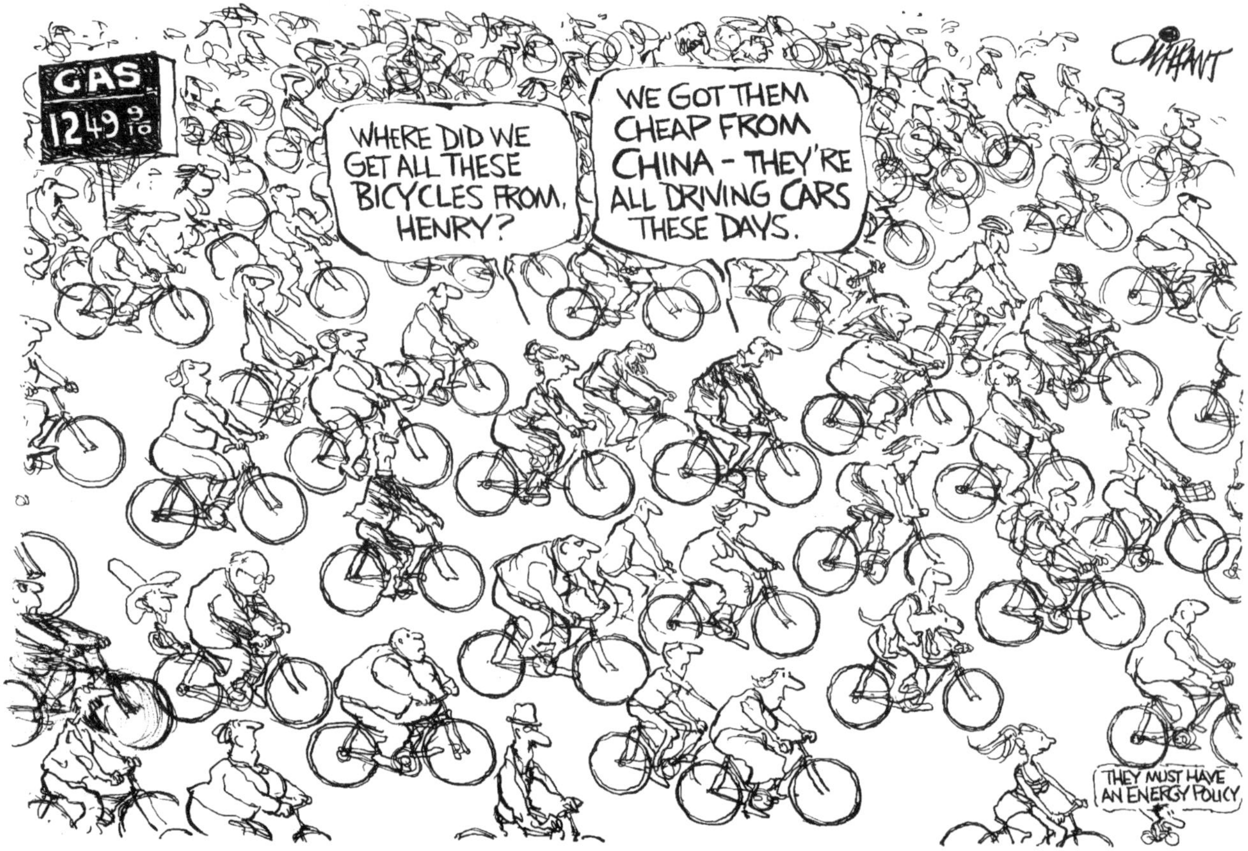
GAS
12 49 9/10
WHERE DID WE GET ALL THESE BICYCLES FROM, HENRY?
WE GOT THEM CHEAP FROM CHINA - THEY'RE ALL DRIVING CARS THESE DAYS.
THEY MUST HAVE AN ENERGY POLICY
OLIPHANT

49.

Don't Rush Over

May 23, 2006

The brutal treatment of black Africans by the Arab-dominated Sudanese government in Khartoum, and an exhausted environment that can no longer support the number of people who live there, was made worse by the resultant famine ravaging the country. Relief is on the way, said the world . . .

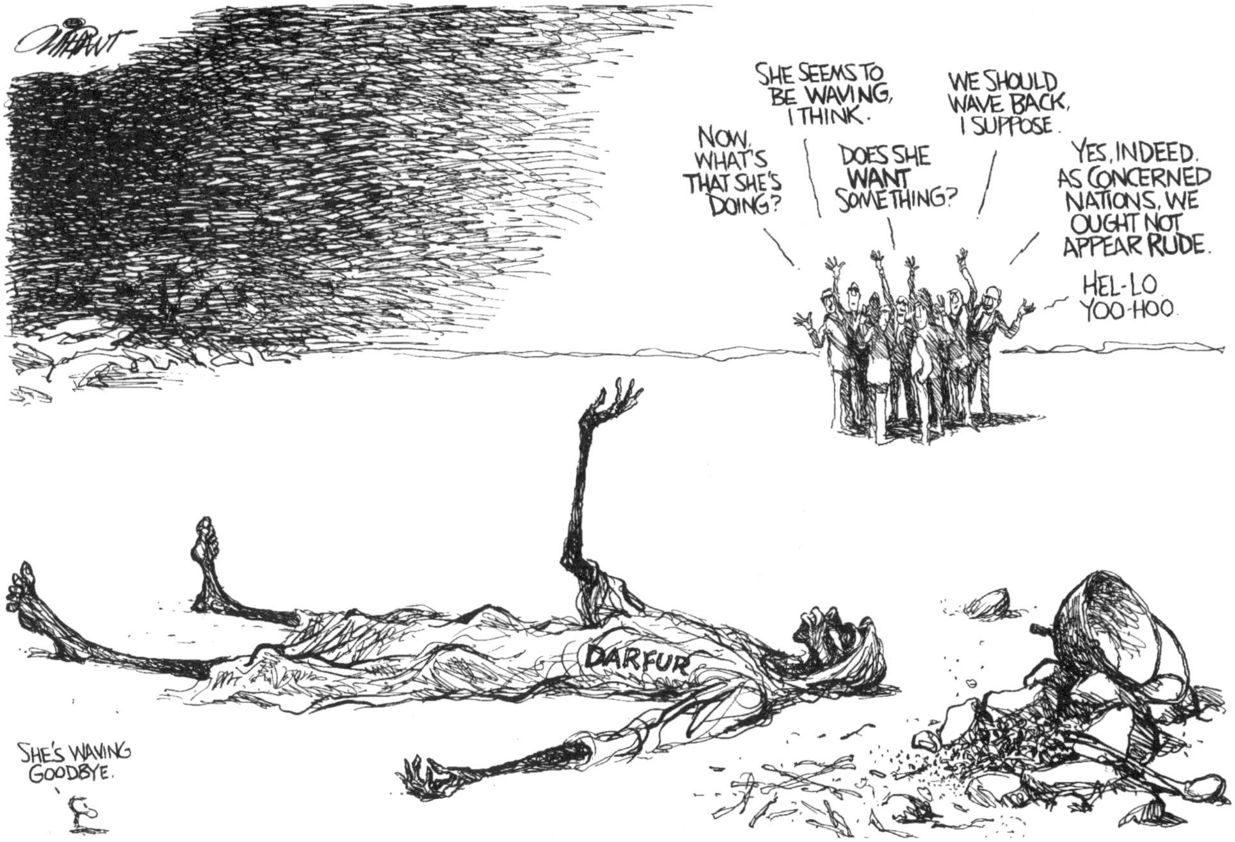
NOW, WHAT'S THAT SHE'S DOING?
SHE SEEMS TO BE WAVING, I THINK.
DOES SHE WANT SOMETHING?
WE SHOULD WAVE BACK, I SUPPOSE.
YES, INDEED. AS CONCERNED NATIONS, WE OUGHT NOT APPEAR RUDE.
HEL-LO YOO-HOO
DARFUR
SHE'S WAVING GOODBYE.

50.
Handy Diversion
June 8, 2006

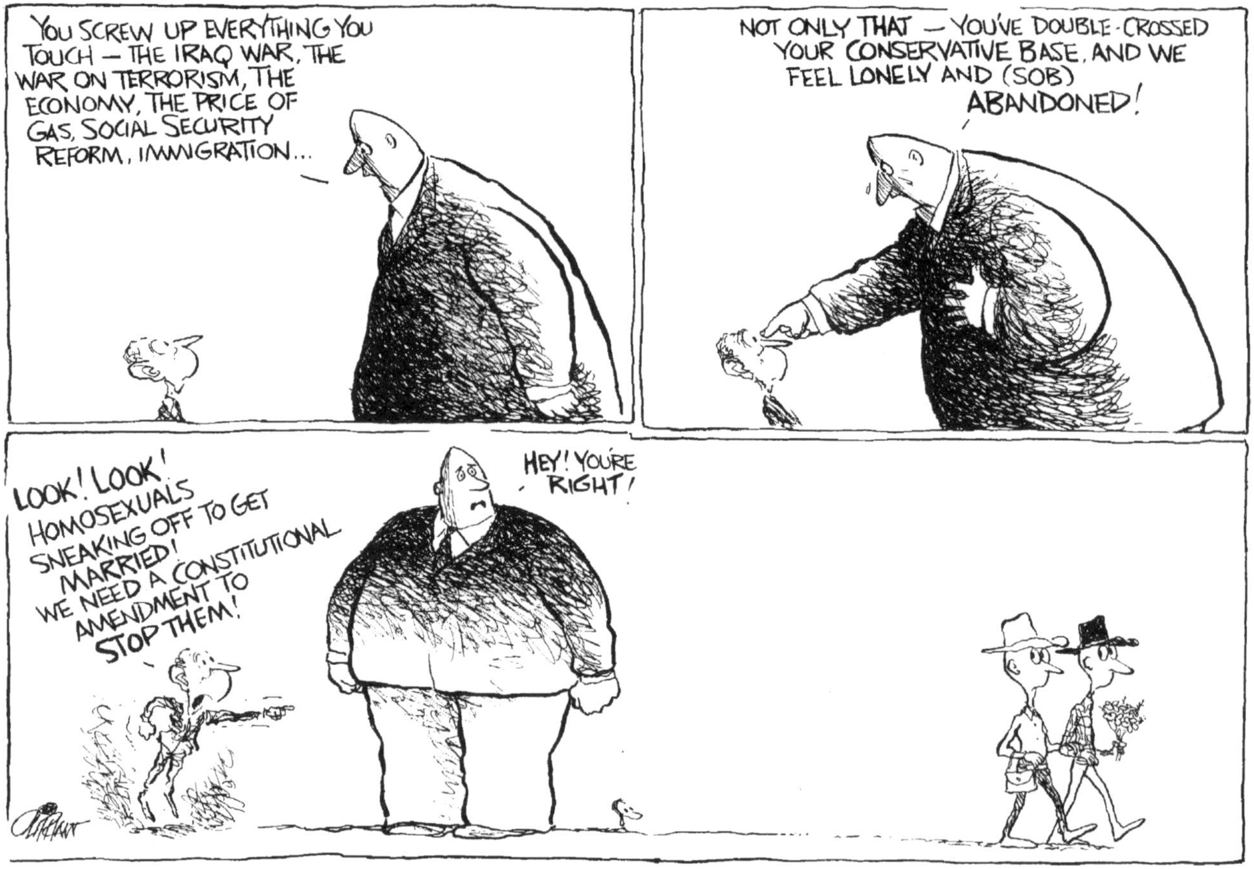
YOU SCREW UP EVERYTHING YOU TOUCH — THE IRAQ WAR, THE WAR ON TERRORISM, THE ECONOMY, THE PRICE OF GAS, SOCIAL SECURITY REFORM, IMMIGRATION...
NOT ONLY THAT — YOU'VE DOUBLE-CROSSED YOUR CONSERVATIVE BASE, AND WE FEEL LONELY AND (SOB) ABANDONED!
LOOK! LOOK! HOMOSEXUALS SNEAKING OFF TO GET MARRIED! WE NEED A CONSTITUTIONAL AMENDMENT TO STOP THEM!
HEY! YOU'RE RIGHT!

51.
Donkey Panic
June 15, 2006

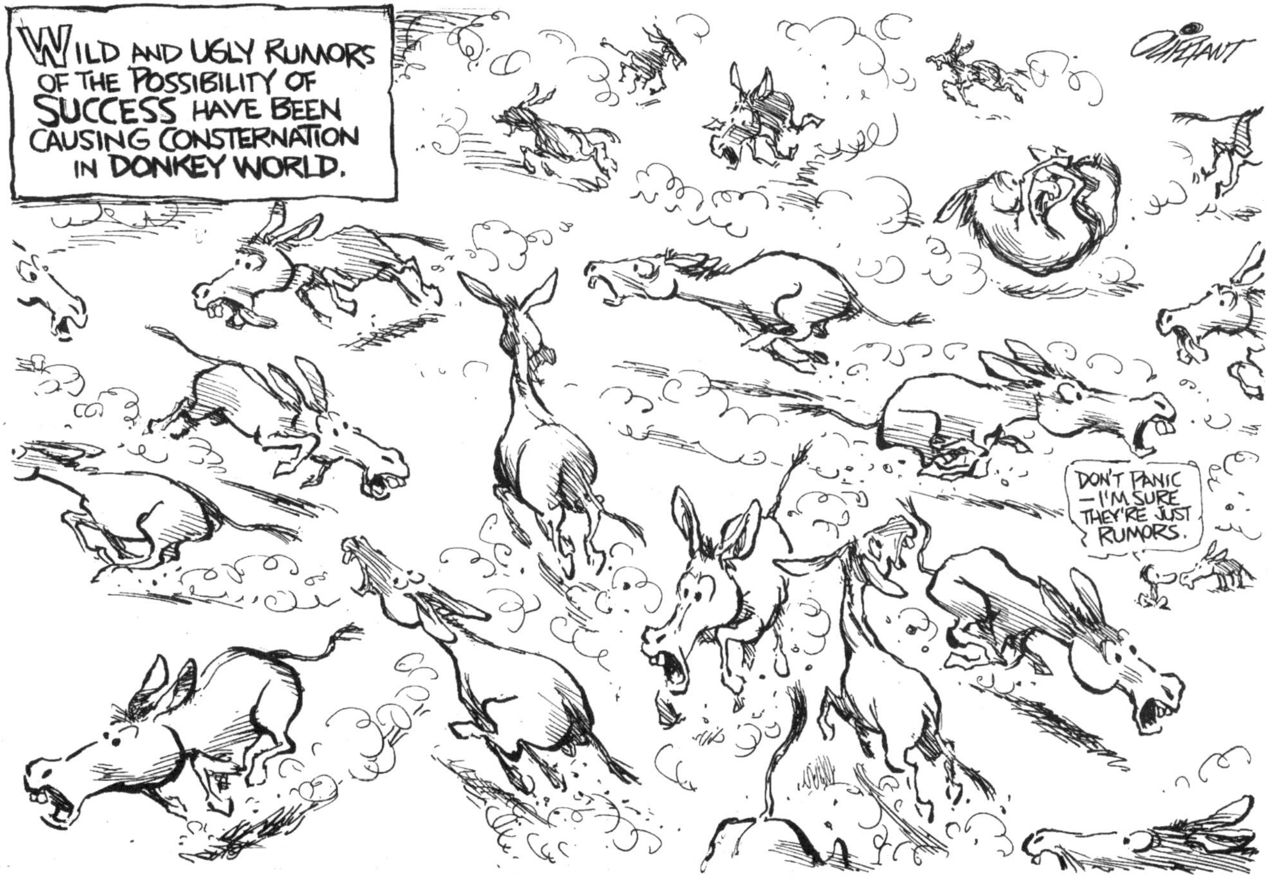
WILD AND UGLY RUMORS OF THE POSSIBILITY OF SUCCESS HAVE BEEN CAUSING CONSTERNATION IN DONKEY WORLD.
OLIPHANT
DON'T PANIC —I'M SURE THEY'RE JUST RUMORS.

52.
Exchange of Fire
August 1, 2006

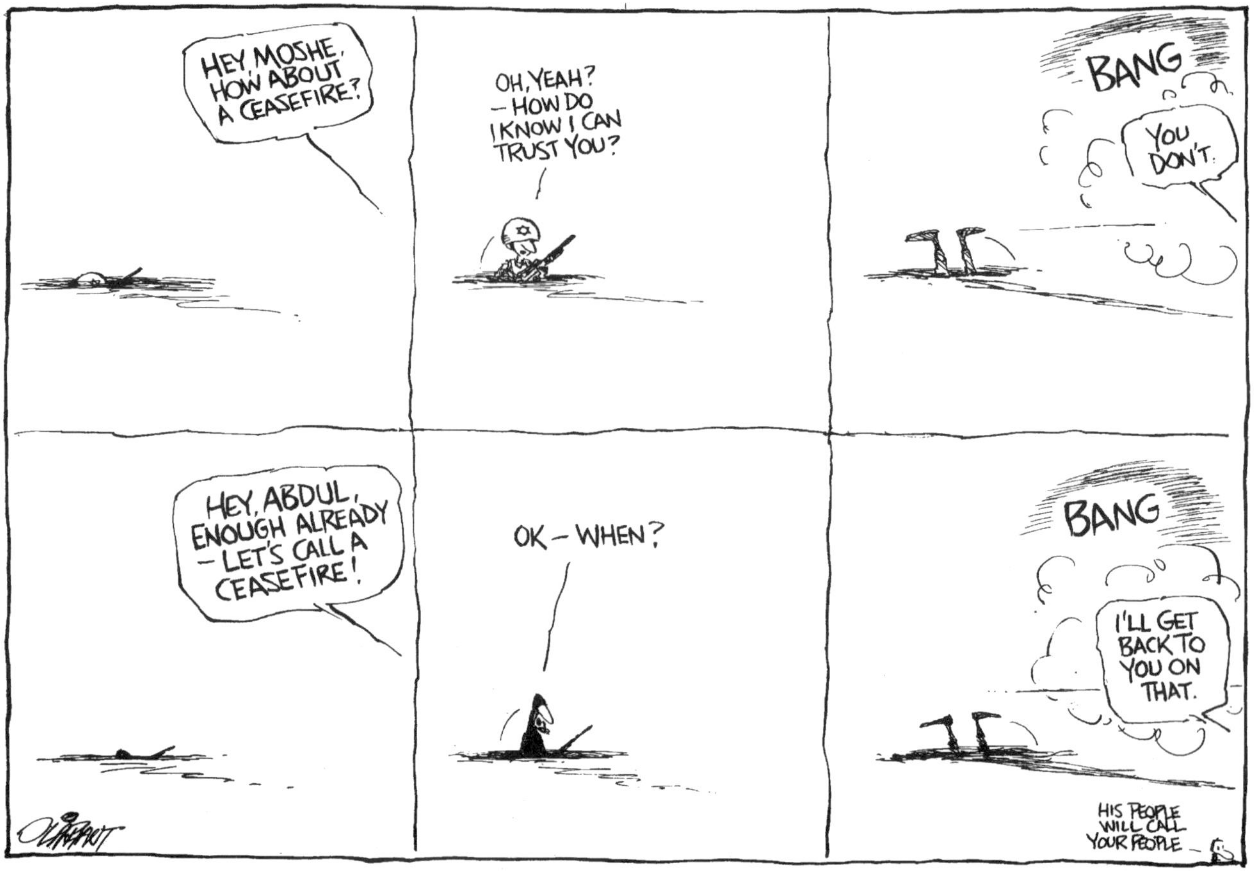
HEY, MOSHE, HOW ABOUT A CEASEFIRE?
OH, YEAH? – HOW DO I KNOW I CAN TRUST YOU?
BANG
YOU DON'T.
HEY, ABDUL, ENOUGH ALREADY – LET'S CALL A CEASEFIRE!
OK – WHEN?
BANG
I'LL GET BACK TO YOU ON THAT.
HIS PEOPLE WILL CALL YOUR PEOPLE –
OLIPHANT

53.

Oh, Yeah?

September 1, 2006

Iran insisted its nuclear research is for peaceful purposes only. Iran also has oil. Why don't we give Iran another chance? Iran is also run by a mad man.

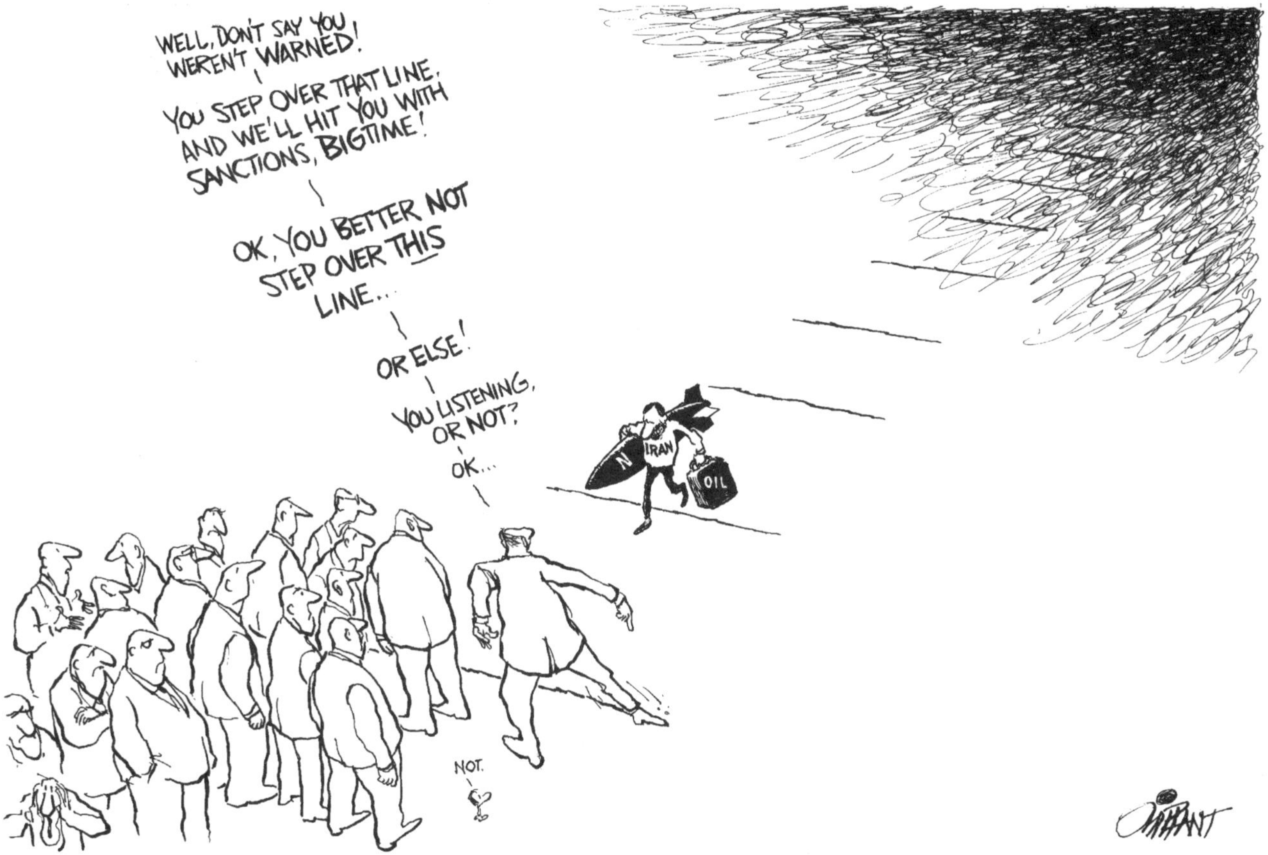
WELL, DON'T SAY YOU WEREN'T WARNED!
YOU STEP OVER THAT LINE, AND WE'LL HIT YOU WITH SANCTIONS, BIGTIME!
OK, YOU BETTER NOT STEP OVER THIS LINE...
OR ELSE!
YOU LISTENING, OR NOT?
OK...
N
IRAN
OIL
NOT.

54.
Right-Wing Jesus
October 13, 2006

What would Jesus sing,
supposing he would attend
in the first place?

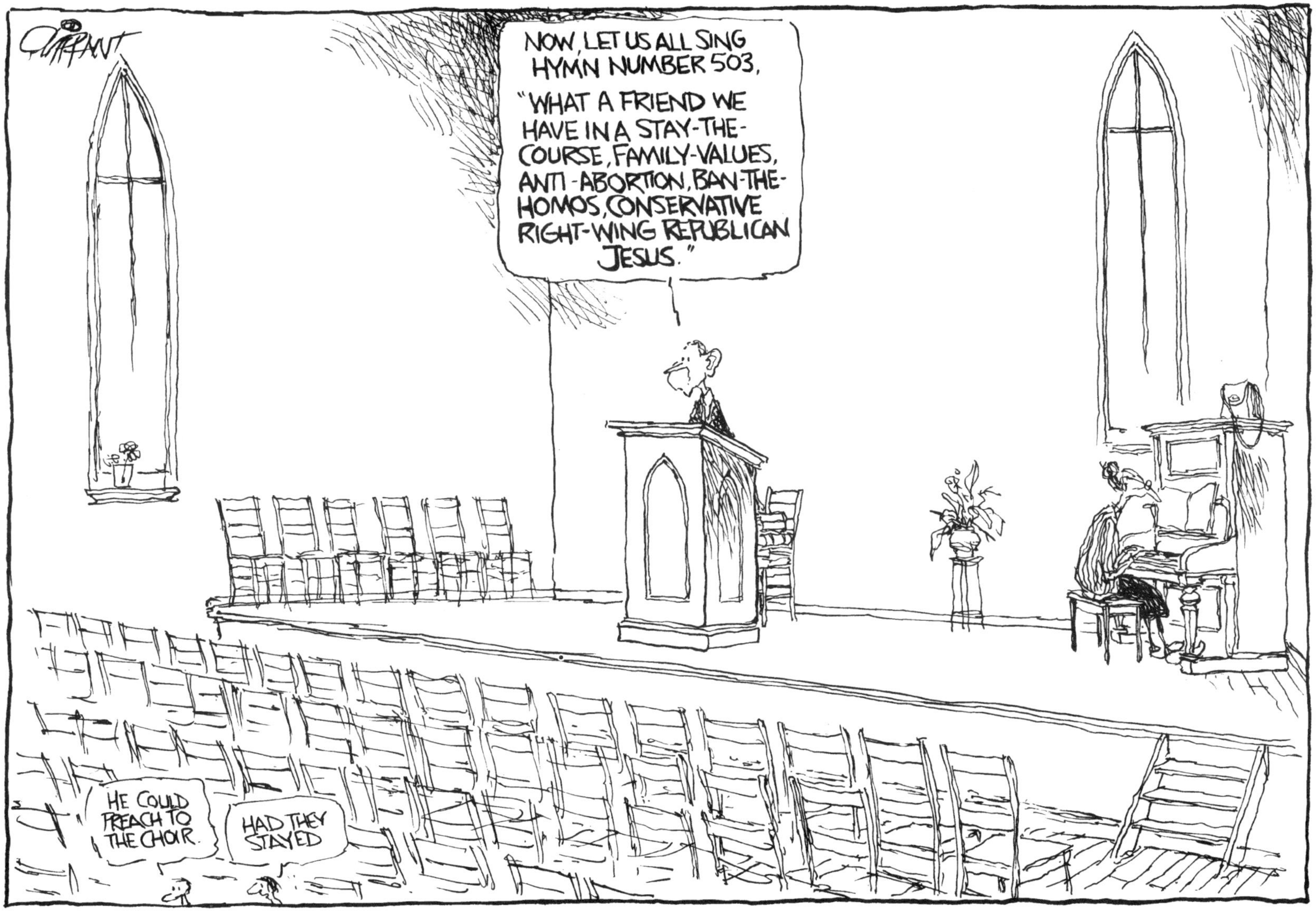
OLIPHANT
NOW, LET US ALL SING HYMN NUMBER 503, "WHAT A FRIEND WE HAVE IN A STAY-THE-COURSE, FAMILY-VALUES, ANTI-ABORTION, BAN-THE-HOMOS, CONSERVATIVE RIGHT-WING REPUBLICAN JESUS."
HE COULD PREACH TO THE CHOIR.
HAD THEY STAYED

55.
Welcome!
October 19, 2006

Timing is everything—
however, before we are
overcome by enthusiasm,
we would like to add a
few caveats to that initial
statement.

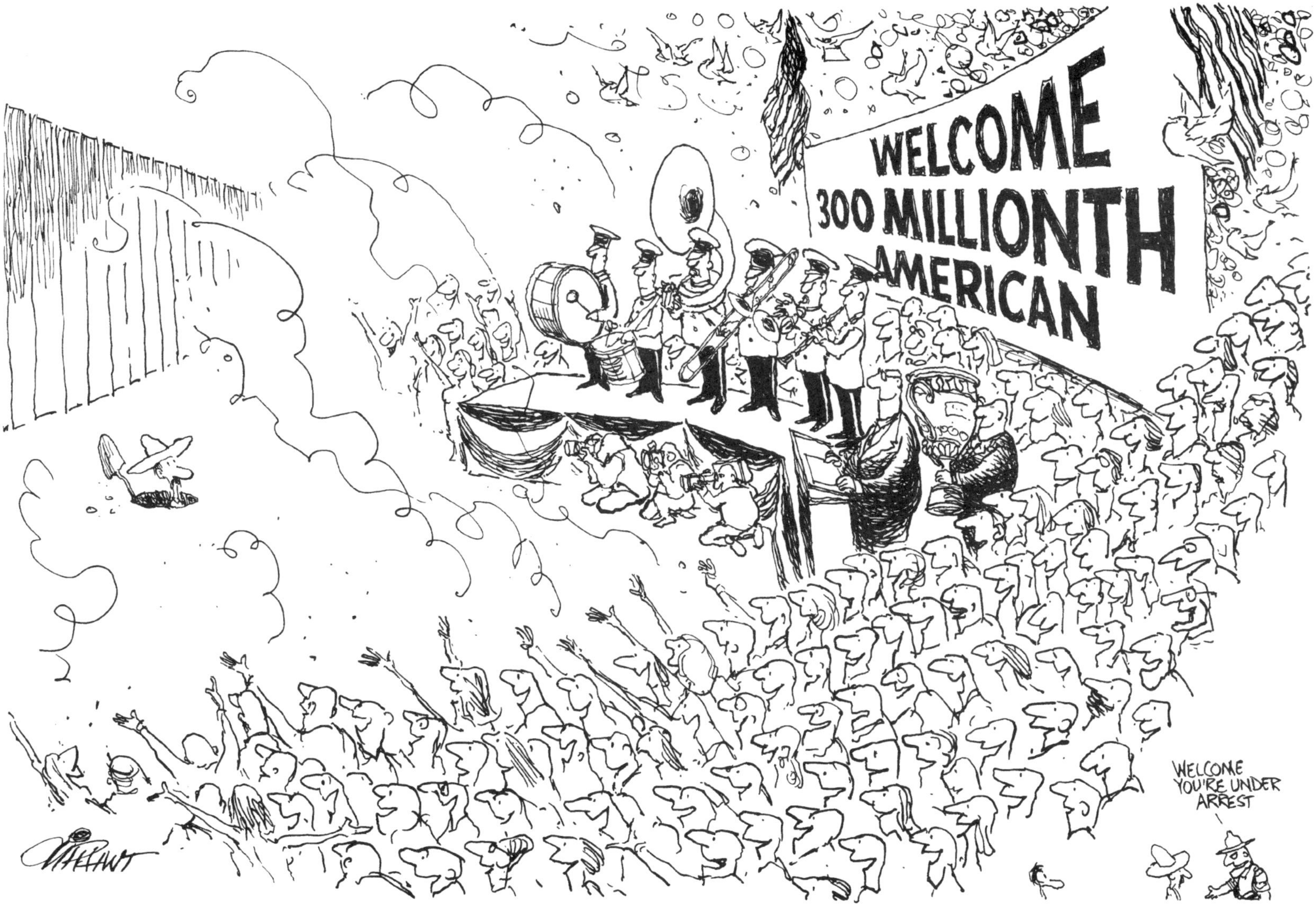
WELCOME
300 MILLIONTH
AMERICAN
WELCOME
YOU'RE UNDER
ARREST

56.
All Hail, Obama
October 23, 2006

So thirsty were we for change. So appalled, scared, and disgusted were we at the thought of four more Republican years. So apprehensive were we of the dreaded Hillary . . .

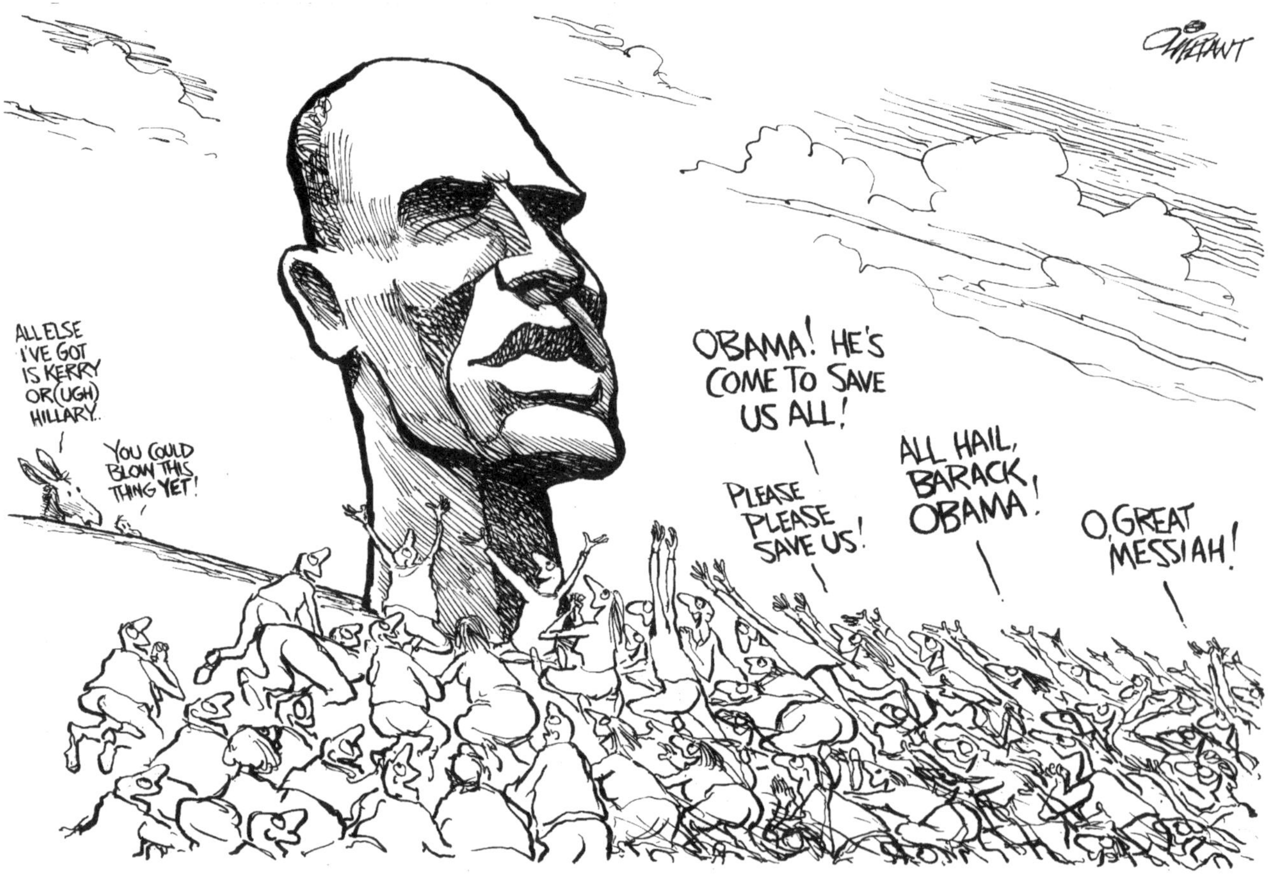

ALL ELSE I'VE GOT IS KERRY OR (UGH) HILLARY..
YOU COULD BLOW THIS THING YET!
OBAMA! HE'S COME TO SAVE US ALL!
PLEASE PLEASE SAVE US!
ALL HAIL, BARACK OBAMA!
O, GREAT MESSIAH!

57.
The Next Move
October 30, 2006

Oh, that's right, we gave away habeas corpus to the needy.

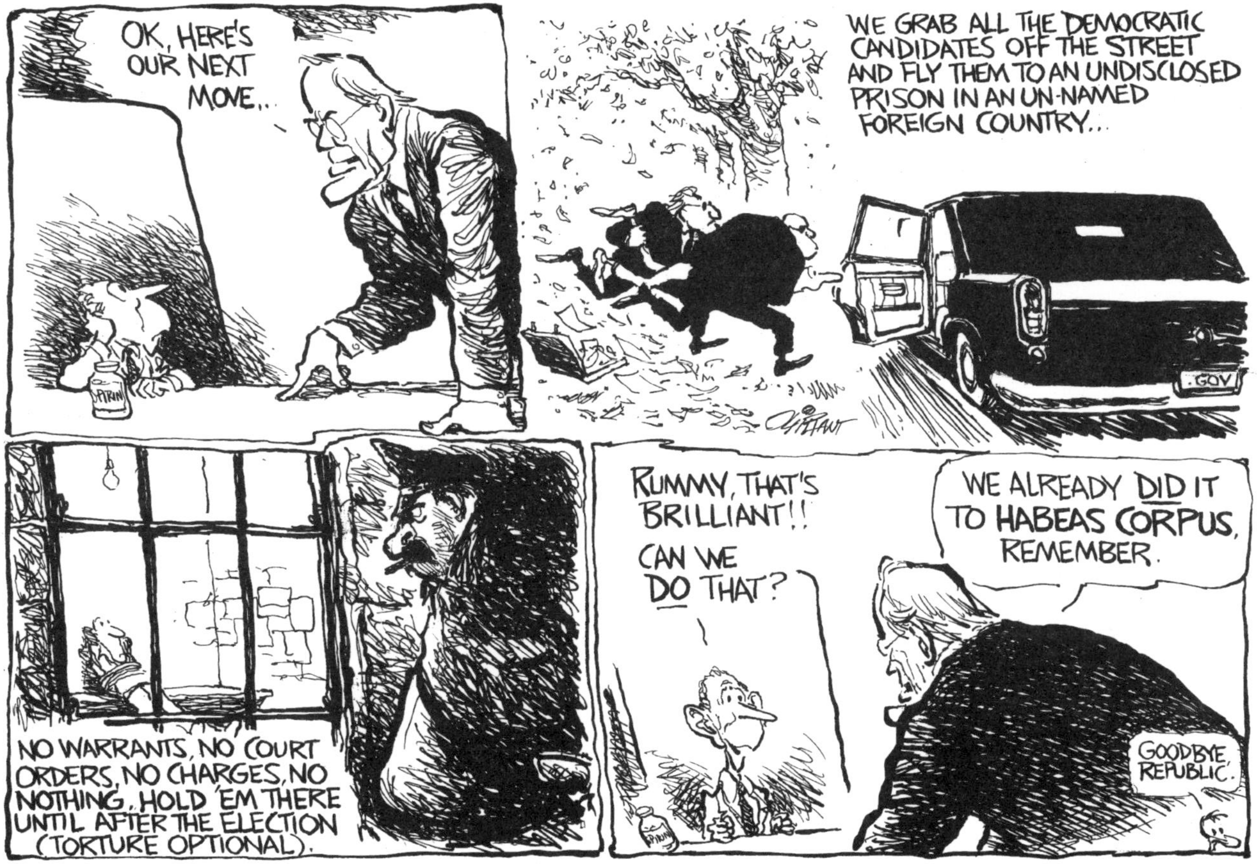

OK, HERE'S OUR NEXT MOVE...
WE GRAB ALL THE DEMOCRATIC CANDIDATES OFF THE STREET AND FLY THEM TO AN UNDISCLOSED PRISON IN AN UN-NAMED FOREIGN COUNTRY...
.GOV
NO WARRANTS, NO COURT ORDERS, NO CHARGES, NO NOTHING. HOLD 'EM THERE UNTIL AFTER THE ELECTION (TORTURE OPTIONAL).
RUMMY, THAT'S BRILLIANT!! CAN WE DO THAT?
WE ALREADY DID IT TO HABEAS CORPUS, REMEMBER.
GOODBYE, REPUBLIC.

58.
Sympathy
November 7, 2006

The Republicans got hammered in the midterm elections.

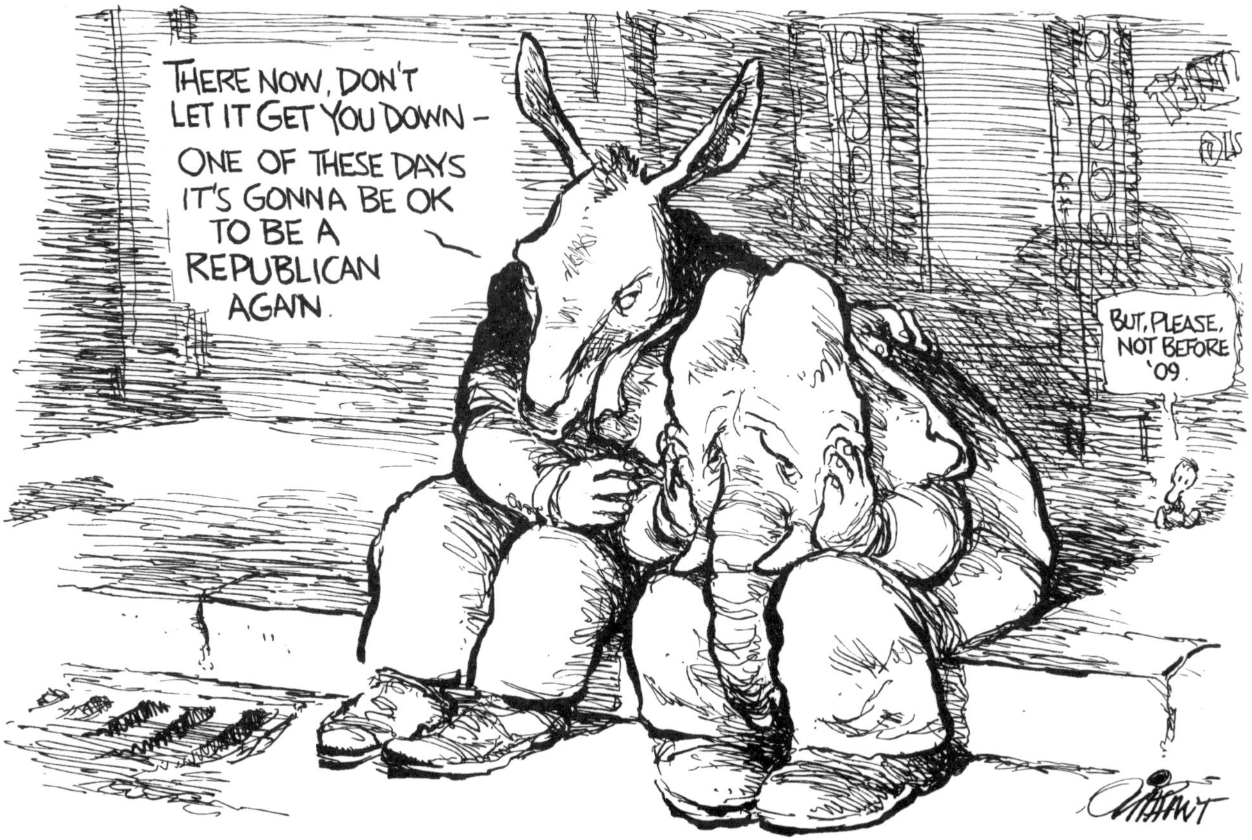
THERE NOW, DON'T LET IT GET YOU DOWN - ONE OF THESE DAYS IT'S GONNA BE OK TO BE A REPUBLICAN AGAIN.
BUT, PLEASE, NOT BEFORE '09.

59.
The Fall
November 9, 2006

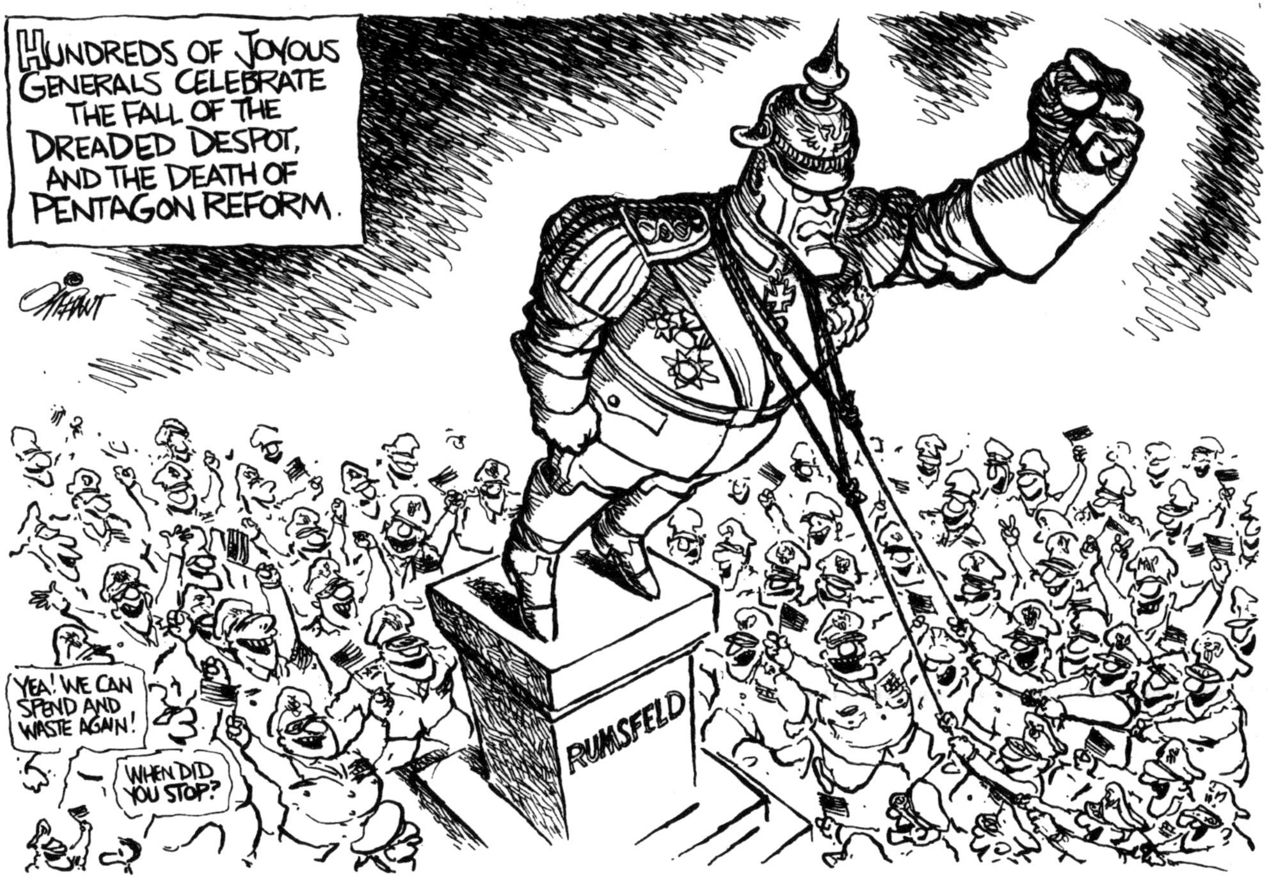
HUNDREDS OF JOYOUS GENERALS CELEBRATE THE FALL OF THE DREADED DESPOT, AND THE DEATH OF PENTAGON REFORM.
YEA! WE CAN SPEND AND WASTE AGAIN!
WHEN DID YOU STOP?
RUMSFELD

60.
The Lecture
November 29, 2006

Congresswoman Nancy Pelosi became Speaker Pelosi. On the right is Iraq's Prime Minister Malaki. In the middle is the president of the United States. Many would say that none of them should be running anything.

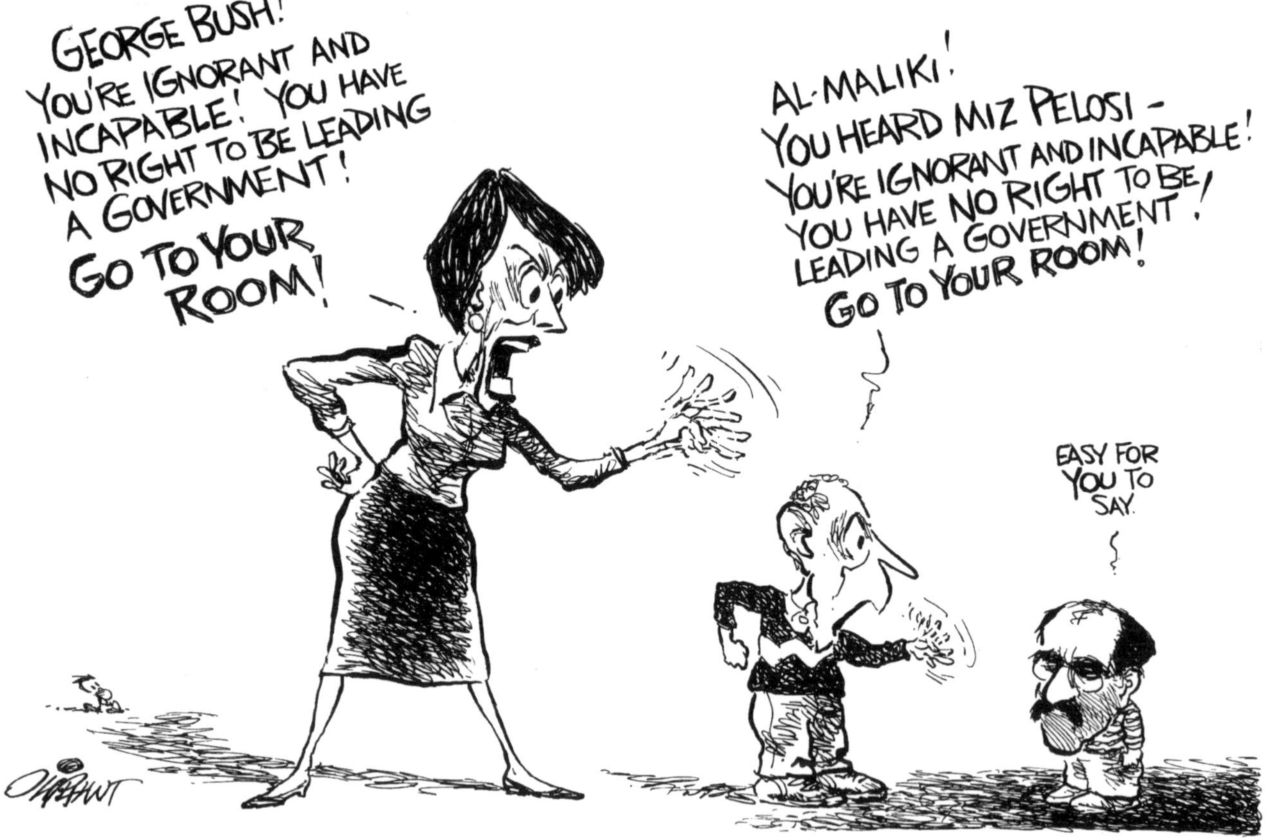
GEORGE BUSH! YOU'RE IGNORANT AND INCAPABLE! YOU HAVE NO RIGHT TO BE LEADING A GOVERNMENT! GO TO YOUR ROOM!
AL-MALIKI! YOU HEARD MIZ PELOSI - YOU'RE IGNORANT AND INCAPABLE! YOU HAVE NO RIGHT TO BE LEADING A GOVERNMENT! GO TO YOUR ROOM!
EASY FOR YOU TO SAY.
OLIPHANT

61.

Gerald Ford Remembered

December 27, 2006

Because of his perceived penchant, quite undeserved, for banging his head on helicopters and falling down stairs, I habitually depicted President Gerald Ford wearing a large Band-Aid across his forehead. In June of 1996, I was surprised to find myself providing the amusement at a heavily Republican gathering which was, in fact, the party regularly given in Washington, D.C., by the ex-president for the alumni of his White House.

They were a reassuringly relaxed group, and I was encouraged to draw and remark on people and incidents of the Nixon-Ford years, working in charcoal on paper under a TV camera while the image was projected on a huge screen behind me as I drew. With this setup in place, I caricatured, with varying degrees of politeness, such luminaries as Nixon, Kissinger, Schlesinger, Rumsfeld, Cheney and so on, and eventually (wait for it) Gerald Ford himself, complete with Band-Aid. The president joined in the reaction with great roars of laughter, and at that I quickly finished my presentation, relieved it was over.

Some say you should not encourage cartoonists too much as they are given to overreacting to applause, which may be the explanation for what I did next, but whatever the case, I have a set of Kennerly photos to prove it. Leaving the podium, I crossed the room to President Ford and with the charcoal drew a large Band-Aid on his forehead. The photos show me in the act while the president stands perfectly still, his eyes rolled upward, wearing a huge, expectant smile. A Secret Service agent appeared at my shoulder just then and muttered, "You do that one more time and you'll never cartoon in this town again..." I was glad to note he was grinning when he said that.

So I offer this drawing of President Gerald Ford, sans Band-Aid, as a farewell gesture of respect. He was a gentleman of generous good humor and one heck of a good sport. I have drawn many presidents, but he is the only one I ever drew ON.

Pat Oliphant

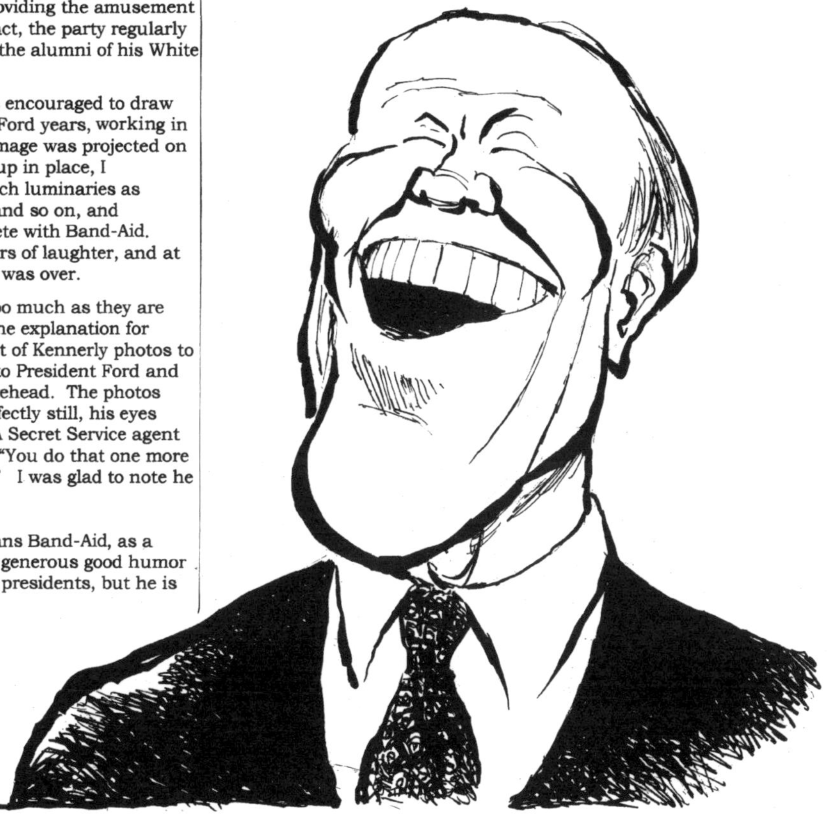

62.
Meat Grinder
January 8, 2007

The Great Surge Plan to end the Iraq war—20,000 to 30,000 extra troops will be needed, says the president. Why, some would say, there must be that many generals there right now, doing TV appearances and strategy assessments and the like, why not enlist some of them to fill the ranks?

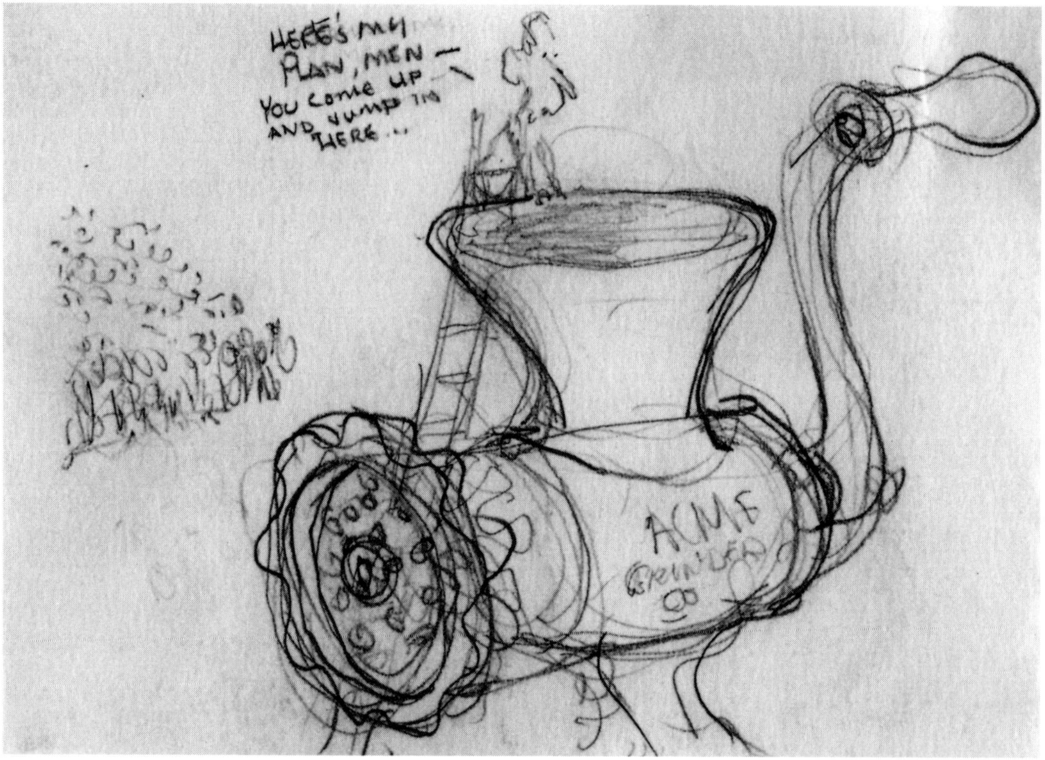
HERE'S MY PLAN, MEN — YOU COME UP AND JUMP IN HERE...
ACME GRINDER

Preliminary sketch for
Meat Grinder
Graphite on paper

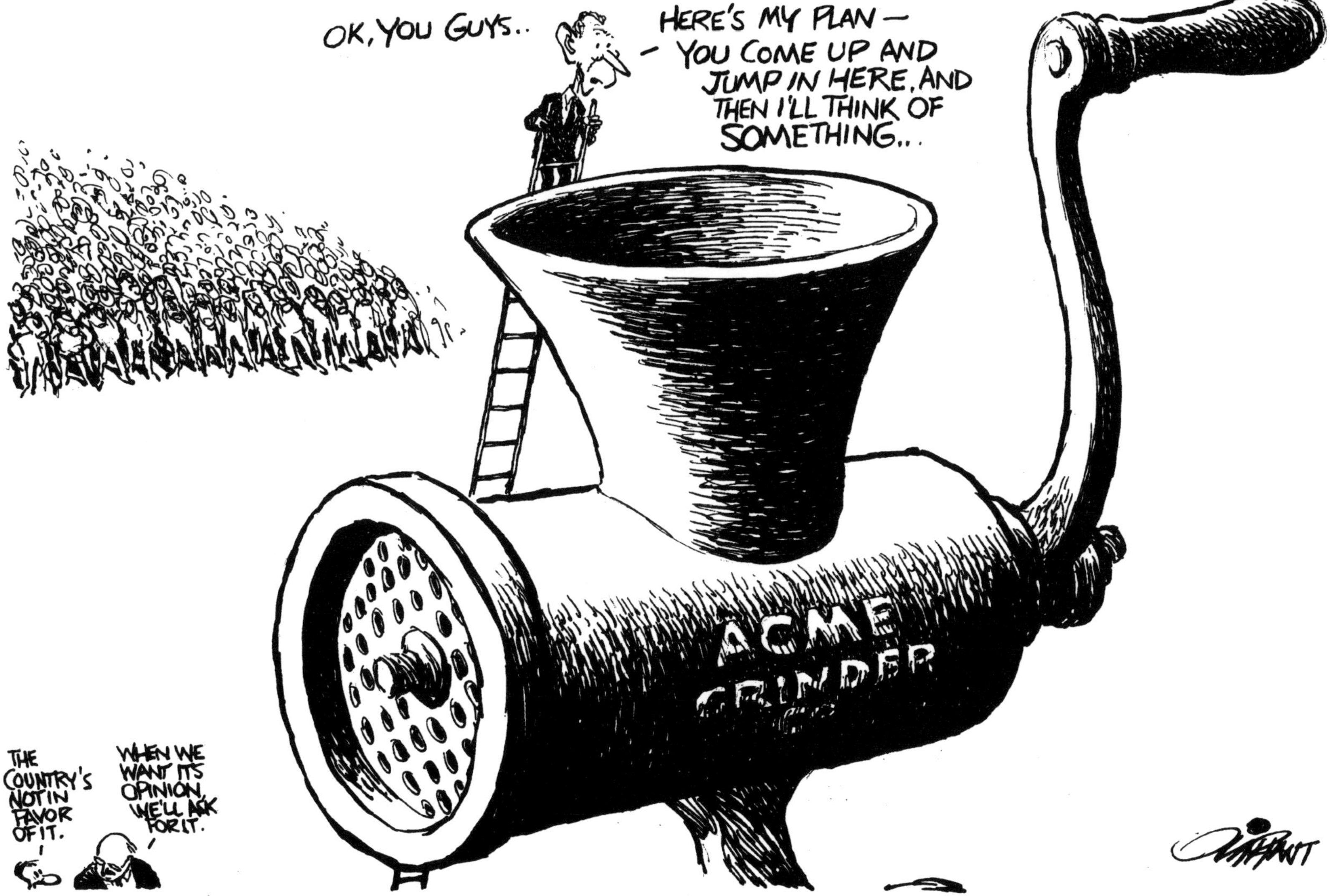
OK, YOU GUYS..
HERE'S MY PLAN — — YOU COME UP AND JUMP IN HERE, AND THEN I'LL THINK OF SOMETHING...
ACME GRINDER
THE COUNTRY'S NOT IN FAVOR OF IT.
WHEN WE WANT ITS OPINION, WE'LL ASK FOR IT.
OLIPHANT

63.
Oh, Incidentally . . .
February 20, 2007

Oh, incidentally . . . Television news has become, and still is, little more than a breathless recitation of the mindless doings of celebrities interspersed with a scattering of what used to be called Hard News.

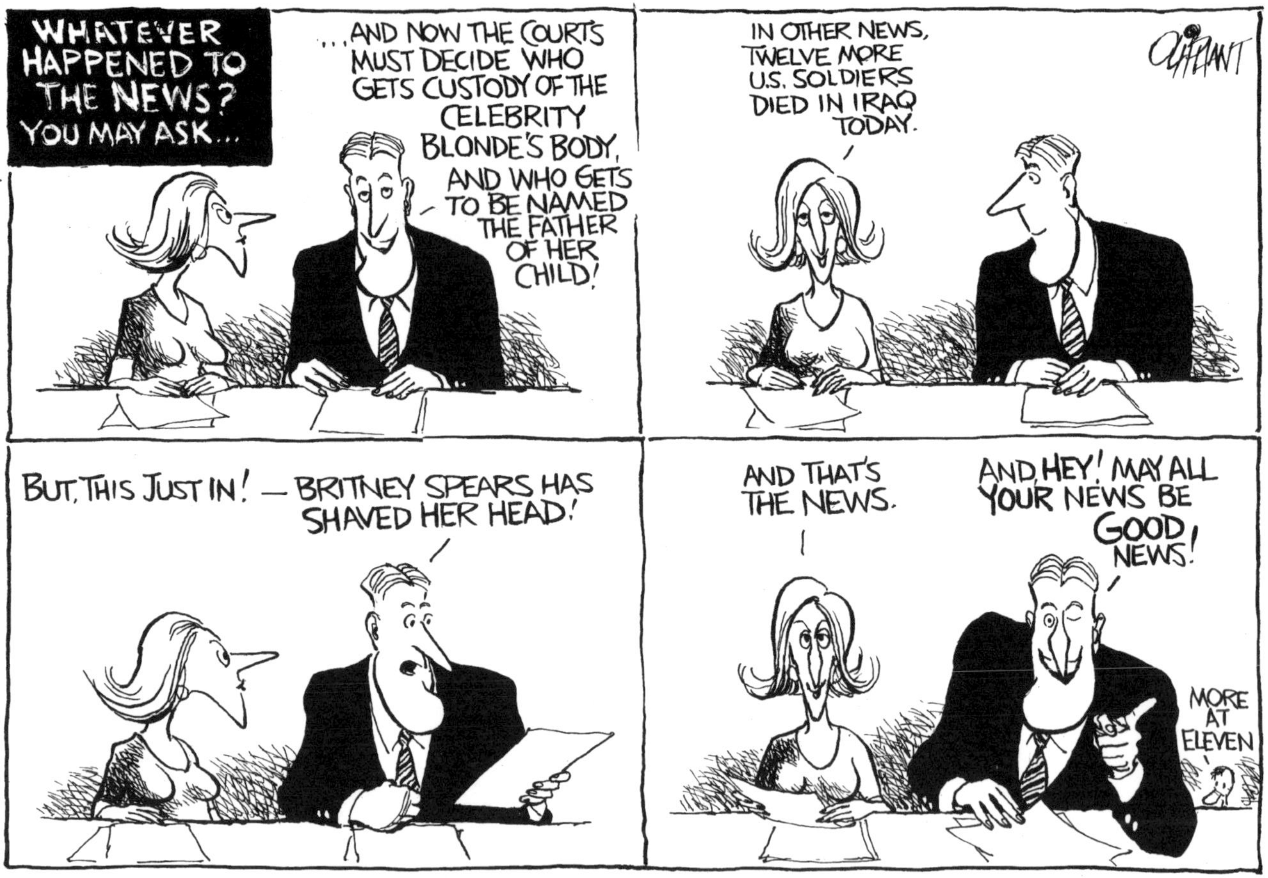
WHATEVER HAPPENED TO THE NEWS? YOU MAY ASK...
...AND NOW THE COURTS MUST DECIDE WHO GETS CUSTODY OF THE CELEBRITY BLONDE'S BODY, AND WHO GETS TO BE NAMED THE FATHER OF HER CHILD!
IN OTHER NEWS, TWELVE MORE U.S. SOLDIERS DIED IN IRAQ TODAY.
OLIPHANT
BUT, THIS JUST IN! — BRITNEY SPEARS HAS SHAVED HER HEAD!
AND THAT'S THE NEWS.
AND, HEY! MAY ALL YOUR NEWS BE GOOD NEWS!
MORE AT ELEVEN

64.
The Cleanup
March 1, 2007

Wounded veterans of the Iraq War are returned for medical attention to the rodent-ridden grime and squalor of Walter Reed Army Medical Center outside Washington, D.C. A grateful nation's stomach turns.

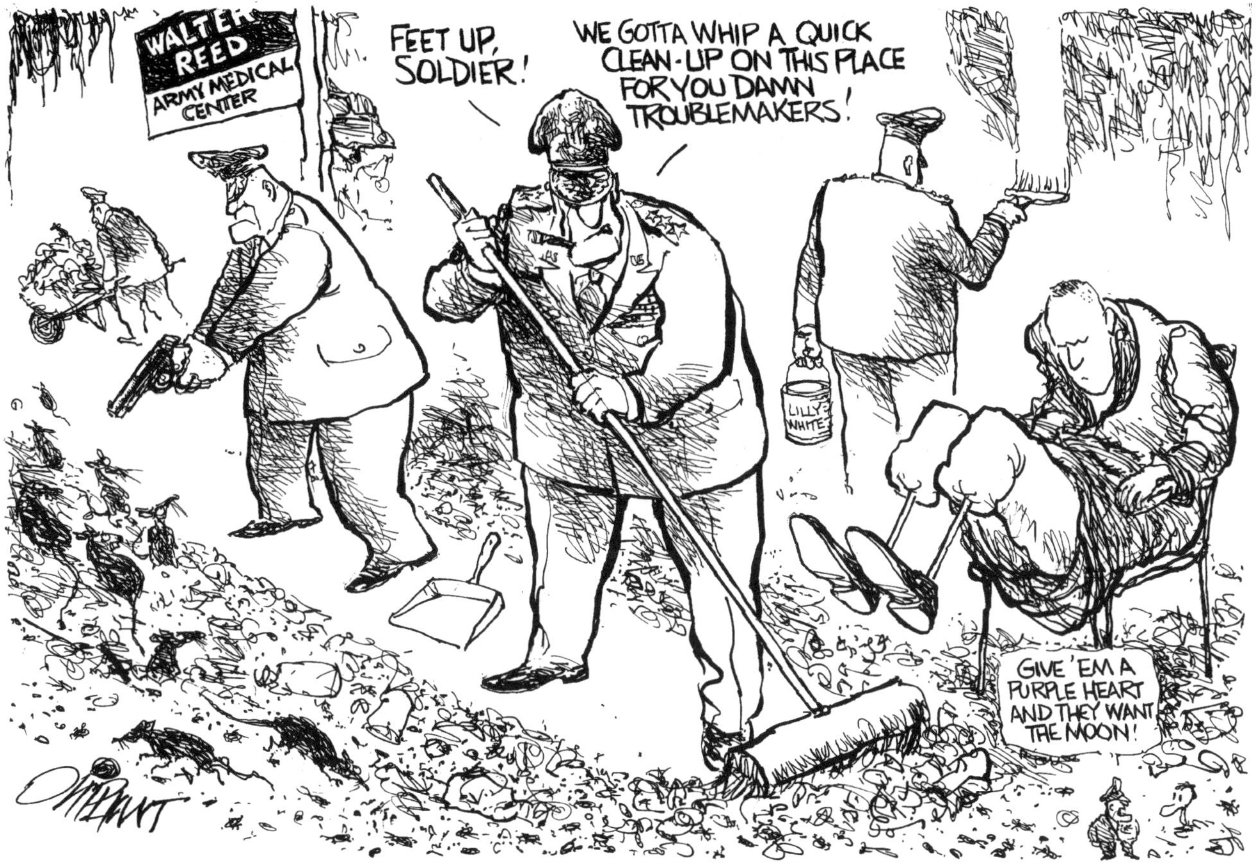
WALTER REED
ARMY MEDICAL CENTER
FEET UP, SOLDIER!
WE GOTTA WHIP A QUICK CLEAN-UP ON THIS PLACE FOR YOU DAMN TROUBLEMAKERS!
LILLY WHITE
GIVE 'EM A PURPLE HEART AND THEY WANT THE MOON!

65.
Ownership
March 5, 2007

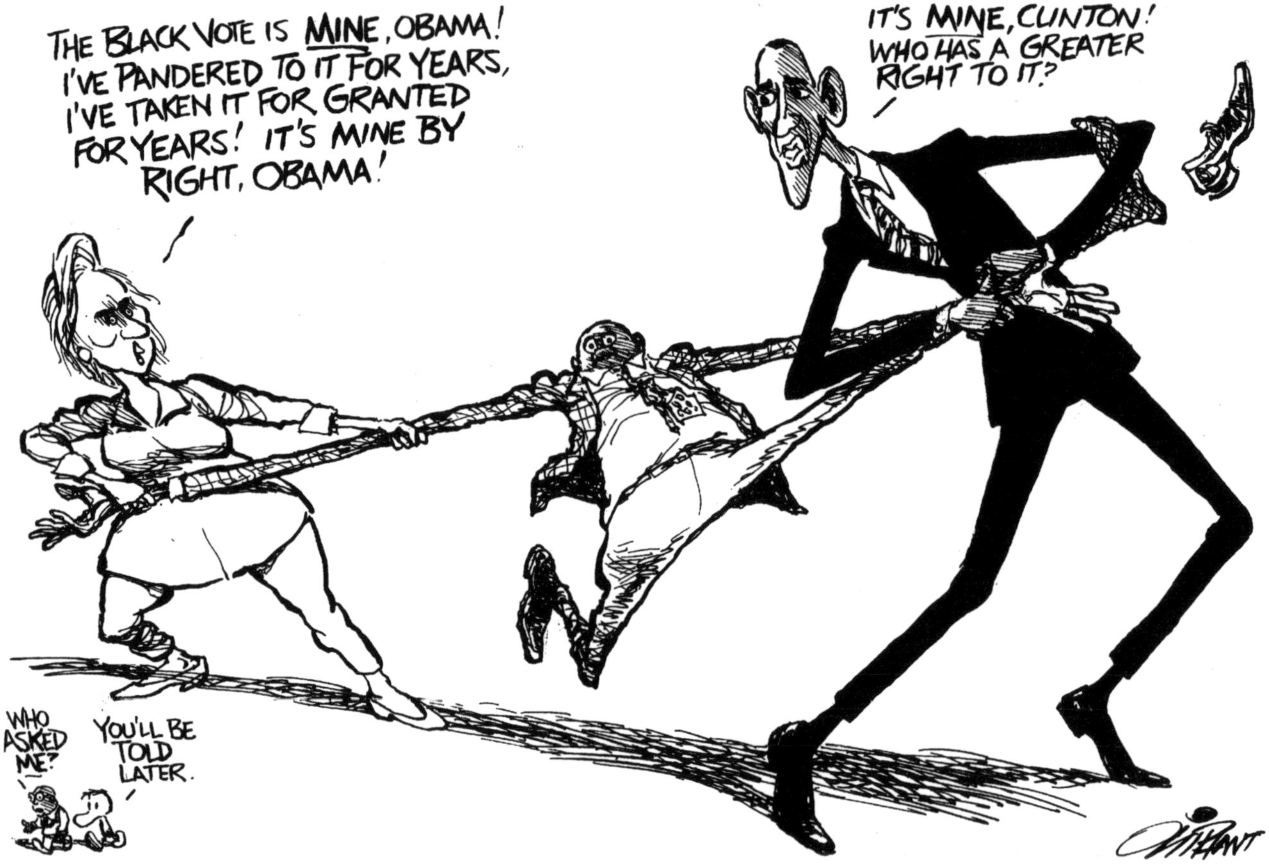

THE BLACK VOTE IS MINE, OBAMA! I'VE PANDERED TO IT FOR YEARS, I'VE TAKEN IT FOR GRANTED FOR YEARS! IT'S MINE BY RIGHT, OBAMA!
IT'S MINE, CLINTON! WHO HAS A GREATER RIGHT TO IT?
WHO ASKED ME?
YOU'LL BE TOLD LATER.

66.
Mistakes Were Made
March 14, 2007

"Mistakes Were Made": Attorney General Alberto Gonzales wrote memos endorsing the use of torture in the interrogation of terror suspects, took a lead role in justifying warrantless wiretaps by the Bush Administration, and developed the list that resulted in a purge of United States attorneys to make way for eager young Republican Bush loyalists. Mistakes were made.

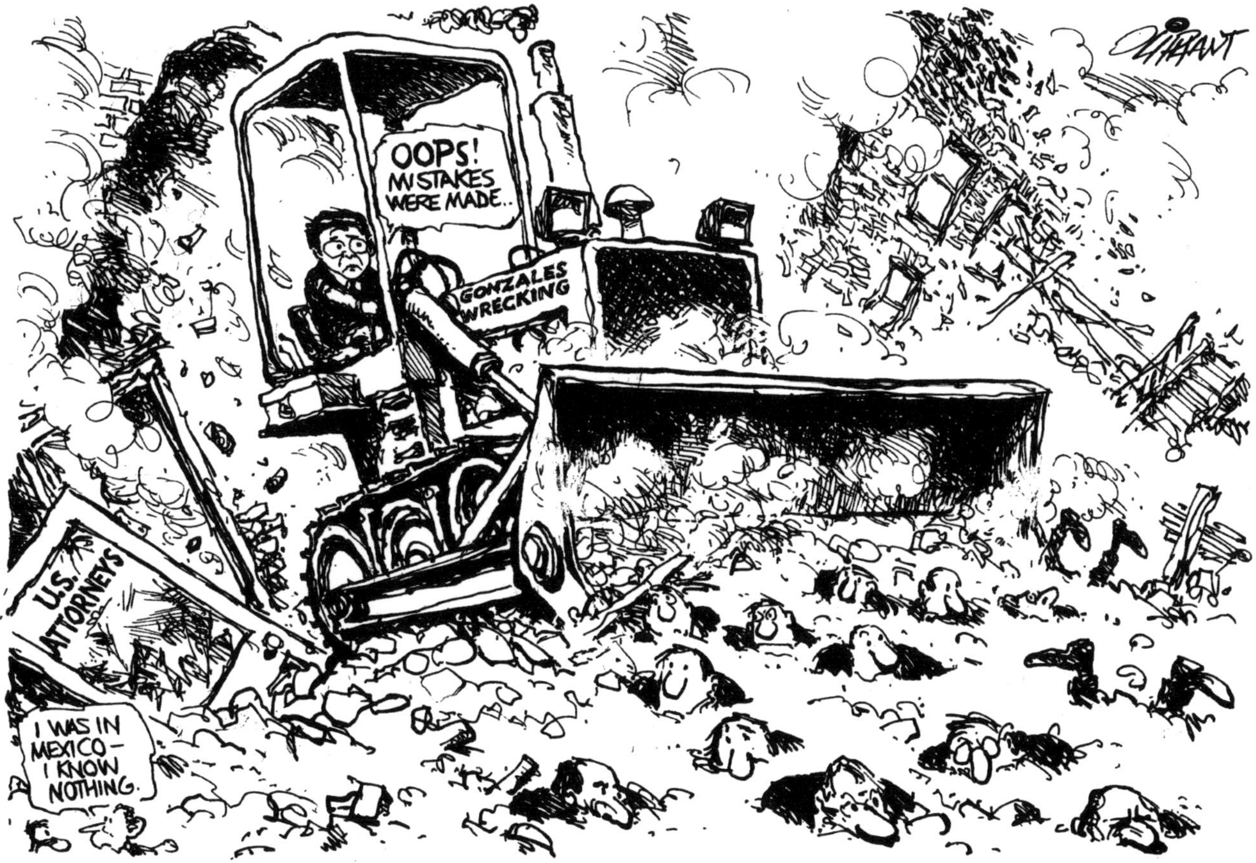
OOPS! MISTAKES WERE MADE..
GONZALES WRECKING
U.S. ATTORNEYS
I WAS IN MEXICO - I KNOW NOTHING.

67.
The Rove Brilliance
March 20, 2007

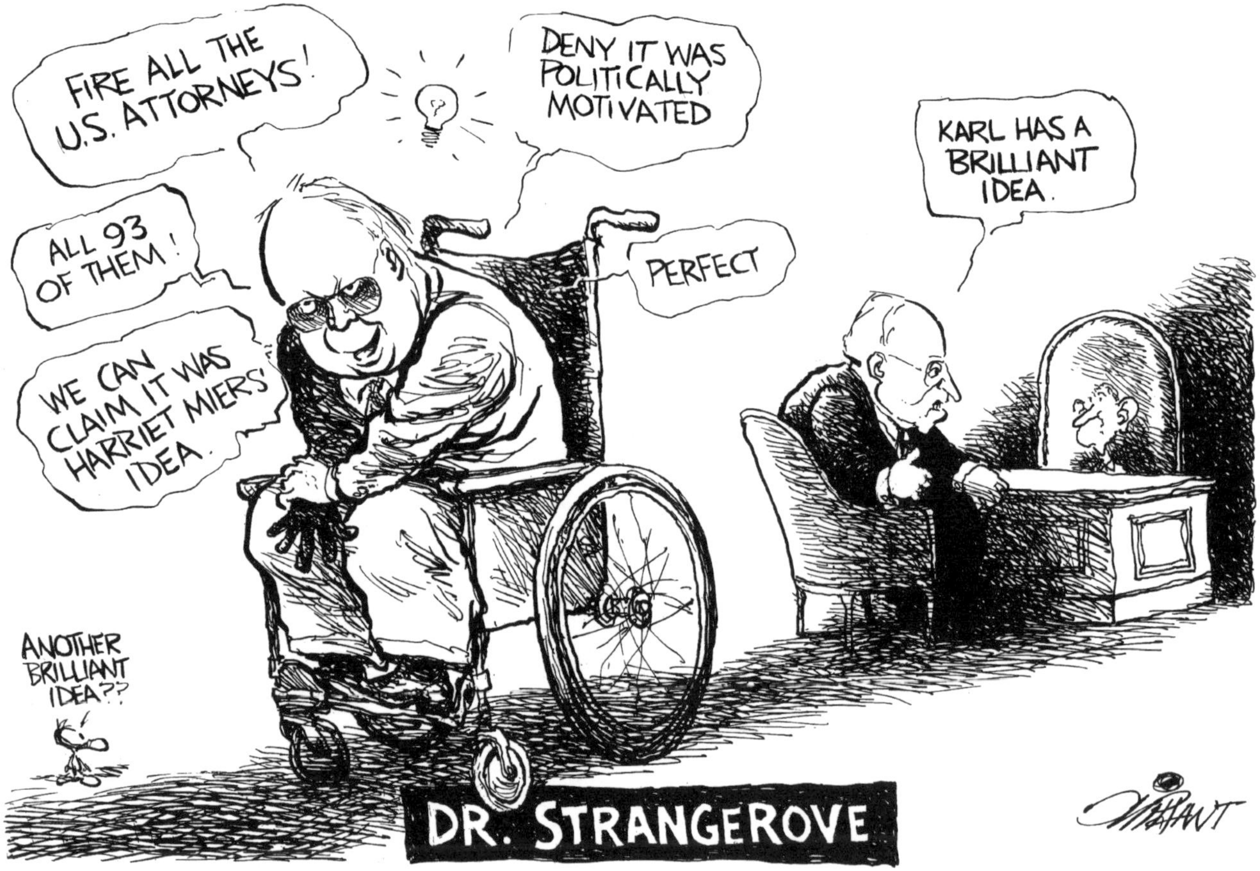
FIRE ALL THE U.S. ATTORNEYS!
ALL 93 OF THEM!
WE CAN CLAIM IT WAS HARRIET MIERS' IDEA.
DENY IT WAS POLITICALLY MOTIVATED
PERFECT
KARL HAS A BRILLIANT IDEA.
ANOTHER BRILLIANT IDEA??
DR. STRANGEROVE
OLIPHANT

68.
This Is a Demonstration
March 29, 2007

This Is a Demonstration: Breathe deeply. Do not show distress. They can smell fear.

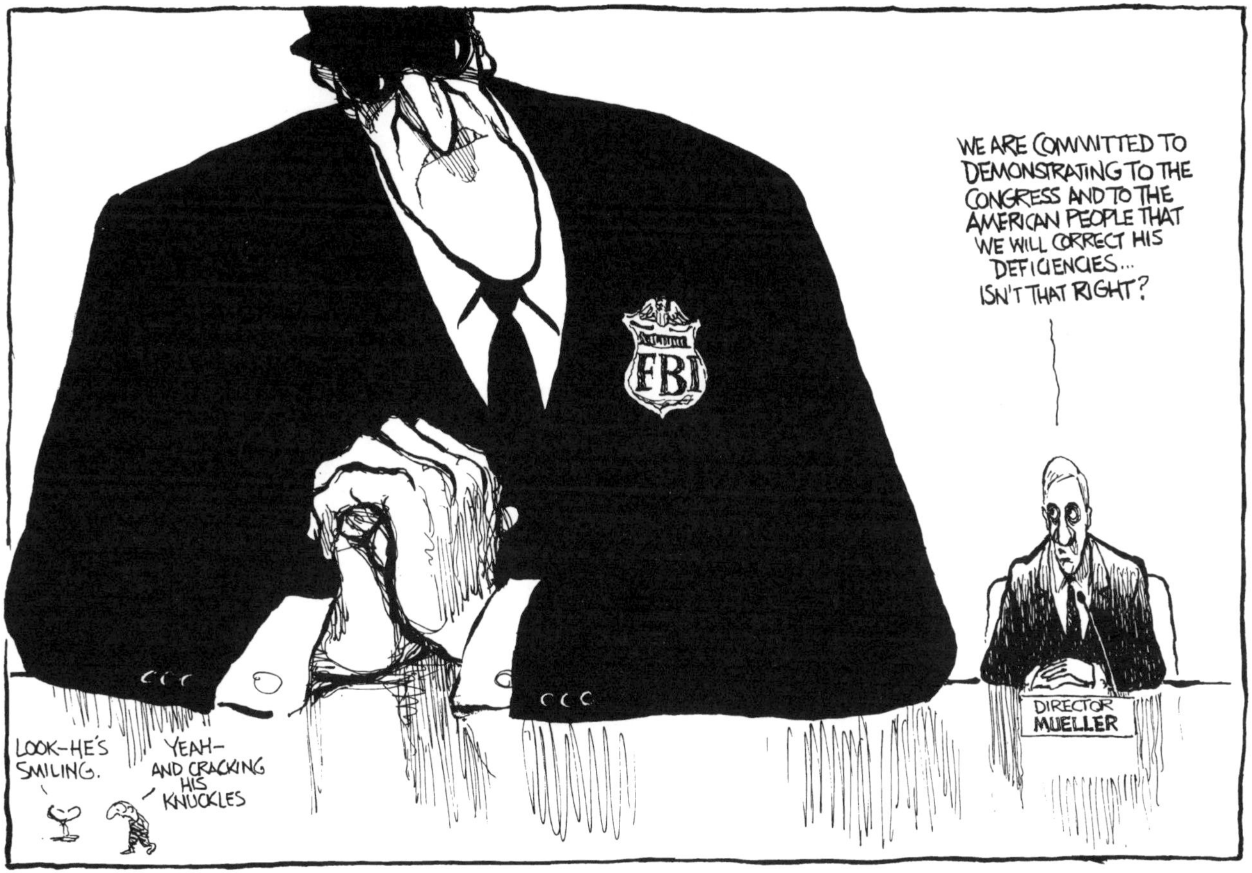
WE ARE COMMITTED TO DEMONSTRATING TO THE CONGRESS AND TO THE AMERICAN PEOPLE THAT WE WILL CORRECT HIS DEFICIENCIES... ISN'T THAT RIGHT?
FBI
DIRECTOR MUELLER
LOOK-HE'S SMILING.
YEAH- AND CRACKING HIS KNUCKLES

69.

Later . . .

April 10, 2007

Later: Britain threatened military action against Iran after fifteen British sailors were arrested and held by Iran on charges of having illegally entered Iranian waters. Iranian officials said they would discontinue broadcasting the crew's "confessions" on Iranian television due to positive changes in Britain's attitude. Iranian President Ahmadinejad strutted accordingly.

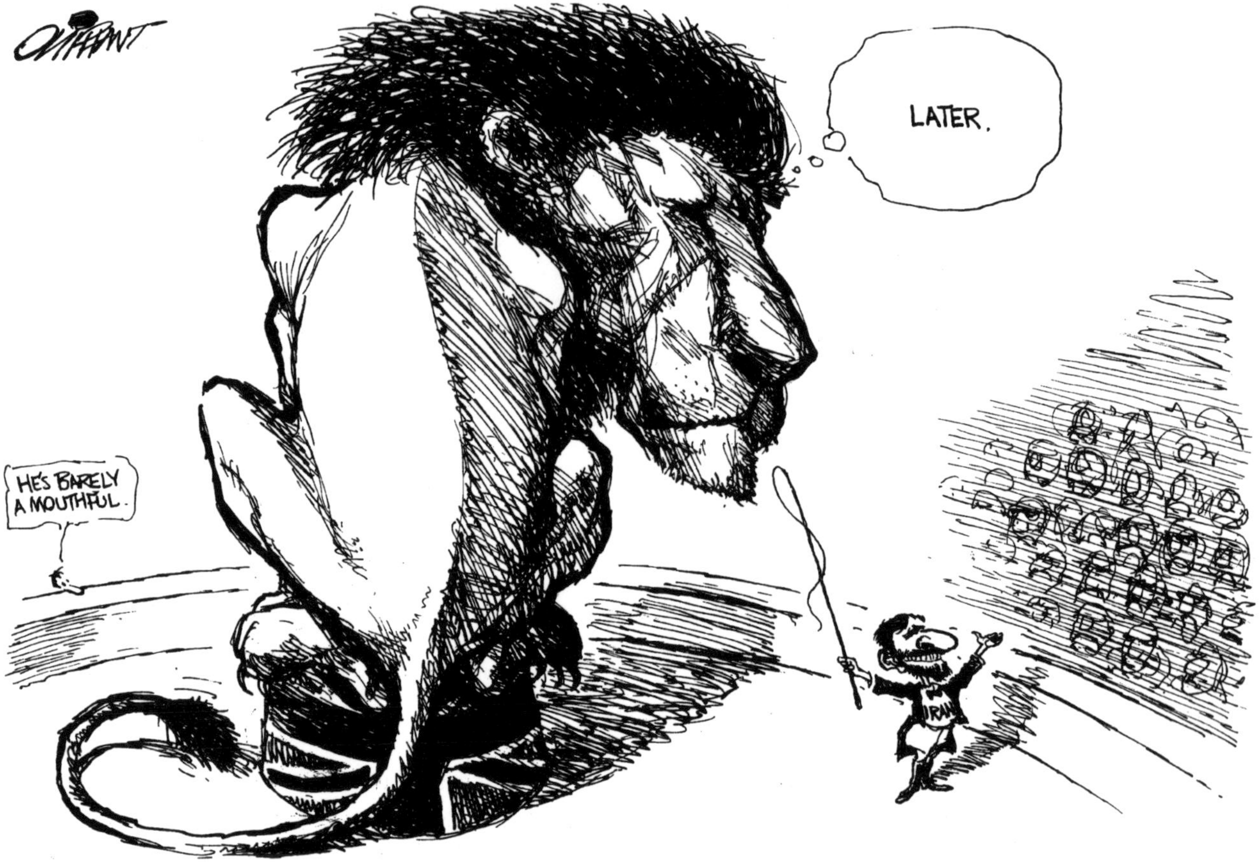
LATER.
HE'S BARELY A MOUTHFUL.
IRAN

70.
Der Bunker
April 13, 2007

The Senate Judiciary hearings were giving Attorney General Alberto Gonzales a rough time. The federal investigation into the political activities of the Royal Bush Handler, Karl Rove, continued. The news from Iraq continued from bad to worse. The mood in the bunker was glum. BUT, the public's minuscule attention span fell exhausted,. then picked itself up and went dancing off after the story of talk radio personality—dare we say celebrity?—Don Imus, who had made certain unrestrained racist remarks on air, and who was fired by CBS Radio as a result. What luck!

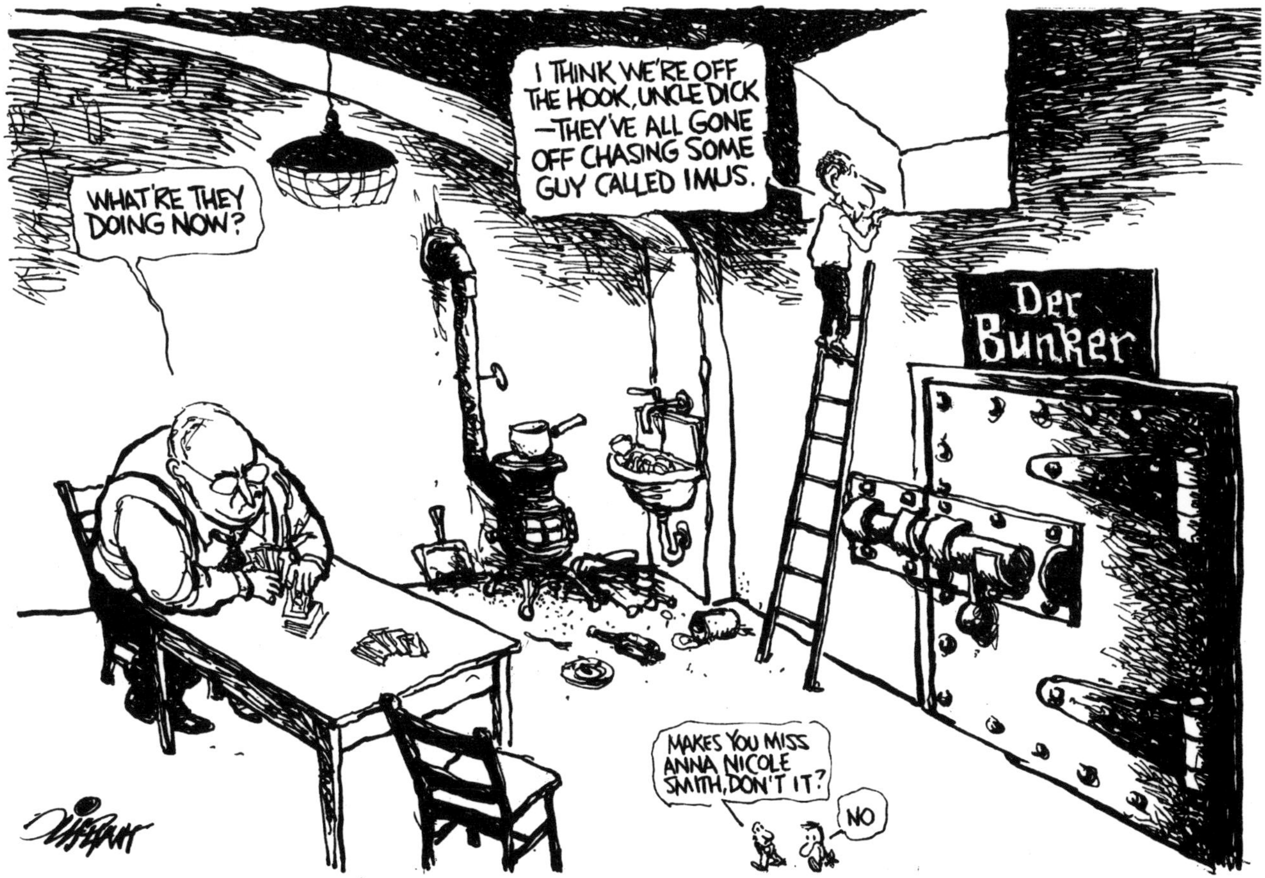
WHAT'RE THEY DOING NOW?
I THINK WE'RE OFF THE HOOK, UNCLE DICK —THEY'VE ALL GONE OFF CHASING SOME GUY CALLED IMUS.
Der Bunker
MAKES YOU MISS ANNA NICOLE SMITH, DON'T IT?
NO

71.
Wangler
April 16, 2007

Paul Wolfowitz, former
Iraq War Architect for the
White House, made the
most of his subsequent
appointment as head of
the World Bank when he
arranged for his girlfriend
a promotion to the State
Department and a large
salary increase. As a result,
Girlfriend would have
been making more than her
boss, Condoleezza Rice.
Mr. Wolfowitz no longer
runs the World Bank.

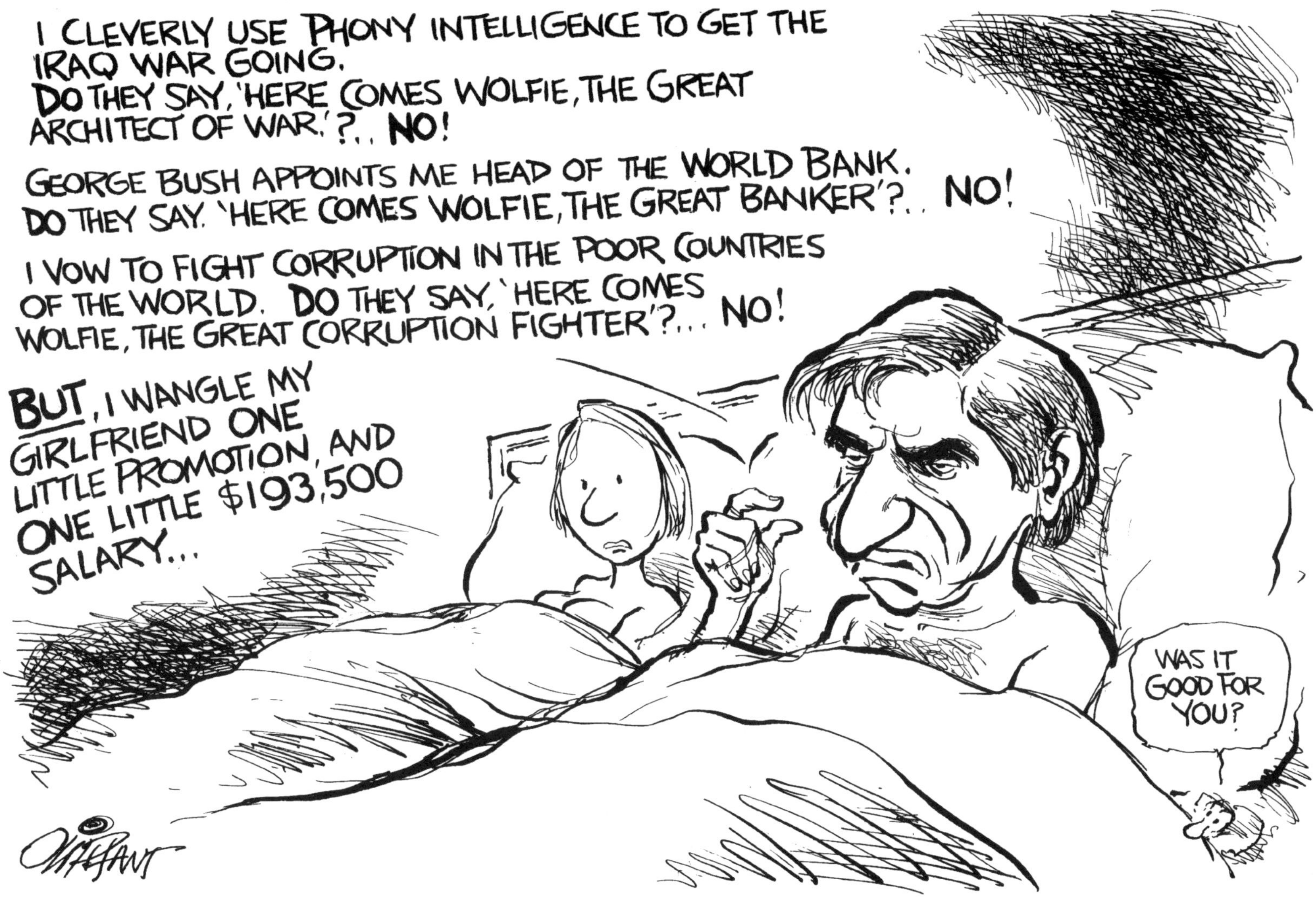
I CLEVERLY USE PHONY INTELLIGENCE TO GET THE IRAQ WAR GOING.
DO THEY SAY, 'HERE COMES WOLFIE, THE GREAT ARCHITECT OF WAR.'?.. NO!
GEORGE BUSH APPOINTS ME HEAD OF THE WORLD BANK.
DO THEY SAY. 'HERE COMES WOLFIE, THE GREAT BANKER'?.. NO!
I VOW TO FIGHT CORRUPTION IN THE POOR COUNTRIES OF THE WORLD. DO THEY SAY, 'HERE COMES WOLFIE, THE GREAT CORRUPTION FIGHTER'?... NO!
BUT, I WANGLE MY GIRLFRIEND ONE LITTLE PROMOTION, AND ONE LITTLE $193,500 SALARY...
WAS IT GOOD FOR YOU?
OLIPHANT

72.
Horrors!
May 2, 2007

While we're on the subject of leadership, let us consider this. On the death of his father in 1952, Rupert Murdoch inherited a fly-blown little rag called *The News* in Adelaide, Australia. Rupert closed the newspaper years ago but its spirit lives on in the name of News Corp. and in all the publications he has acquired and altered to his taste in the past fifty-five years—large, out-of-proportion headlines over three short paragraphs of story; slanted, far-right articles of dubious value; puzzles, contests, and naked girls; all the trash that's fit to print. Now, with promises not to meddle in the daily running of the paper, he acquired the *Wall Street Journal*. There is a story, most probably not apocryphal, related to his acquisition of the *New York Post*, when Rupert approached the owners of one of the city's mammoth department stores with a request that they advertise in his paper. "But, Mr. Murdoch," they answered laughing, "your readers are our shoplifters!" With Rupert, the road of leadership has always led down-market.

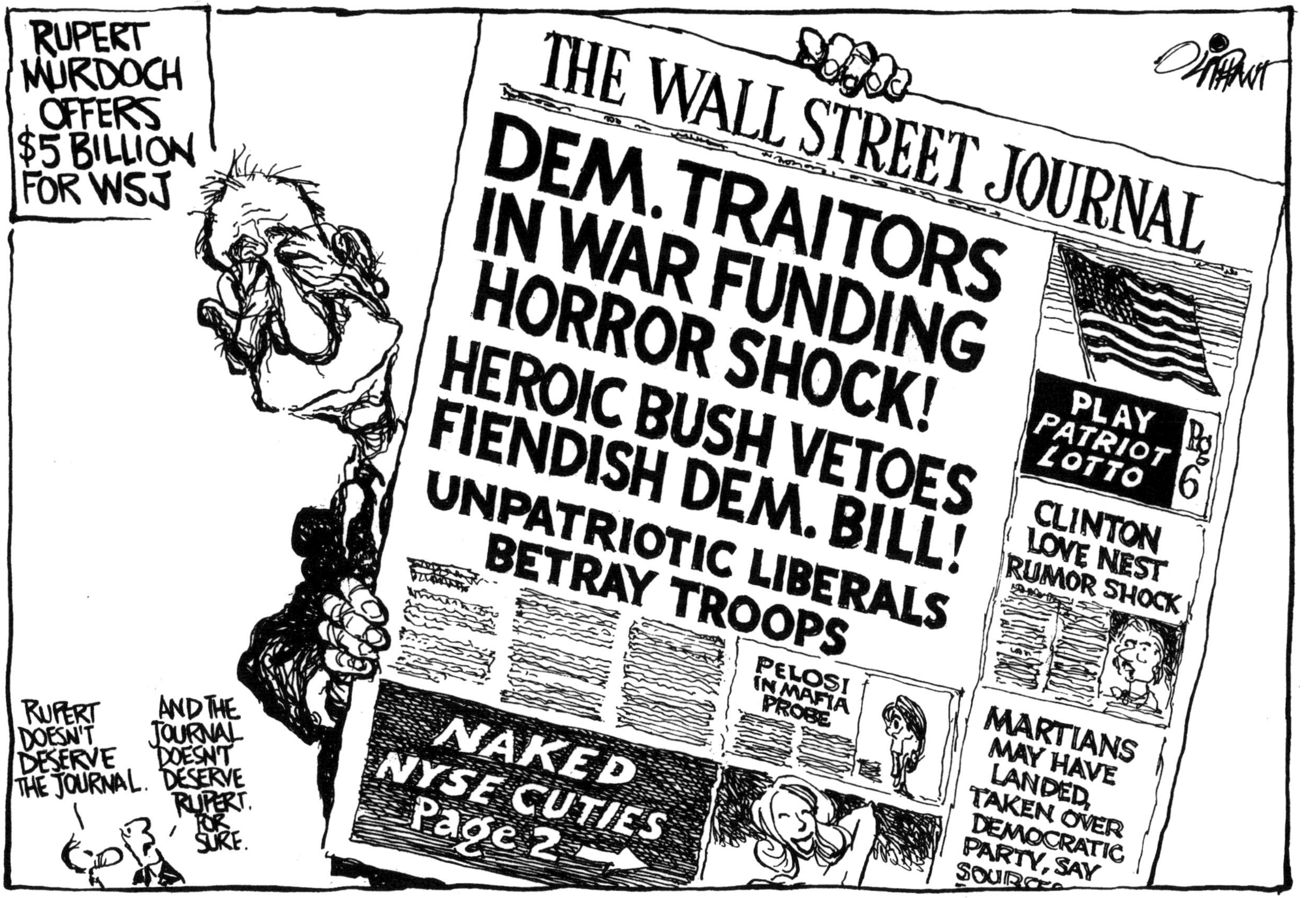
RUPERT MURDOCH OFFERS $5 BILLION FOR WSJ
THE WALL STREET JOURNAL
DEM. TRAITORS IN WAR FUNDING HORROR SHOCK!
HEROIC BUSH VETOES FIENDISH DEM. BILL!
UNPATRIOTIC LIBERALS BETRAY TROOPS
PLAY PATRIOT LOTTO
Pg 6
CLINTON LOVE NEST RUMOR SHOCK
PELOSI IN MAFIA PROBE
NAKED NYSE CUTIES Page 2
MARTIANS MAY HAVE LANDED, TAKEN OVER DEMOCRATIC PARTY, SAY SOURCES
RUPERT DOESN'T DESERVE THE JOURNAL.
AND THE JOURNAL DOESN'T DESERVE RUPERT. FOR SURE.

73.
Window Shopping
May 14, 2007

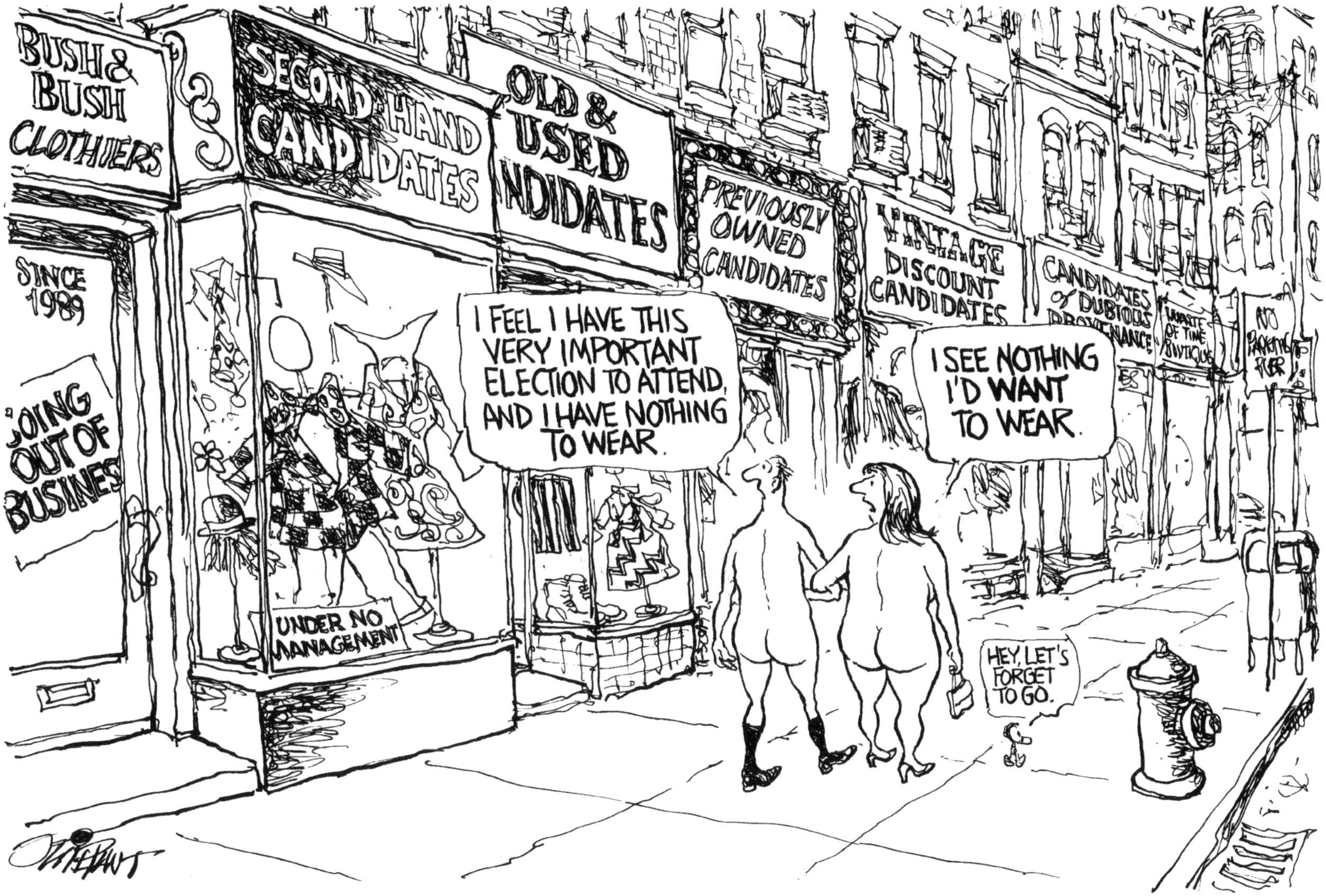
BUSH & BUSH CLOTHIERS
SINCE 1989
GOING OUT OF BUSINES
SECOND-HAND CANDIDATES
UNDER NO MANAGEMENT
OLD & USED CANDIDATES
PREVIOUSLY OWNED CANDIDATES
VINTAGE DISCOUNT CANDIDATES
CANDIDATES of DUBIOUS PROVENANCE
I FEEL I HAVE THIS VERY IMPORTANT ELECTION TO ATTEND, AND I HAVE NOTHING TO WEAR.
I SEE NOTHING I'D WANT TO WEAR.
HEY, LET'S FORGET TO GO.

74.
Cookies
May 15, 2007

Hillary Clinton noisily
declared in 1992 that she
wasn't much at staying
home and baking cookies.
Well, somebody has to
do it, Bill . . . or not. Just do
as she says and let her
take the free ride. You
have nothing to lose but
domestic tranquility.

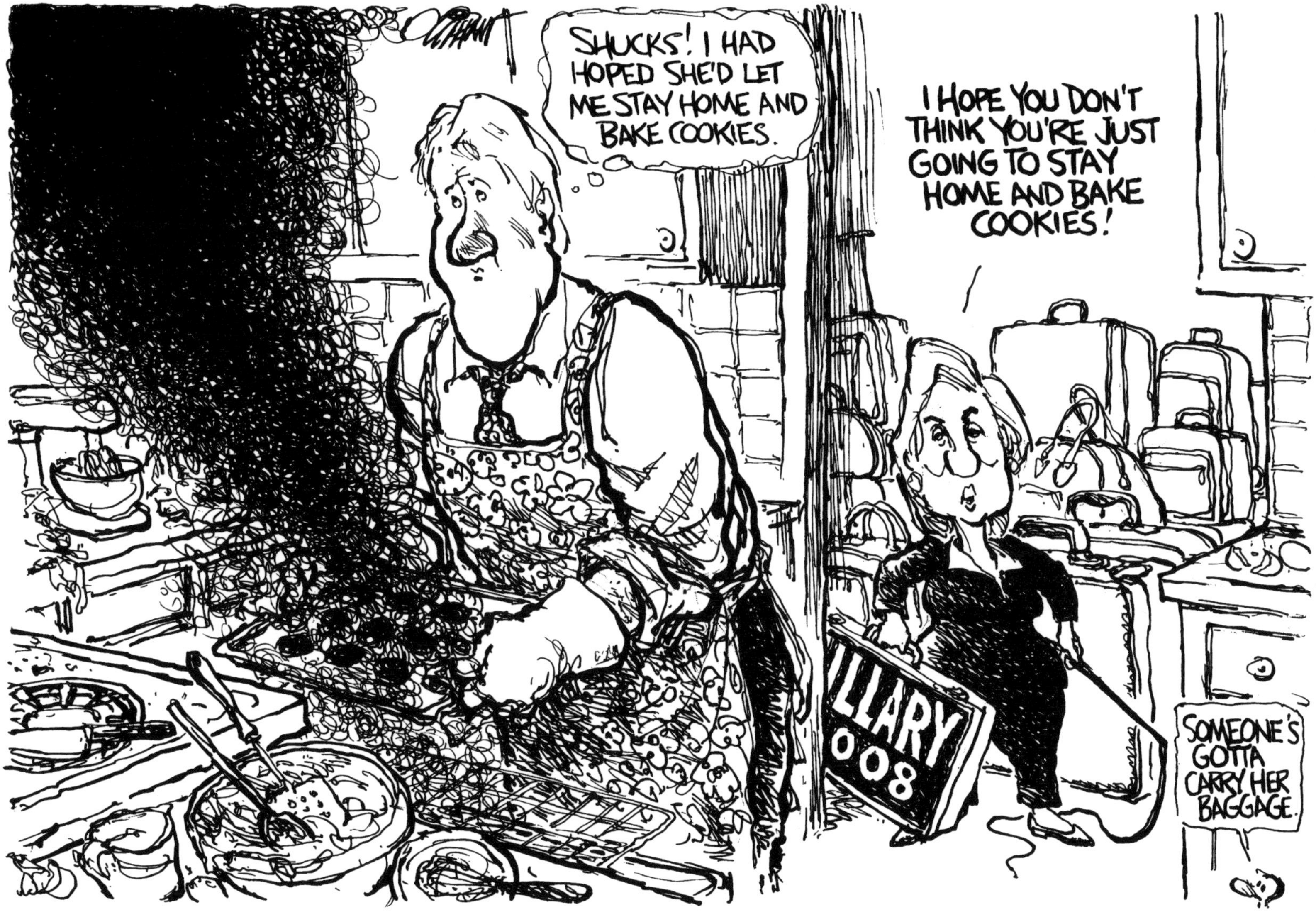
SHUCKS! I HAD HOPED SHE'D LET ME STAY HOME AND BAKE COOKIES.
I HOPE YOU DON'T THINK YOU'RE JUST GOING TO STAY HOME AND BAKE COOKIES!
LLARY
008
SOMEONE'S GOTTA CARRY HER BAGGAGE.

75.
Rise and Fall
May 30, 2007

Jimmy Carter, ranking up
there with the weakest
presidents, rose up and
boldly declared George W.
Bush to be the worst
president in the history of
this country. There was
little argument, and many
admired this former limp
noodle coming forward and
boldly speaking his mind on
our behalf at a time of obvi-
ous national need. But then,
Jimmy drowned himself in
denials that he had ever
meant such a thing and the
Democrats, having folded
on the vote to deny G.W.
a troop surge in Iraq,
limped away again with
memories of the old Jimmy
Carter. Such is leadership.

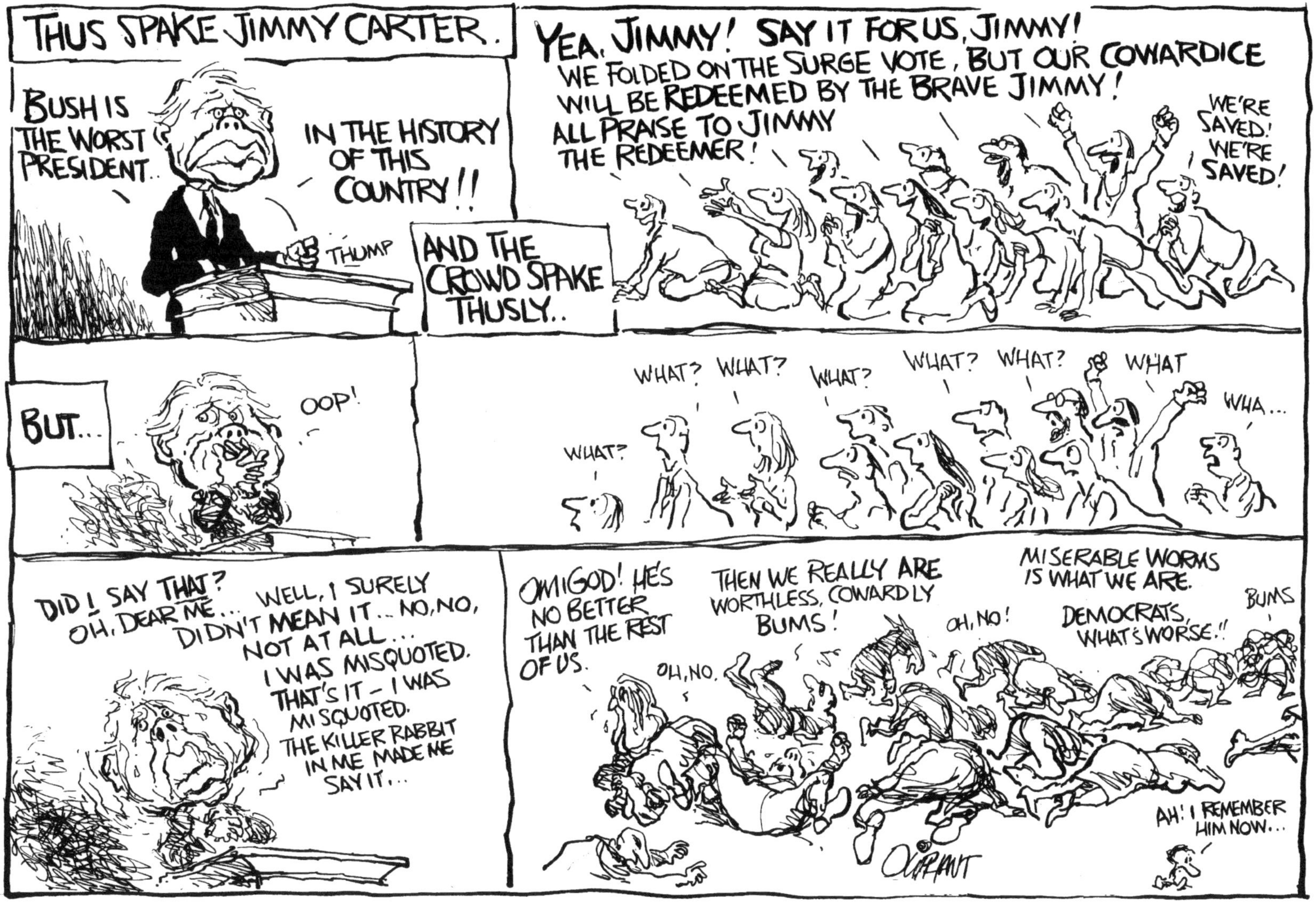
THUS SPAKE JIMMY CARTER.
BUSH IS THE WORST PRESIDENT..
IN THE HISTORY OF THIS COUNTRY!!
THUMP
AND THE CROWD SPAKE THUSLY..
YEA, JIMMY! SAY IT FOR US, JIMMY!
WE FOLDED ON THE SURGE VOTE, BUT OUR COWARDICE WILL BE REDEEMED BY THE BRAVE JIMMY!
ALL PRAISE TO JIMMY THE REDEEMER!
WE'RE SAVED! WE'RE SAVED!
BUT...
OOP!
WHAT?
WHAT?
WHAT?
WHAT?
WHAT?
WHAT?
WHAT
WHA...
DID I SAY THAT? OH, DEAR ME...
WELL, I SURELY DIDN'T MEAN IT... NO, NO, NOT AT ALL...
I WAS MISQUOTED. THAT'S IT - I WAS MISQUOTED.
THE KILLER RABBIT IN ME MADE ME SAY IT...
OMIGOD! HE'S NO BETTER THAN THE REST OF US.
OH, NO.
THEN WE REALLY ARE WORTHLESS, COWARDLY BUMS!
OH, NO!
MISERABLE WORMS IS WHAT WE ARE.
DEMOCRATS, WHAT'S WORSE!!
BUMS
AH! I REMEMBER HIM NOW...

Exhibition Checklist

CARTOON DRAWINGS

Pen and India ink on archival
hot press paper
11 × 14 inches each (sheet)

1.
The Departure
January 24, 2001

2.
Knock, Knock
June 26, 2001

3.
Nine Eleven
September 13, 2001

4.
Celebration of Spring
March 20, 2002

5.
Stop Arguing and Charge
August 27, 2002

6.
Good Doggie!
October 7, 2002

7.
And the Winner Is...
April 8, 2003

8.
Right On, Mr. Blix
June 17, 2003

9.
The Deprived
June 18, 2003

10.
A Son to Be Proud Of
June 26, 2003

11.
Take a Number
March 2, 2004

12.
Inspiration
May 24, 2004

13.
Say What?
May 17, 2004

14.
Last Role
June 7, 2004

15.
The Eulogizer
June 8, 2004

16.
Legacies
June 15, 2004

17.
Easy
June 22, 2004

18.
Rhymes with Duck
June 28, 2004

19.
The Vows of Poverty
July 8, 2004

20.
Pietà
July 12, 2004

21.
Apocalypse
August 11, 2004

22.
The Leaderer
November 3, 2004

23.
Medals, Medals, Medals
December 15, 2004

24.
Tsunami Aid
January 3, 2005

25.
Explain It Again...Slowly
January 12, 2005

26.
Here Comes Democracy
January 31, 2005

27.
Brain Check
March 29, 2005

28.
The Education President
April 5, 2005

29.
No! No! Not the Woods!
April 26, 2005

30.
Spear Carriers
May 9, 2005

31.
Democratize!
June 21, 2005

32.
Comparative Greatness
July 5, 2005

33.
On the Road
August 23, 2005

34.
The Perils of Overwork
September 5, 2005

35.
Ship of Fools
September 9, 2005

36.
The Responsibility of the Irresponsible
September 14, 2005

37.
The Righted
October 11, 2005

38.
A Study in Pliancy
October 17, 2005

39.
Dominatrix
December 8, 2005

40.
Poor Devil
December 27, 2005

41.
You Have to Believe
December 26, 2005

42.
Hunter
February 15, 2006

43.
Medicare Explained
March 16, 2006

44.
Third Anniversary
March 20, 2006

45.
The Great Wall
March 29, 2006

46.
Lucky All Round
March 22, 2006

47.
Don't Hit on Her
May 1, 2006

48.
Transition
May 3, 2006

49.
Don't Rush Over
May 23, 2006

50.
Handy Diversion
June 8, 2006

51.
Donkey Panic
June 15, 2006

52.
Exchange of Fire
August 1, 2006

53.
Oh, Yeah?
September 1, 2006

54.
Right-Wing Jesus
October 13, 2006

55.
Welcome!
October 19, 2006

56.
All Hail, Obama
October 23, 2006

57.
The Next Move
October 30, 2006

58.
Sympathy
November 7, 2006

59.
The Fall
November 9, 2006

94.
Clinton as Billy the Kid, 1999
Bronze, 12 × 8 × 5 inches

60.
The Lecture
November 29, 2006

61.
Gerald Ford Remembered
December 27, 2006

62.
Meat Grinder
January 8, 2007

63.
Oh, Incidentally...
February 20, 2007

64.
The Cleanup
March 1, 2007

65.
Ownership
March 5, 2007

66.
Mistakes Were Made
March 14, 2007

67.
The Rove Brilliance
March 20, 2007

68.
This Is a Demonstration
March 29, 2007

69.
Later...
April 10, 2007

70.
Der Bunker
April 13, 2007

71.
Wangler
April 16, 2007

72.
Horrors!
May 2, 2007

73.
Window Shopping
May 14, 2007

74.
Cookies
May 15, 2007

75.
Rise and Fall
May 30, 2007

WORKING SKETCHES

Graphite on archival
sketch book paper
4 × 6 inches each (sheet)

76.
The Departure*
2001

77.
Knock, Knock*
2001

78.
Nine Eleven*
2001

79.
Apocalypse*
2004

80.
Brain Check*
2005

81.
Democratize!
2005

82.
Hunter*
2006

83.
The Great Wall*
2006

84.
Rumsfeld*
(for sculpture)
2007

85.
Leadership*
(for cover art)
2007

86.
Memorial for a Small War*
(for sculpture)
Archival ink on paper
2007

SCULPTURE

87.
Lyndon Johnson
Bronze
18 × 7½ × 14 inches
1985

88.
Nixon on Horseback*
Bronze
17¾ × 19¾ × 5½ inches
1985

89.
Reagan on Horseback*
Bronze
12 × 10¾ × 11½ inches
1985

90.
George Bush*
Bronze
28½ × 43½ × 12⅛ inches
1989

91.
Jimmy Carter*
Bronze
6¾ × 3¾ × 4¼ inches
1989

92.
Gerald Ford*
Bronze
10 × 6¼ × 5¼ inches
1989

93.
Alan Greenspan*
Wax
10 × 7 × 7 inches
1991

94.
Clinton as Billy the Kid
Bronze
12 × 8 × 5 inches
1999

95.
**Leadership—Bush, Cheney,
and a Horse**
Bronze
17 × 26 × 13 inches
2007

96.
Hillary's Free Ride*
Wax
22 × 9¾ × 11 inches
2007

97.
Rumsfeld
Bronze
22½ × 9 × 9 inches
2007

98.
Memorial for a Small War
Bronze
8¾ × 4 × 4½ inches
2007

OTHER WORKS

99.
Forever the Cowboy*
Charcoal on gray paper
83½ × 53 inches
1993

100.
Bush of Arabia*
Charcoal on gray paper
85 × 47 inches
1993

101.
Seven Presidents*
Graphite, charcoal, and
watercolor on paper
17 × 15 inches
1995

102.
**Leadership—Bush, Cheney,
and a Horse**
Watercolor and colored inks
on archival paper
12 × 16 inches
2007

*Not included in this book.

87.
Lyndon Johnson, 1985
Bronze, 18 × 7½ × 14 inches

Afterword   by Wendy Wick Reaves

How exactly does an editorial cartoonist of Pat Oliphant's caliber have such an impact in the national discourse about politics and people? With unflagging energy and passion, Oliphant has been troubling the waters of bureaucratic and political heedlessness for decades. I had a chance to ponder his magic when I curated the exhibition "Oliphant's Presidents" for the National Portrait Gallery in 1990. His present exhibition skewers national leaders with the same zeal and wisdom. In addition to his skills as a satirist and political commentator, Pat is an accomplished sculptor and a master draftsman. His drawings and sculpture help us understand how artistic and journalistic abilities have merged in his cartoons to create powerfully effective messages.

First, a little bit of bio. Pat is a native of Adelaide, Australia, but, in 1964, he moved to the United States to become the political cartoonist for the *Denver Post*. Within the next few years, he had become syndicated nationally and then internationally and had won a Pulitzer Prize for cartooning. He is now the most widely syndicated political cartoonist in the

world and arguably the dean of his profession. In fact, he has become so respectable, he is invited to the Davos world economic summit. I trust he doesn't do there what he sometimes does here if you meet him for dinner, which is to pass around the table cocktail napkins with hilarious sketches of *extremely* questionable taste just to keep certain friends on their toes. On the other hand, maybe the cocktail napkin trick is exactly what he does at Davos, which is why they keep inviting him back...

So, what is it about an Oliphant cartoon or sculpture that makes it work in the political arena; how does it influence us? Consider, for instance, his depiction of presidents from Johnson to G. W. Bush as a form of portraiture: how it communicates information about those particular men in the oval office. I found in going through his sketchbooks chronologically that the portrayal of a president that emerges from successive cartoons gathers strength as a cumulative form of persuasion. Our first response to a cartoon is assessing how the artist has editorialized on a newsworthy issue. An Oliphant cartoon featuring Lyndon Johnson, for example, seems to be "about" a neutral site for the Vietnam peace talks but the caricature of the beleaguered president is unforgettable. If we are seeing such images regularly, they become indelibly imprinted in our minds. I expect some of you can still envision an Oliphant Nixon. So, often, it is not a single cartoon about a public figure that influences us so much as the building up over time of a memorable, amusingly damning, characterization.

There are three elements of a cartoon that I like to keep in mind in assessing the impact of that cumulative portrait: the caricature of the figure, the analogous situation he is placed in, and the verbal wit in the captions, titles, and speeches of the cartoon. If you look carefully you'll find that Oliphant is a master at each component, and few other cartoonists integrate those three with such forceful impact. Habitually he hones a distinctive, repeatable caricature of each incoming president, for instance. His regular distortion of Johnson, for example, featured a large nose and a protruding, double-knobbed chin; Nixon had huge jowls and squinty eyes. Although no president has a real honeymoon with Oliphant, the exaggerations immediately after an election are funny but minimal. But, fortunately for the art of satire, each president goes to hell quite quickly in his view, and the caricature evolves. LBJ sags and ages; George H. W. Bush weakens; Carter shrinks; Clinton sweats, Nixon bloats. It is an unforgettable cast of characters.

And their small symbolic accessories also wield increasing power in repetition. How do intelligent leaders develop a reputation for being dumb? How do we come to perceive strong, athletic men as bumbling or weak? Surely Oliphant's permanent Band-Aid on President Ford's forehead or the ever-present lady's handbag accompanying Bush Sr. are as influential as TV coverage of a ski slope tumble or journalists' discussion of the "wimp" factor.

When it comes to the analogous imagery of the cartoon, Oliphant is, once again, unparalleled. Of course he bemoans the present ignorance about once usable sources, including the Bible, Shakespeare, myths, and literary classics. "No more 'Alas, poor Yorick!,'" he has complained. "No more ravens quothing 'Nevermore!'. . . Send not to see for whom the bell tolls." Nobody would get it. Nonetheless, Oliphant's imagery from our popular culture, evoking a cowboy, for example, a drag queen, or a short-order cook, seldom misses its mark, and he doesn't shy away from emotionally loaded references: homelessness, surrogate motherhood, assisted suicide. "The Cardboard Messiah" visualized Reagan, during his unsuccessful 1976 campaign, as a shallow, Hollywood cutout. A sketch of a candidate Bush Sr. depicts him as a pregnant surrogate mother, suggesting that the Iran-Contra scandal he is carrying really "belongs to Reagan." Aesop's Fables served to cast Jimmy Carter as the busy, complaining little ant to Ted Kennedy's fiddling grasshopper. Like the distortions of the caricature, the allusions often become more negative as presidential terms progress. Images of a doctor, athlete, or ship's captain—all analogous to power—are replaced by imagery of insanity, diminution, or corruption in a Mad Hatter, an ant, or a pirate.

The third cartoon element is the verbal one. Oliphant is a remarkable wordsmith, aiming additional satiric thrusts not only through titles and captions but dialogue balloons, lettered signs, and sassy remarks in small print by Punk the penguin, a tiny but outrageous on-site observer. Carter's dialogue as Aesop's ant captures the whining of an insignificant player: "Aw, Jeez, Jody, do I have to be the Ant?" The caption for "Shopping for a Special Prosecutor," sets a chillingly dictatorial tone for Nixon, as he searches a pet shop for a polite parrot who will "speak when he's spoken to." I love the Reagan caption where he is called a "Giant Replica of a Statesman." And, when Oliphant alludes to the Emperor's New Clothes to satirize Bush Sr.'s unfulfilled campaign promises, he extends the humor by having Punk confront the skinny naked figure with the comment, "You need a tie to go with that?"

Keep these three elements in mind as you glance through any collection of Oliphant's work; consider his draftsmanship, imagination, and verbal wit and how forcefully they can work together. For pure caricature drawing, Condi Rice as a whip-wielding dominatrix may be my favorite, although the cowboy in pearls is pretty wonderful. For analogous imagery, the *Washington Post* as a bloated W. C. Fields robber baron gets my vote, although the sculptures we own

at the Portrait Gallery of Lyndon Johnson as a cowboy-satyr and Nixon as a returning Napoleon are right on the mark. As for verbal wit, it will be a long time before I will forget the Catholic Church named St. Paedophilia's. But think, too, how subtle this powerful influence can be. Of course, we recognize when he is being outrageous, when he is manipulating our emotions. But often humor disguises the power the cartoonist wields. We do absorb information subconsciously while we laugh. So, Patrick, congratulations on another wonderful exhibition, thank you for setting us straight about all these charlatans we once probably admired, and please do continue to show us how the hell you do it.

Wendy Wick Reaves is Curator of Prints and Drawings at the National Portrait Gallery, Smithsonian

Acknowledgments

With great appreciation to P. J. O'Rourke, author and humorist, and to Wendy Wick Reaves, Curator of Prints and Drawings, National Portrait Gallery, Smithsonian, for their enormous talents and essay contributions; to Harry Katz, author and cartoon historian, for his help with the selection of cartoons; to Steven High, Director, and Holly McCullough, Curator, at the Telfair Museum of Art, for their early enthusiasm and commitment; to Samuel Sachs, Director Emeritus, The Frick Collection, for his encouragement; to Anne Kathryn Stokes for her countless contributions; to Barbara Harrelson for her attention to detail; and to Amy Pyle and Marcus Ratliff for their design integrity. We are indebted and grateful to Louis Atkin for his long-standing generosity and spirit and friendship. We also want to thank John McMeel and Dorothy O'Brien at Andrews McMeel Universal for their continuing support, and for the quality of this publication and its distribution.

Pat Oliphant and
Susan Corn Conway

The publication, exhibition, and tour of *LEADERSHIP: Oliphant Cartoons & Sculpture from the Bush Years* have been organized and produced by:
Susan Conway Gallery
Santa Fe, NM
SConwayGly@aol.com